THE
home furnishings
workbook

THE
home furnishings
workbook

MAUREEN WHITEMORE

I would like to thank my wonderful family Kevin, Joe, Shelley, Louie, Sarah, Anna, my mother and my
friends for their love and support throughout the years.
And to my two Alwyns, father and son.

First published in the United States in 1999 by
Randall International
PO Box 1656, Orange, CA 92856
Phone: 714-771-8488
Toll free: 800-882-8907
E-mail: sales@randallonline.com
Internet: http://www.randallonline.com

First published in Great Britain in 1999 by Collins & Brown Limited

1 3 5 7 9 8 6 4 2

Library of Congress Cataloging-in-Publication Data
is available from Randall International

ISBN 1 890379 00 X

Editor: Kate Haxell
Design conceived by: Janet James
Designer: Roger Daniels
Photography: Matthew Dickens

Reproduction by Hong Kong Graphic & Printing Ltd
Printed and bound in China by Sun Fung

contents

The Techniques

The Techniques

The Projects

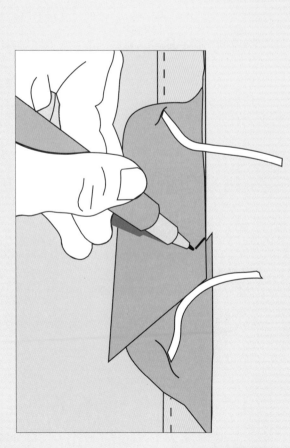

Introduction

Although fashions in the way in which we use fabric in our homes change, good, sound basics will never alter. During the many years (that sounds terribly ageing) I have spent in the furnishing industry I have seen trends come and go, but there will always be a call, for instance, for traditional swags and tails. Regardless of current fashions, wonderful, tall, elegant windows in traditional rooms will always look their best dressed in this style.

I was trained to expect that curtains should look as good in ten years time as the day they are made. Providing they are well made, lined and even interlined, hung on a good quality track and well-maintained by gentle vacuuming (with muslin over the brush end) they will indeed look as good in a decade.

This does not necessarily always mean purchasing the most expensive fabrics – we all have a budget to work to – but good-quality workmanship will make even the simplest fabrics and styles into something of which you can be justly proud. If you fall in love with a fabric that is beyond your budget, use it in small quantities in, say, a Roman blind. Work of the quality shown in this book is, because of its high standard, expensive, as it is time consuming and labour costs are high. However, by following the careful instructions and detailed illustrations, you too can achieve these standards, with a little practise.

Training in the traditional apprentice situation involved working on one particular section until you were sufficiently proficient to move onto the next. I can still remember the many weeks I spent making up curtain linings and boiling piping cord ready for using in loose covers (the smell will live with me forever). I can also remember the day I was first allowed to help in a customer's house on a loose cover cutting. Strange what sticks in your memory, but I remember the house and the fabric too. I like to use the phrase 'professional shortcuts to perfection' to describe the way in which I train my students. Over the last twenty years or so I have come up with my own techniques, enabling me to train people in much less time than that traditional apprenticeship, hence the term 'shortcuts'. Wherever I have been running a class or a training session and found that a student has problems, I have tried to come up with a better technique. This book is based on those techniques. I hope you will enjoy using them, and most of all, I hope you will enjoy the transformation they can make in your home or workroom.

Maureen Whitemore

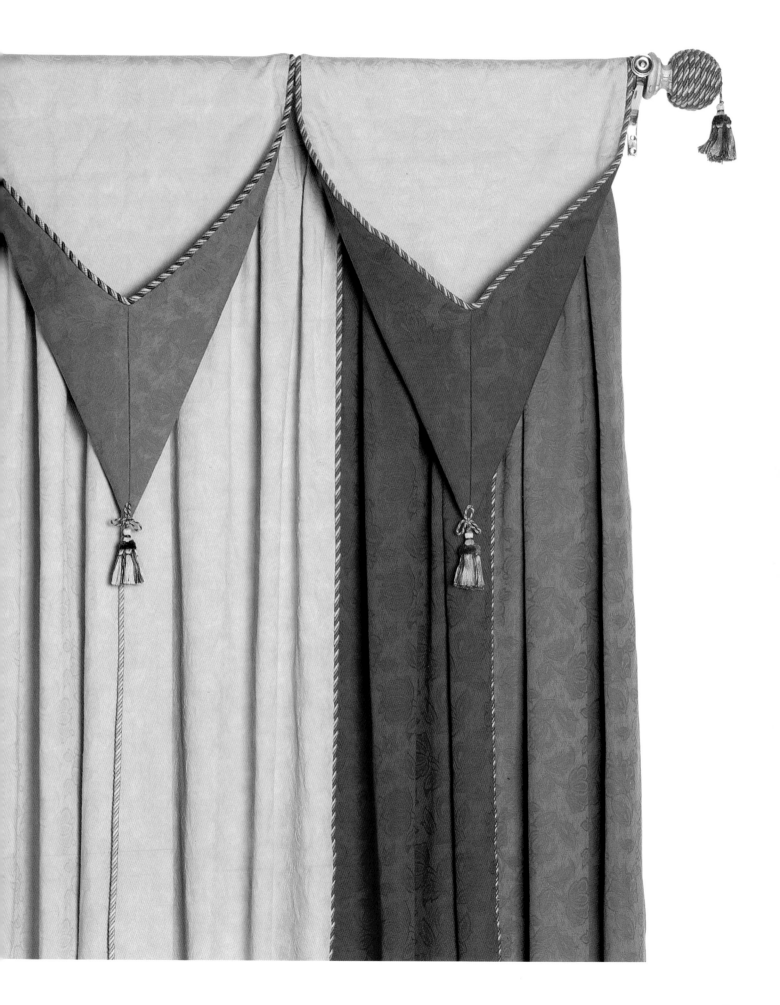

Tools and equipment

I recommend that you start with a straight-forward sewing machine, preferably one that can blind hem and has a reasonable zigzag stitch; scissors; pins; long fine needles; four covered house bricks; a small ruler; some kind of marker and a metal tape measure. When you start a project buy a large reel of good-quality thread. In a short time you will have a collection of useful colors. Small reels work out to be more expensive and you are often left with useless amounts of thread. In time, all the items on these pages will prove invaluable.

One item not shown is a cutting table. You could make a wooden top to go over your dining table, with thin foam between for protection. The top should ideally be 150cm (59in) by 250cm (100in), or longer. Strips of wood underneath, fitting up to the table, stop it moving. The top can be in two pieces, with two strips of wood and wing nuts to connect them underneath, near the edges. An alternative is a folding table tennis table. Eventually, if you are setting up a workroom, a worktable at the correct working height for you is critical.

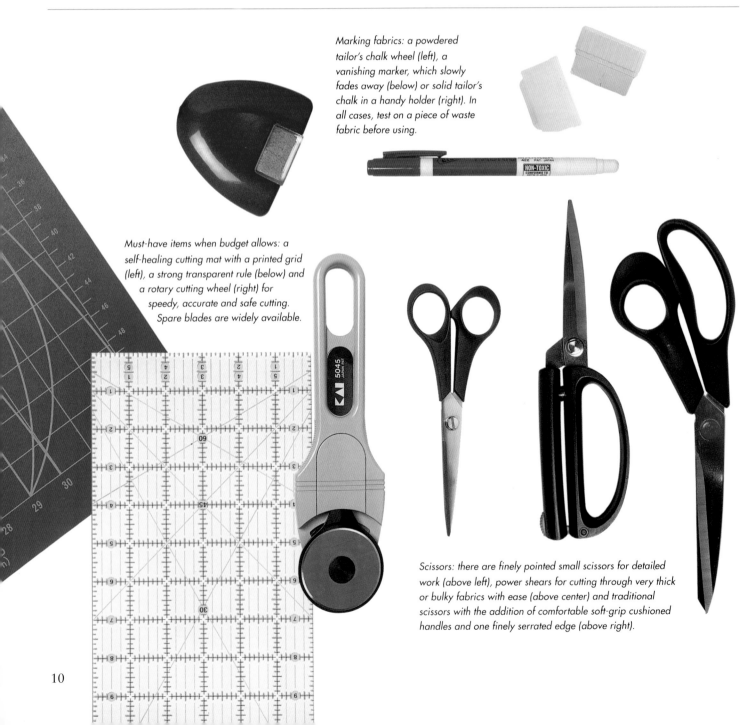

Marking fabrics: a powdered tailor's chalk wheel (left), a vanishing marker, which slowly fades away (below) or solid tailor's chalk in a handy holder (right). In all cases, test on a piece of waste fabric before using.

Must-have items when budget allows: a self-healing cutting mat with a printed grid (left), a strong transparent rule (below) and a rotary cutting wheel (right) for speedy, accurate and safe cutting. Spare blades are widely available.

Scissors: there are finely pointed small scissors for detailed work (above left), power shears for cutting through very thick or bulky fabrics with ease (above center) and traditional scissors with the addition of comfortable soft-grip cushioned handles and one finely serrated edge (above right).

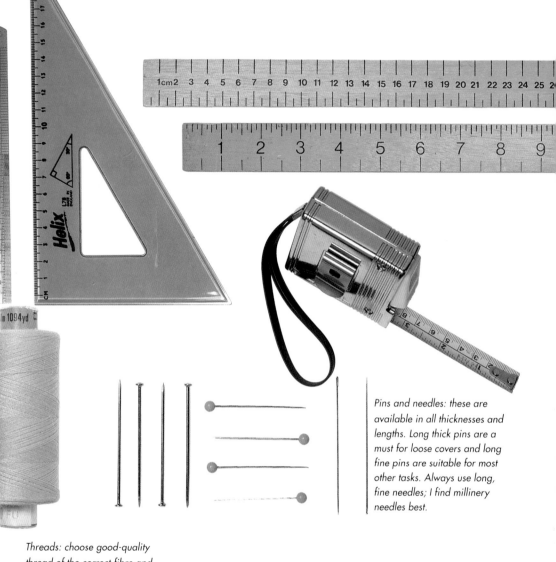

Measuring: a must for so many workroom tasks is a metre or yardstick. A metal measuring tape is essential for accurate curtain making. This one has a specially adapted hook (see Technique 22) which fits into the curtain glider or ring. You need a set square with a 60° angle for mitred curtain corners. One of the products I just couldn't be without is a small metal engineer's ruler, with both metric and imperial measurements. Its big advantages are that it doesn't melt when touched accidentally with the iron and that it starts at zero on both sides.

Pins and needles: these are available in all thicknesses and lengths. Long thick pins are a must for loose covers and long fine pins are suitable for most other tasks. Always use long, fine needles; I find millinery needles best.

Threads: choose good-quality thread of the correct fibre and type for the fabric you are making up. A 120 1s thread for the machine and 45 1s or 75 1s for hand stitching: the numbers are an indication of the thickness and the strength of the thread.

Holding fabrics: when an extra pair of hands is needed these clamps are invaluable. Ideal when cutting, measuring, pressing and hand sewing. It is preferable to have a minimum of four clamps when making up curtains.

A simple and cheap alternative to clamps are house bricks, washed and covered in thick fabric with tape sewn on as a handle. Useful if you are working on the floor.

1 How to draw to scale

The advantages of drawing to scale are firstly, that it is so much easier to gauge the correct proportions and position of tracks, cornice boards etc. Secondly, it is an accurate way of assessing if a particular treatment will suit your window.

Graph paper makes designing your window treatment simple. If you want to see the effect of different designs, draw each one on transparency film so that you can lay them over the drawing of the window on the graph paper.

- *Where do you start?*
- *How can you visualise what your window will look like?*
- *How long should your valance, cornice or curtains be?*
- *Where should you fit your curtain track or pole?*
- *Should you use long or short curtains?*
- *How do you avoid costly mistakes?*

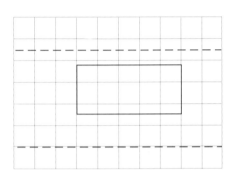

First of all, draw a line to indicate the ceiling and another line for the floor. (For the sake of clarity I have shown the large squares only and have used a dotted line to indicate the floor and ceiling.) To place these lines in the correct position you need to decide a scale. In most instances one large square will represent either 10cm (4in) or 50cm (20in) according to the size of the window you are drawing. So if you are working on a scheme for a very large window, you will need to make each square equal to 50cm (20in), which is what I have done in this scale drawing. Following this rule you can see that the ceiling is 225cm (88in) from the floor.

Draw in the outline of the window in the correct position and to scale. Again, following the same principles you can see that the window is approximately 110cm (43in) high and the bottom of it is 75cm (29½in) from

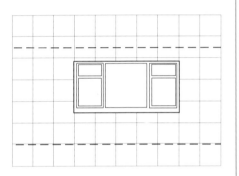

the floor. Of course, on real graph paper there are many more divisions so it is easy to be very accurate.

Draw in any divisions within the window itself, as this may effect the number of blinds you decide to use, the placing of the swags or the shape of a valance or pelmet.

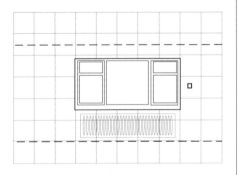

Lastly, draw in any other factors, such as radiators and light switches, which may influence the way you dress the window.

Planning your window treatment

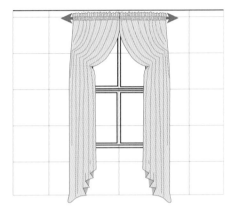

Tall, elegant proportions

With the scale drawing of the window in the background, you can add a pair of curtains on a pole. They can be Italian strung to draw them back from the window and let in light. You could also use an asymmetric treatment on this style of window.

See Project 23, Grampol Swag, page 163.

This Grampol swag uses a form of Italian stringing to draw it up.

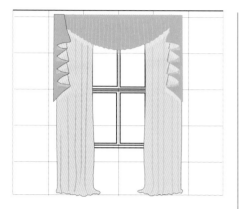

Adding width and letting in light

Taking the cornice board past the edge of the window allows the curtains to be drawn back to let in light, and makes the window look larger. The treatment above uses a wide, hand-gathered fabric valance.

See Technique 66, Making Hand-gathered Headings, page 65.

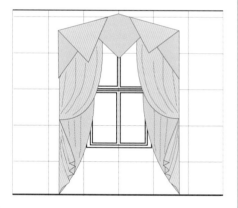

Changing the shape of the window

To completely change the look of the window you could add a shaped top to the cornice board and hook the curtains back to show a contrast lining. You can calculate the dimensions of the pelmet sections using a ruler.

See Project 34, Cornice with a Shaped Top, page 184.

Proportions

Drawing to scale can also help you see if the proportions you want to use are correct. For curved valances, such as the one shown in the following illustrations, the centre of the valance should be approximately one-fifth of the total measurement of the whole window treatment, which should be measured from the top of the cornice board or track to the bottom of the curtain.

If you are using a trim such as bullion, where light can be seen through the fringe, measure the valance from its top to the top of the fringe. If you are using a solid trim such as a frill, it should be included in the depth of the valance.

A straight valance should be approximately one-sixth of the total measurement of the whole window treatment.

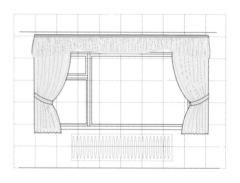

Short curtains

These will make the window look wide and the ceiling look low, and all the heat from the radiator will be lost behind the curtains.

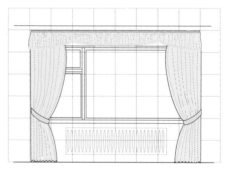

Long dress curtains with a short valance

The curtains help to make the window look taller, though the valance is much too short for the proportions of these curtains. People often ask for a short valance in the mistaken belief that it will cut out less light. In fact, it makes little difference, other than spoiling the whole effect of the

window treatment. Another advantage of drawing this treatment to scale is that it becomes apparent that if the valance were made to these dimensions, you would see the top of the window frame.

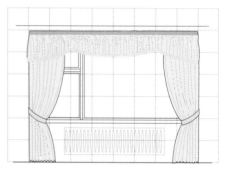

The correct proportions

Full-length dress curtains over a valance of the correct depth add height to the room. Short working curtains or blinds could be hung within the recess to ensure that the heat from the radiator is retained within the room.

2 Dealing with wall mounted heaters

These are traditionally placed under windows in order to heat draughts as they enter a room. The major drawback to this is that curtains often hang over the heater, so the heat goes up the back of the curtains and the room is cold, with a wonderful warm area behind the curtains.
Another drawback is that the heat is not good for the fabrics. Also, double glazing, luxurious window dressings and insulated linings and interlinings mean that most of us have relatively draft-proof windows.

Having weighed up the pros and cons, my suggestion would be to move the heater. This is not as expensive as it sounds, so if you intend staying in your home it is worth the investment. Alternatively, I can show you some ways of dressing a window that help to get over the problem.

- *What should you do if you have wall mounted heaters beneath, or right next to, your window?*
- *Do the heaters need to be there?*
- *What styles of curtain will preserve the most heat and look good at the same time?*

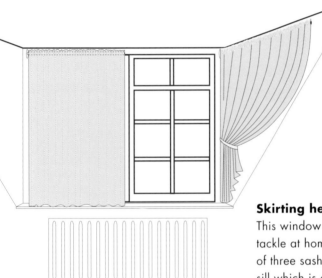

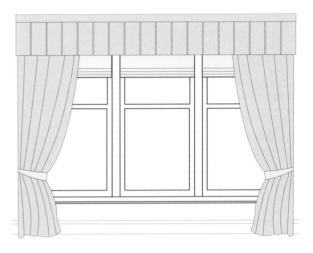

A dormer window

A common problem is a wall mounted heater beneath a dormer window. Short curtains which hang just below the sill will cause some loss of heat, while full-length curtains will cut out virtually all the heat. Normally, curtains set within the recess will cut out too much light. However, you can use swing arms: during the day the arms are swung back and the curtains are held in a tieback. They look extremely attractive as well as solving all the heat and light problems. The same solution could be used for a cottage window set in a very deep recess.

Skirting heaters

This window is one I had to tackle at home. It is made up of three sash windows, has a sill which is only about 50cm (20in) from the floor and there is virtually no wall space at either side. The window is extremely draughty and beneath it there is a long skirting heater. I solved these problems by using three separate Roman blinds, a box-pleated valance with a stiffened top band and dress curtains. Everything is interlined for a luxurious look, and for added insulation the blinds were lined with a thermal lining. As the curtains themselves do not close it would be wasteful to use the thermal lining on them.

An offset wall mounted heater

If you have a wall mounted heater which has been placed too close to the edge of the window it is difficult to use normal full-length curtains. If you want to make the window treatment really special, or want to use swags and tails, here is a great solution – an asymmetric window treatment. The curtain could be simply for effect or, if you want to use it at night, run a small, neat track set below the dip in the swag.

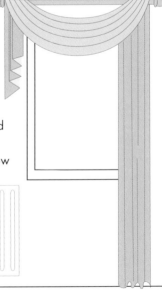

3 Windows in a corner

A window in the corner of a room needs handling with a little caution, but don't worry too much about trying to make it look balanced. Give it either an asymmetric treatment, as in the illustration below, or just dress it as though it was in the centre of the room. If you are bold enough you can get away with anything.

- If you have a window right in the corner of a room, what is the best way to treat it?
- Which styles of curtain or blind will make the most of a long, narrow shape?
- How can you achieve a luxurious effect in a small space?

A simple treatment

Whereas a Roman blind will emphasise the long, narrow shape of this window, a fan blind (see Project 11, page 141) adds a little extra interest, as well as being very practical. This blind also has the advantage of being very easy and inexpensive to make.

If you require privacy, a Slouch Curtain (see Project 29, page 172) with a matching voile is a lovely asymmetric treatment. Like the tab-top, this is primarily a static heading, but it can be drawn back if necessary.

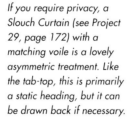

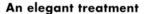

An elegant treatment

This stylish but informal swag needs to be made in a soft cotton, silk or muslin to look its best. The curtains are static and are suspended from a short piece of track concealed behind the swag. If privacy is needed, a voile curtain can be hung behind the dress curtains.

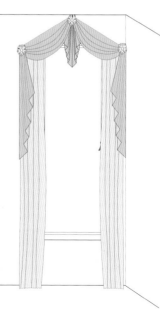

A striking yet practical treatment

These curtains have a static tab-top heading, but by releasing the tiebacks the curtains can be lowered to cover the window completely. The pole is quite high so the length of the window is emphasised, but the draping of the fabric softens the narrow shape and adds a touch of luxury. (Remember, in this situation you can only have one finial on the curtain pole.)

4 Wide, shallow windows

This type of window is often combined with modern low ceilings, so one of the prime aims is to add height to the room. The following diagrams will, I hope, show yet again the enormous advantages of drawing to scale.

- *What can you do to make this fairly standard style of window look more unusual?*
- *What can you do to make the room seem higher?*
- *If you dress this window with a pole will it look boring?*
- *Although the window is modern in style can you make it look a little more traditional?*

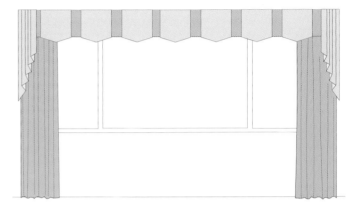

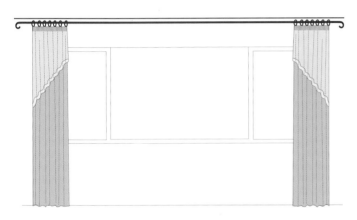

Adding height

Curtains suspended from a pole without tiebacks add immediate visual height. Take the pole almost to the ceiling and you will improve the proportions dramatically. The over-valance is cut at an angle to draw the eye in and upwards.

See Project 30, Cut-away Goblet-headed Curtain, page 174, for instructions on making an over-valance.

A traditional look

If you would prefer something with a little more fabric, try combining a fabric-covered cornice with different-coloured, separate banners and tails. This cornice only just covers the top of the window frame and long tails always help to add visual height.

See Project 4, The Classic Cornice, page 109; Project 16, Banner Valance, page 150 and Project 6, The Classic Swag and Tail treatment, page 118.

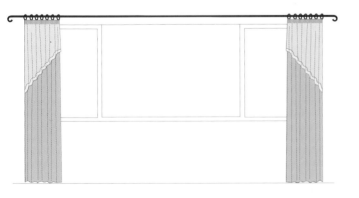

Low, wide treatment

Here the curtain pole is lower and the curtains are shorter, and you can really see the difference it makes to the window. This is a cheaper treatment to do as you need less fabric, but the pole should always be positioned high enough so that the curtain heading doesn't show from outside the window.

Softer lines

This particular combination of a fabric-covered cornice and swags softens some of the straight lines, taking the eye away from the wide, rather uninteresting window.

See Project 31, Bordered Cornice with a Cover and a Swag, page 177.

5 Full-length windows

French windows and patio doors are found in many modern homes and they present their own problems when it comes to window treatments. As there is such a large area to curtain, it is important that the treatment is visually interesting, though in a contemporary setting it doesn't want to look fussy or cluttered.

- *French windows with blinds can look boring, so how can you dress up the top of the window?*
- *Which treatments will sit happily in a modern setting yet still suit a traditional french window?*
- *How can you make curtains for patio doors look more interesting without using a valance or a cornice?*

See Project 34, Cornice with a Shaped Top, page 184.

A traditional look

Traditional french windows can be so elegant, and I love to see them dressed with a really luxurious window treatment. This double-shaped valance has heavily draped curtains below it. For extra privacy you could fix voile curtains with small brass rods to the doors themselves, or hang small, cotton holland roller blinds.

Patio windows

Patio windows tend to have their own problems in that they often have very little wall space above the doors. If there is virtually no space at all, use a small corded track, attached directly to the ceiling, with pinch pleat curtains to obtain the best stack back. For this window, which has sufficient space for a curtain pole, I have used a simple, though very effective, slouch heading.

See Project 29: Slouch Curtain, page 172.

A modern look

For a more modern look I have used banner valances that are contrast-lined and hung over a decorative pole. Small roller or Roman blinds beneath can be made to complement the valances perfectly by using the same shape for their bottom hem.

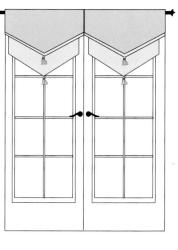

See Project 16: Banner Valance, page 150.

6 Dealing with sloping floors

If your want your curtains to draw, but the measurements from floor to ceiling across the window are not consistent, you have two choices: you can cut and make the curtains themselves at a slope. However, although the curtains will look fine when they are drawn across the window, when they are drawn back during the day they will look uneven, unless of course they are held in a tieback.

Alternatively, you can adjust the track so that it is parallel to the floor; if you have a severely sloping floor and a sloping ceiling, this is the best solution. The track is fitted straight on to the wall in a position that is parallel to the floor, and the cornice board is fitted parallel to the ceiling.

- *How do you hang curtains in a room where the floor slopes?*
- *What if both the floor and the ceiling slope?*

The dotted line indicates the true horizontal, and the solid line the actual floor and ceiling.

Beside the window, measure from the floor to the track position to ensure that the track is parallel with the floor. Then measure from the top of the cornice board to the ceiling to ensure that they are parallel. When you attach the valance or cornice to the board, the track is covered and everything looks square.

7 Multiple windows

The main point to decide upon is whether you want to dress the whole wall or simply the separate windows, as shown in the two drawings below. The first example is grand and adds height to the room – wonderful for a drawing room. The second example would be perfect for a child's room, as the windows are smaller and the wall space between them could be used for pictures.

- *If you have several windows close together, should you treat them as one or dress them separately?*
- *Can you use blinds on multiple windows for a more modern look?*
- *If you have quite plain windows, what treatment will make them look grander?*

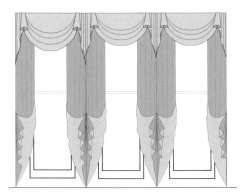

A luxurious look

These curtains have a contrast lining and are simply hooked back with a loop or ring placed on the leading edge of each curtain. The swags can be made as formal swags, with the addition of small tails, or they can be made in a less formal fashion, like eyelet swags.

See Project 6, The Classic Swag and Tail Treatment, page 118 and Project 20, Eyelet Swag, page 158.

A simple look

These windows are dressed with a simple ruffle-headed valance, which is contrast lined. The heading above the slot is arranged to show glimpses of the lining. Reefed blinds complete the window treatment.

See Project 27, Reefed Blind, page 169 and Project 14, Ruffle-headed Curtain, page 146

An informal look

Three separate windows can be joined together with a cornice for a more unified look. A double-layered treatment with a simple sheer gives a lighter, airier look to the room. The main curtains can be hooked over holdbacks when they are not in use.

See Project 4; The Classic Cornice, page 109.

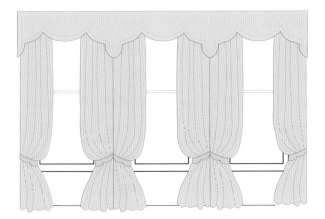

A traditional look

For something much grander, you could use the same cornice with a contrast trim and one pair of curtains for each window, each with a contrast leading edge. Tiebacks also add to the more formal look.

See Project 31, Bordered Cornice with a Cover and a Swag, page 177; Technique 101, Making Contrast Leading Edges, page 92 and Project 5, The Classic Tieback, page 115.

8 Arched windows

Arched windows can be decorated in almost any style as you can see from the designs shown below. They do take a little more thinking about than ordinary rectangular windows, but don't be put off as the finished effects can be spectacular.

- *What are the best styles to use if you want to show the shape of the arch rather than simply fitting a track straight across to top of the window. Can swags be used in some way?*
- *Will blinds work at arched windows?*

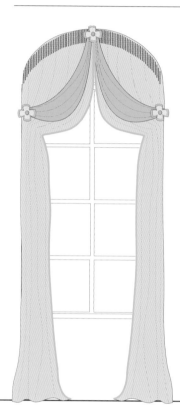

Swags at an arch

Separate over-swags can be attached by Velcro to small pieces of wood fitted to the inside of the recess, in front of the curtains. Maltese crosses complete the picture.

See Project 31, Bordered Cornice with a Cover and a Swag, page 177 and Technique 97, Making Maltese Crosses, page 89.

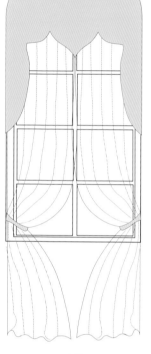

Accentuating the shape of the arch

A lambrequin or cornice made by covering 6mm (¼in) plywood. The window shape lends itself beautifully to this cornice design over soft muslin drapes.

See Project 4, The Classic Cornice, page 109; Project 33, Voile Curtains with Informal Pleats, page 182 and Technique 38, Cutting Sheer Fabrics, page 42.

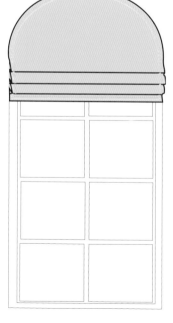

A formal blind

A simple Roman blind can be enhanced with a millinery petersham ribbon border or decorative braid.

See Project 7, The Classic Roman Blind, page 124; Project 27, Reefed Blind, page 169 and Project 19, Eyelet Blind, page 156.

Softening the shape of a blind

A softer, traditional style of blind with decorative cord and key tassels makes for a more relaxed treatment. A fan blind is another style which gives a less formal look and which can be accessorised easily.

See Project 11, Fan Blind, page 141.

9 Bay windows

Bay windows can offer quite a challenge, both from the point of view of the actual design and in terms of the hardware needed (curtain tracks etc). Also, the way in which you dress a bay can change its proportions dramatically.

- *What is the simplest way to curtain a bay window?*
- *How should you dress a bay window to minimise heat loss?*
- *What do you do if the bay ceiling is lower than the ceiling of the room?*

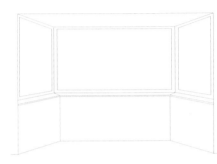

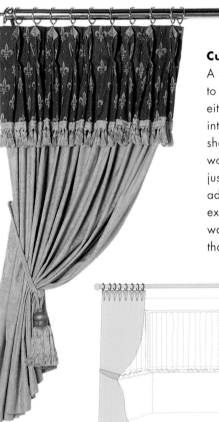

A low-ceilinged bay window

This is very typical of bays in smaller houses. The ceiling of the bay is lower than the ceiling in the rest of the room, and there is very little space between the top of the window frame and the bay ceiling. It also has a deep window ledge, though sadly it is not at a height that could be useful in creating a window seat.

Curtaining-off the bay

A very simple way of dressing this window is to use a pole on the outside of the bay with either working or dress curtains with an interesting heading, like the cut-away goblet shown, left. Simple sheers or secondary working curtains on the inside of the bay can just skim the sill. This design really helps to add height to the room, though to some extent it cuts off the bay. This is also a good way of keeping heat in the room, assuming that there isn't a radiator in the bay itself.

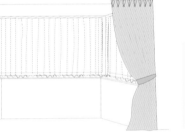

See Project 30, Cut-away Goblet-headed Curtain, page 174.

Dressing the bay

If you unite the bay with a narrow cornice that is in the correct proportion to the short curtains, you can achieve the look of a fully dressed window. It never ceases to amaze me how curtains can change a room. In this example I have also used purchased roller blinds to add another element to the window and to visually fill the bay.

A traditional bay

This very traditional bay has an extremely attractive valance, with pleats that almost form jabots. Classically elegant proportions give a fairly simple and uncluttered look, while retaining a traditional feel.

See Project 4, The Classic Cornice, page 109.

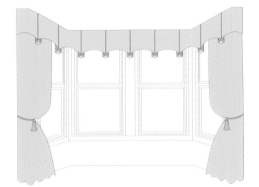

See Project 13, Pleated Valance, page 144.

10 Designing swag and tail treatments

The design element of swags and tails is perhaps the most daunting part of the whole operation. The only way to get it right is to make a scale drawing like the one shown below: it will solve all your problems.

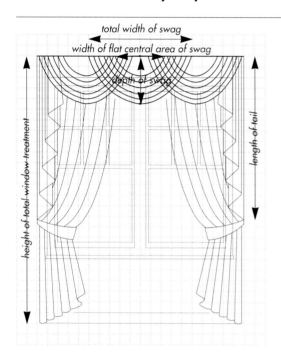

- How long should you make the tails?
- How deep should the swags be?
- How far should the separate swags overlap each other?

These slightly pointed swags have a more contemporary feel than traditional, gently rounded ones.

Classic swag and tail treatment

A treatment made from the scale drawing on the left will look like the illustration on the right.

See Project 6, The Classic Swag and Tail Treatment, page 118.

Here are some guidelines that will help you when you are making your scale drawing.

1 The deepest part of the swag is usually one-fifth of the depth of the total window treatment.

2 The longest part of the tail is normally twice as long as the deepest part of the swag. You will see many examples that are shorter than this, but they tend to look a little 'chopped off'. The tails can of course be even longer, up to two-thirds of the whole window treatment, which will look very dramatic. Long tails also add height to a room and make your window look much more elegant.

3 In most cases, I prefer the shortest part of the tail to be approximately the same length as the deepest part of the swag.

4 To make a window look wider, put the swags on top of the tails. To make a window look taller, place the tails on top of the swags.

Stripes on swags

I have read, and been told many times, that you cannot use stripes on swags if you are going to cut them on the cross. I disagree with this statement; I think that if you spend time working out the placing of the template on the fabric before cutting they can look very interesting.

I would probably only use stripes as shown for equal numbers of swags on a single window. If you are making swags for two adjacent windows, you can have the stripes running in opposite directions on each window, then you can have as many swags as you like.

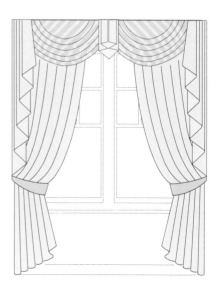

11 Making cornice boards

Cornice boards undoubtedly offer the simplest way of suspending a valance, cornice or swags and tails. They are substantial, so they do not allow anything to sag; they prevent dust from soiling the very top of the curtain, and they do not allow the light to shine up the back of the curtains onto the ceiling. This is especially useful if you hate being woken by sunlight!

For full-length lined or interlined curtains, I would make the cornice board to the dimensions below. The board must be deep enough to allow the curtains to be drawn without disturbing the valance. If the curtains are smaller, and perhaps not interlined, you can adjust the measurements accordingly. If you wish to give a good square corner to a long valance, the side pieces could be extended in length.

17.5cm (6½in)

15cm (6in)

Assembling the board

I normally make cornice boards from 2.5cm (1in) planed softwood. They don't take any great joinery skills to make, especially if your local wood yard will cut the pieces to size. You will need the top piece, two side pieces and eight 4cm (1½in) countersink screws.

Screw down through the top piece into the edges of the side pieces, with four screws at each end, being careful not to split the wood. If you have a drill, use a small drill bit to make pilot holes for the screws. As the wood is soft, if you do not have a drill you will probably be able to manage by using a bradawl or even a nail tapped into the wood and then removed, leaving a hole in which to insert your screw.

Using netting staples

The least expensive method of attaching a valance to a cornice board is with netting staples. They provide a firm fixing for standard curtain or pin-on hooks. The hooks are dropped into netting staples hammered into the front edge and returns of the board. As hooks have to line up with the staples, it is easier to put the hooks in the curtain when you are up the ladder.

Using Velcro

The method of fixing I use most often is Velcro. This makes it so simple to attach the valance to the cornice board and equally easy to remove it for cleaning.

Stick adhesive hook Velcro to the front edge and returns of the cornice board with a staple at each end to secure it. Sew loop Velcro to the back of the valance instead of curtain tape, or use Velcro-compatible tape, which simply presses onto the Velcro on the board.

Velcro for top bands

Using adhesive-backed Velcro on top of the board is particularly suitable for hanging heavy or bulky valances and where you do not want to see machine lines attaching Velcro to the valance. Sew-on loop Velcro is machined to a fabric band, which is divided for a snug fit at the corners.

See Technique 69, Making Top Bands, page 67.

Fitting the board

Fasten the cornice board to the wall with angle brackets. Screw a bracket to the wall, 10cm (4in) in from the edge of the board. Then rest the board on the brackets and screw up into it. You should have a bracket every metre (yard), so for a 200cm (78in) cornice board you should have three brackets. If you are hanging very heavy curtains from the cornice board, you may need extra brackets.

12 Placing cornice boards, tracks or poles

Placing a track if you have already fitted a cornice board is an easy matter, unless you have a sloping floor.

See Technique 6, Dealing with Sloping Floors, page 17.

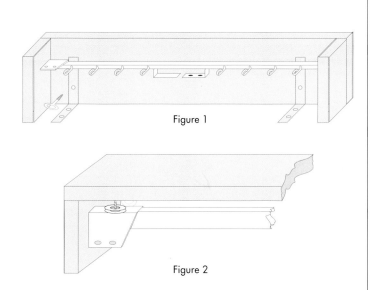

Figure 1

Figure 2

A corded track, preferably one made of metal with nylon gliders, is always helpful in maintaining the good looks of your curtains. It ensures low maintenance and trouble-free curtain drawing. The track should be fitted to the centre of the underside of the cornice board (Figure 1). To allow a gap for the angle brackets to pass under the track, spacers or washers may be required for the track-fitting screws (Figure 2).

To complete the end of the treatment, a "vine eye" can be screwed into the cornice board, level with the gliders and with the end bracket of the curtain track (Figure 1). The last hook of your curtain would be placed into this vine eye to return the curtains snugly to the wall.

The actual position of a track, pole or cornice board can be accurately assessed from your scale drawing, but as a guide the lowest part of the ring or glider should be placed a minimum of 15cm (6in) above the window. This is not always possible due to architectural restrictions, but it does ensure that curtain tapes and hooks are neatly hidden, which will improve the view of the room from outside the building.

I also recommend that tracks, poles and cornice boards are positioned a minimum of 15cm (6in) past the edge of the window on each side. The larger the window the greater the distance you will need if you wish to draw the curtains well back from the window to allow maximum light into the room.

13 Fittings for arches

There are a number of methods of attaching curtains, valances, cornices, blinds and even swags and tails to an arch. Probably one of the cheapest and most effective ways is to take a template of the arch and use this to cut out a wooden curve to fit the arch exactly. You could use ply, blockboard or MDF, and to save on wastage I would tend to cut the curve in two halves, joining them together in the centre.

See Technique 14, Making Templates for Arches, page 24.

The curve can be fitted in place either with small angle brackets attached to the back or, if you are using 2.5cm- (1in-) thick wood, you can drill and screw directly through the wooden curve into the wall, which gives a really neat appearance. If the wood is painted to match the recess it will be barely noticeable from outside the window.

The wooden curve can be positioned either at the front of the recess (Figure 1) or set back within it (Figure 2). I would not recommend putting it too close to the glass as you may have problems with moisture staining the curtain lining. The window treatment is attached to the curve with Velcro or netting staples. Stick adhesive hook Velcro to the wood, notching it to fit to the curves. An occasional staple will ensure that the Velcro stays permanently in place.

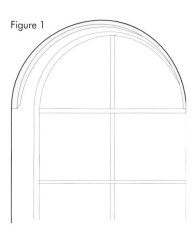

Figure 1

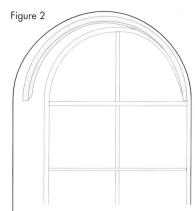

Figure 2

14 Making templates for arches

In almost all cases, to make a blind or a curtain, or simply to order a bent-to-measure track, you will have to make a template of the arch you want to dress.

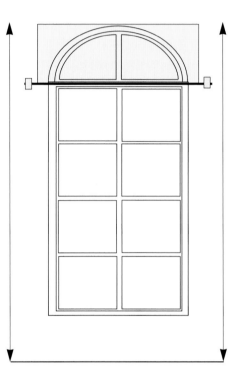

To make the template, first measure from the floor to the base of the arch and mark the position of the base with a piece of masking tape. Using the same measurement, mark the base of the arch on the opposite side of the window. Place a piece of string across the window running from one piece of tape to the other. The string should be parallel to the floor, unless the floor slopes badly.

Using masking tape to secure it in position, place a piece of thick polythene over the arch with its lower edge against the string, as shown. An alternative to polythene is brown paper.

Using a permanent marker pen, trace the shape of the arch on the polythene. After the ink has dried, remove the template and cut out the shape. (This is sound advice from someone who once marked a customer's wallpaper by taking down the template before the marker-pen ink had dried.) If you are using brown paper, you can simply run your nail around the edge of the arch to mark the paper before cutting the template out.

Now you have an exact template of the arch. In an ideal world this will be exactly symmetrical and each curtain can be worked out from the same calculations, but as we all know, windows in buildings old or new are rarely ideal. As a double check, put the cut-out template back up to the arch, in the position where you are placing the rail, to check that the width of the arch does not taper in any way.

15 Making templates for window seats

Making a template for a window seat is most important if there is any shaping. For a straightforward rectangular window seat you can simply take measurements.

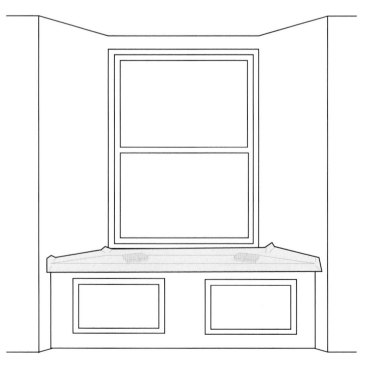

Cut a piece of brown paper to the largest dimensions possible for the seat then place it roughly in position. To prevent the paper moving too much, I usually place a couple of covered bricks (see Equipment, page 10) on top of the paper; they really help to make life easier.

Run your thumbnail (this is not a job for nail-biters) along the edges of the seat where the cushion will sit. Remove the template, cut away the excess paper and place the template back in position. As a double check I usually turn the template over, as often the cushion shape is not completely reversible. If this is the case, mark the template to show which is the top and the bottom.

16 Making templates for wooden, fabric-covered cornices

For a straightforward cornice shape, which will be covered with a plain or all-over patterned fabric, draw out the shape on brown paper or wallpaper lining paper. Sometimes the cornice shape is dictated by the design or pattern on the fabric itself, in which case thick polythene is the ideal material for making a template.

Cut and join fabric strips together, making sure you have enough depth and width to be able to manoeuvre the pattern, and to give you a minimum of 4cm (1½in) seam allowance around all sides. Cut a piece of polythene to the width of the cornice board, including the returns, and to the maximum depth you require from top to bottom.

Place the polythene shape over the fabric until you see exactly how you would like to place the pattern on the finished cornice. Using a permanent marker, draw the shape of the cornice around the pattern on the fabric.

Cut along the lines on the polythene and you will have an exact shape to cut both the plywood and your fabric to (with the addition of seam allowances).

17 Making patterns for swags

Swags can vary in shape, but the technique for working them out is almost always the same, no matter what the size or style of the final window treatment. Follow these steps, using your own measurements.

One piece of equipment I find invaluable is a piece of board that I call a swag-board. It is made from heavy fibreboard, which can be covered in fabric to help it to last longer. I wrap fabric around the fibreboard then stitch it securely along the edges using a circular needle, almost like upholstering the board. I usually have three or four swag boards approximately 100 x 20cm (39 x 8in). I can put a single swag onto each board and overlap the boards to see how the swags work together. This allows me maximum flexibility when working on large window treatments. If you prefer to use one large board, it is possible to obtain a piece of board up to 244cm

(96in) long. In a workroom the boards should be placed on a shelf at a good working height – roughly chest height.

The boards we have just mentioned are invaluable when pleating up swags, but they are also useful in helping to calculate measurements. The illustration

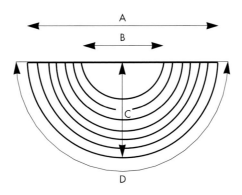

shown is for a single swag of average size and a traditional shape.

A measures 100cm (39in), the overall width of the swag, the outer edges of which may not always be visible as they may be overlapped by other swags or a tail.

B measures 50cm (20in) and is the flat or unpleated area of the swag. This measurement will vary tremendously according to individual design.

C measures 50cm (20in) and is the finished drop, or deepest part, of the swag. The measurement for this is usually one-fifth of the length of the total window treatment. This swag would therefore be suitable for a treatment measuring 250cm (100in) from the top of the cornice board to the floor. If you are using bullion fringe as a trim, its depth is usually added on to the finished length of the swag, as light can be seen through the fringe and so the base line is still the bottom edge of the fabric. However, if you are using a pleated or frilled edge it would be included as part of the total drop because it is solid.

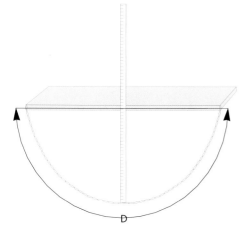

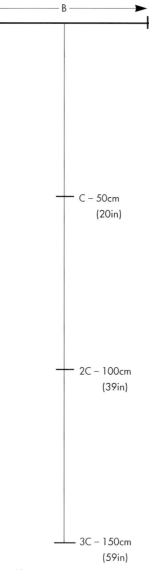

C – 50cm
(20in)

2C – 100cm
(39in)

3C – 150cm
(59in)

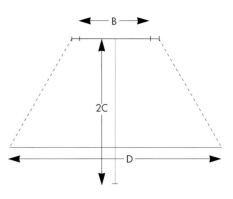

D is the measurement of the curved part of the valance. It is calculated by placing three pins on the swag board. The two outer pins indicate the finished width of the swag, while the third pin is at the centre of the swag. Suspend a piece of lead-weight chain or heavy cord from the outer pin on one side, then loop it across to the outer pin on the other side until the centre of the curve is 50cm (20in) below the board.

From the points where it just touches the board, measure the length of chain suspended between the pins.

Drawing a template
I usually draw templates on brown paper, as they keep their shape and do not tear easily while cutting out the various fabrics. Firstly, draw a horizontal line that measures length B, 50cm (20in), plus 6cm (2½in) at each end. This 6cm (2½in) lies under the first fold on each side.

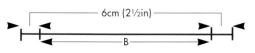

At right angles from the centre of B, draw a line the length you need for the pleating in the swag. This length varies between two and three times C, depending on the fullness you want and the thickness of the fabric. If you are using reasonably thick cotton or satin with an interlining, twice length C will be sufficient. If you are using dupion

silk or a self-lined voile without an interlining, up to three times C would look luxurious without being too full. Here we are using 2C as the depth.

Draw a horizontal line, D, the length of the measured chain, bisecting line C three quarters of the way down.

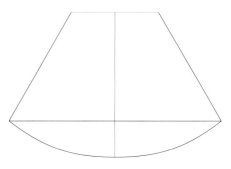

Freehand, or using an adjustable curve, join the lower points of the diagram with a curved line. I cannot give you a specific shape for this curve as it is a matter of choice. However, shown below are three varying curves and illustrations of the different shapes these curves give to the lower edges of the finished swag.

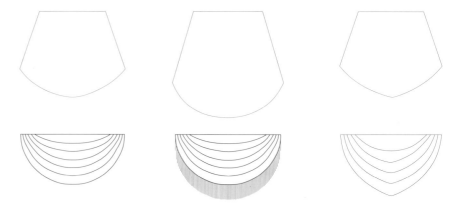

A smooth, evenly curved swag.

A much flatter outer band, suitable for showing off a wonderful trimming.

A rather interesting pointed swag.

18 Making patterns for tails

There are two main styles of tail, geometric tails and curved tails, and each requires a slightly different treatment.

The tail in these examples has a finished length of 150cm (59in) at its longest and 50cm (20in) at its shortest edge. It will use one full width of fabric, as anything less tends to look skimpy. This would be ideal with the swag shown in Technique 17, which measured 50cm (20in) at its deepest.

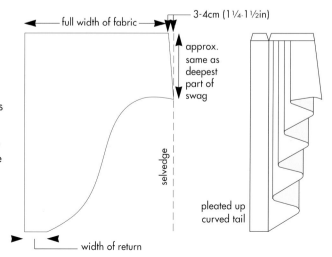

Geometric tails

Geometric tails look much more tailored and dramatic than curved tails. The leading edge should be completely vertical and they are often, though not always, folded so that all the pleats lie one on top of each other. Therefore, where the lining shows, each area of contrast colour should exactly match the others. Staggering the pleats very slightly, as we have done here, reduces the bulk at the top but keeps the clean look.

A geometric tail can look particularly effective when used with a single large swag, or with swags draped over a wooden pole. I prefer these tails on windows that are tall and not too wide, as they enhance these elegant proportions rather than distracting the eye with a cluttered treatment.

It is best to cut a template in brown paper just as you did for the swag. If you are inexperienced this can then be translated onto lining fabric or an old sheet, and hung at the window to see if it drapes correctly.

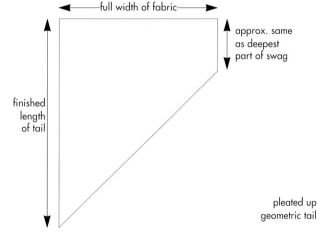

full width of fabric

approx. same as deepest part of swag

finished length of tail

pleated up geometric tail

Curved tails

This type of tail is much softer and more flowing. It looks particularly attractive with less formal fabrics such as cotton prints, or in treatments where there are a number of swags. The sloping leading edge adds a feeling of continuity by literally leading into the swag. Part of its appeal lies in the fact that it offers an individual look now the market has been flooded with mass-produced tails, all very similar. The curves are drawn freehand, which means that the areas where the contrast lining shows will vary in size, but both tails should match exactly. The folds are staggered so that the pleats overlap. On a very large window I would use one-and-a-half widths of fabric in each tail, to allow for a greater finished tail width, in keeping with the proportions of the window.

full width of fabric

3-4cm (1¼-1½in)

approx. same as deepest part of swag

selvedge

width of return

pleated up curved tail

19 Hook positions for curtain tracks

Knowing the curtain-hook position is critical for measuring and calculating quantities of fabric. The most common pencil pleat tapes have three hook positions, though there are many alternatives as there are varying depths of curtain rail. Always choose a curtain tape with a woven pocket as opposed to one with a corded pocket and then your curtains won't sag over time.

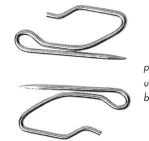

*pin-on hooks –
used with
buckram only*

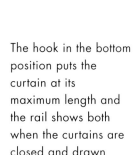

*sew-on hooks –
used with
buckram only*

standard hooks

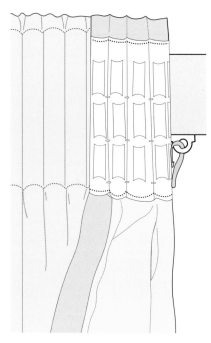

Here the hook is in the bottom hook position, which gives maximum coverage of the rail. This position is used when the track is without a cornice board. If, however, the track is under a cornice board, this position may not give sufficient clearance for the heading, so be cautious.

See Technique 71, Attaching Standard Hooks, page 69.

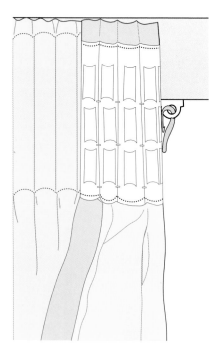

If you have a heading above the tape, putting the hook in the centre position may still bring the curtain level with the top of the track, though this will depend on the make and type of track you use. This hook position is useful as, if you are using the curtains under a cornice board, it is possible to adjust the length of the curtain slightly in either direction simply by moving the position of the hook.

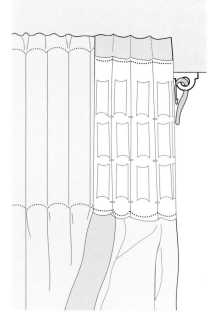

The hook in the bottom position puts the curtain at its maximum length and the rail shows both when the curtains are closed and drawn back. This position would only be used under a cornice board.

If you are using pin-on or sew-on hooks they will be attached in a similar position to the standard hooks, though they will not be restricted to the positions of the tape pockets.

20 Hook positions for curtain poles

If curtain tape is used with a pole, the hook is inserted in the top pocket so that the curtain hangs below the pole. In a similar way, a sew-on or pin-on hook should be positioned to show the pole, though not the small ring into which the hook is inserted.

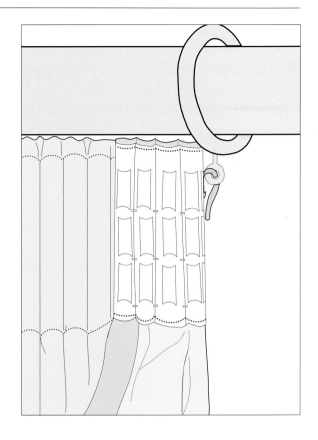

21 Hook positions for cornice boards with netting staples

For tape and hooks, the best solution for fitting either static curtains or a valance to a cornice board is to use netting staples in the edge of the board. Unless you particularly wish to alter the dimensions of the curtain treatment (by placing the hook in the centre pocket) use the hook in the top pocket. If you have used particularly thick wood for the cornice board however, you will need to move the curtain up to cover the board.

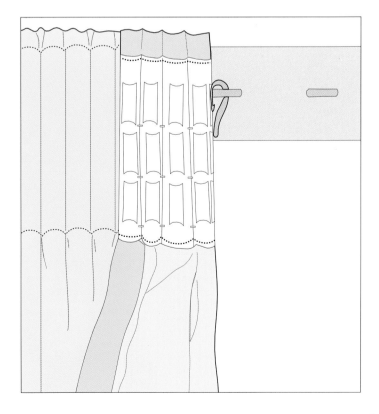

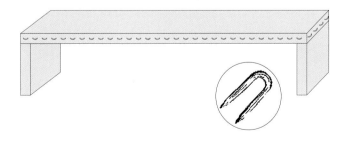

22 Measuring for curtains

The first step in making curtains is to take accurate measurements. This may sound obvious but it is amazing how often people will measure only roughly before cutting into expensive fabric.

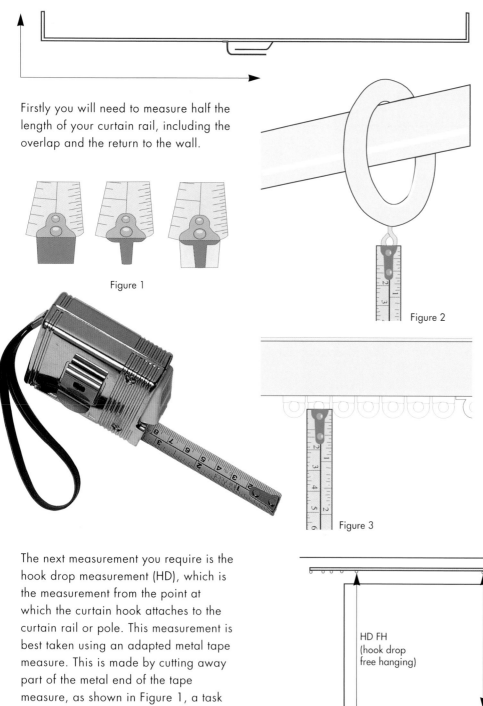

Firstly you will need to measure half the length of your curtain rail, including the overlap and the return to the wall.

Figure 1

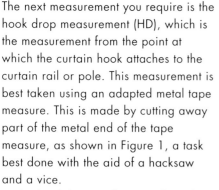

Figure 2

Figure 3

The next measurement you require is the hook drop measurement (HD), which is the measurement from the point at which the curtain hook attaches to the curtain rail or pole. This measurement is best taken using an adapted metal tape measure. This is made by cutting away part of the metal end of the tape measure, as shown in Figure 1, a task best done with the aid of a hacksaw and a vice.

This hook fits into the ring of a pole or to a curtain-rail glider, as shown in Figures 2 and 3. A good quality curtain

track is a worthwhile investment, especially if it is corded. It will prolong the life of your curtains by helping them keep their shape and preventing soiling by greasy hands.

The finished length of your curtains may be governed by many factors. In general the length you make your curtains will be one of the lengths shown in Figure 4.

When you have taken your measurements write them down in a book kept especially for the purpose. It is useful to have all the information together when shopping for the fabrics, as well as during making up. It is best to write the measurements down as follows: this is shorthand but it contains all the information you require and will not be misinterpreted at a later stage.

208cm (81½in) overall length of rail, including the overlap and returns.
239cm (93½in) HD to touch.
190cm (74½in) HD FH.

Once you have decided on the style of the window treatment you want and have taken the measurements required, you can work out the fabric quantities.

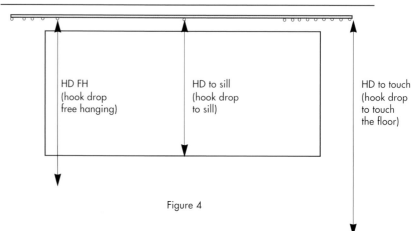

HD FH
(hook drop
free hanging)

HD to sill
(hook drop
to sill)

HD to touch
(hook drop
to touch
the floor)

Figure 4

23 Measuring for blinds

Blinds are frequently fitted in the window recess, which requires very careful measuring. Tiles are often extended into the recess in bathrooms and kitchens and so have to be taken into consideration when taking measurements.

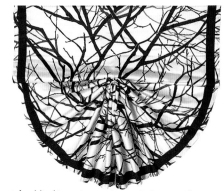

A fan blind is an interesting variation on a Roman blind (see Project 11, page 141).

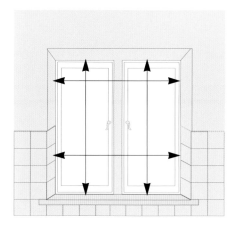
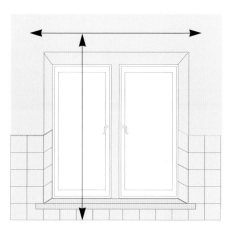

Take measurements in a number of positions, as shown above. The blind should be made to the narrowest dimension.

For blinds on the outside of the recess, make sure you completely cover the window recess, especially if you wish to cut out the light as much as possible. When placing a blind outside the recess you may prefer to use a narrower wooden batten measuring 2.5 x 2.5cm (1in x 1in) to hang the blind from.

A forward rolling reefed blind with decorative tabs (see Project 27, page 169).

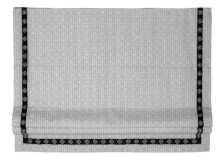

The classic Roman blind can be decorated with borders and trimmings (see Project 7, page 124).

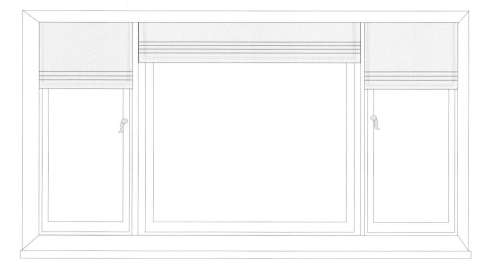

Larger windows can be covered with one single blind or the width can be divided according to the structure of the window. Each division should be measured accordingly and as small a gap as possible left between the blinds.

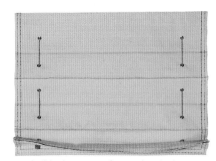

An eyelet blind gives a softer modern look (see Project 19, page 156).

24 Measuring for loose covers

Before you measure, place a strip of masking tape round the legs of the chair at the piping line, a quarter to a third of the height from the seat to the floor, plus making-up allowances. Use a cloth tape to measure curved parts and a metal tape or rule for the remainder.

A wooden chair

This type of chair is ideal for a beginner to work on. A cover will completely transform it, giving you the inspiration and encouragement to progress further. A chair with a very curved back or a great deal of carving may not be suitable. If in doubt, try cutting and pinning the back of the chair with pieces cut from an old sheet or scrap fabric. You will soon find out if it is possible to cover the shape.

ABBREVIATIONS

I B	Inside Back	S Seat
O B	Outside Back	F B Front Border
I A	Inside Arm	B Border
O A	Outside Arm	A F Arm Facing

A simple chair

In some ways this type of chair is even simpler as you can pin the fabric pieces to the upholstery to hold them in position. This also may be your first introduction to 'tuckaways' – areas of the chair into which a flap of fabric can be pushed to help hold the cover in position. However, not all chairs of this style have a tuckaway where the inside back meets the seat, so don't worry if yours hasn't.

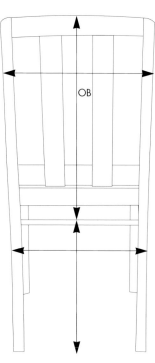

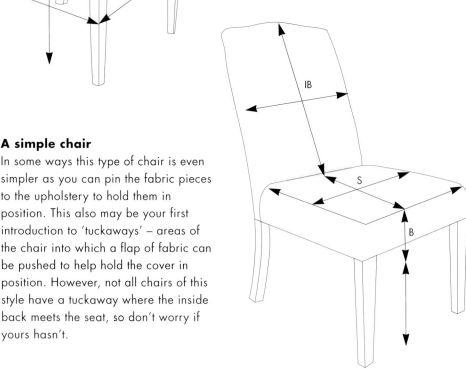

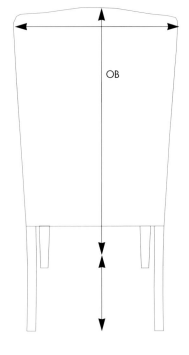

25 Measuring for tiebacks

Obviously the length, shape and position of the tieback are the first priorities. I would rarely determine any of these factors until the curtains are hanging in position, unless I had an identical window in another room, using identical weight of fabric and lining. It is so easy to make a mistake, either over the bulk of the curtains or the tieback position, with the end result that the curtains are held too tightly and therefore crease; or alternatively, that the tieback is too loose and hangs down instead of being held in position or the overall length allows an area of wall to show, which looks extremely unsightly. The overall length is a simple matter to decide: hold a piece of fabric around the curtain until you are satisfied with the effect, then measure the length of the fabric, bearing in mind that this should include the ring or fabric loop which attaches the tieback to the tieback hook.

The position of the tieback is really a personal choice and depends on the size and style of the window you are furnishing. For a standard window the position of the tieback would normally be one-third of the length of the total window treatment up from the floor, but they can be placed in whatever position suits your design. Be aware that if tiebacks are placed at a very high level it may make it impossible to release them to draw the curtains.

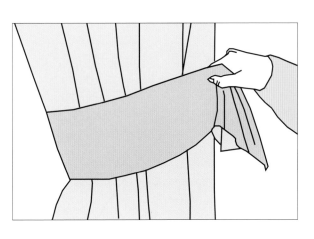
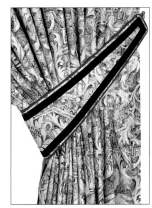

26 Measuring for valances or cornices

Careful measuring is critical, particularly for a valance with a stiffened top or a fabric-covered cornice, as they are very difficult to adjust once completed.

Initially take the straightforward measurements of the front of the board and along the returns. In old houses, a picture rail might interfere with the returns of the cornice. Use a profile gauge, available from DIY shops, to reproduce the shape, then cut the wood for the cornice to fit around it. The gauge is made up of a number of needles that, when pressed against the picture rail or moulding, adjust to the shape.

As well as the measurements of the front of the board and the returns, use a set square to check that the angle between the wall and the board is exactly 90°. If it isn't square, make a thin card template by using loose staples or drawing pins to attach a piece of card to the end of the cornice board as shown. Crease the card to fit exactly against the wall and you will have a perfect template to cut the end of the buckram or wood to. Check both ends in this way.

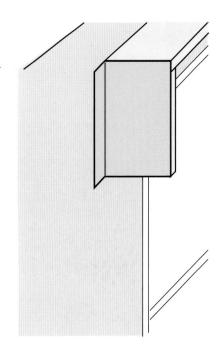

27 Calculating fullness and quantities for curtains

Fullness is always calculated in the same way, whether be it for valances or curtains. Gathered blinds, dressing-table frills and bed valances also use the same basic principles. Use the calculations shown here and refer to the charts for fullness and making-up allowances.

To calculate fullness I will use as an example a window with a 208cm (81½in) overall length of rail, including the overlap and returns, and a 239cm (93½in) HD to touch.

If the fabric is plain, has a vertical stripe or is woven without a repeating pattern, then calculating the amount of fabric is simple.

To find out the number of widths you require if you are using a standard 2.5cm (1in) curtain heading tape with double fullness (see chart), you need to multiply the overall length of the rail by two.

208cm (81½in)	x 2	= 416cm (163in)
length of rail	*double fullness*	*total width of fabric required*

To convert this figure into fabric widths, you need to divide this total width by the width of the fabric, which is usually 120-140cm (48-56in).

416cm (163in)	÷ 120cm (48in)	= 3.466 widths
total width required	*width of the fabric*	*number of widths*

This figure is usually taken up to the next whole figure, giving us four widths of fabric. Depending on the window and your design, the widths would probably be joined to make one pair of curtains with two widths of fabric joined together in each curtain.

To allow for hems at the bottom of the curtain and turnings at the top, you need to add a minimum of 25cm (10in) to each length of fabric (which are usually called 'drops').

239cm (93½in)	+ 25cm (10in)	= 264cm (103½in)
hook drop	*allowances*	*cut length of curtain*

Therefore, to make these curtains we need:

264cm (103½in)	x 4	= 1056cm (414in)
cut length	*number of widths*	*plain fabric*

Of course for a patterned fabric the calculations would be done differently to allow for pattern matching.

See Technique 30, Calculating Quantities for Patterned Fabrics, page 36.

How to Use This Chart

The quantities given are purely a useful guideline as there are so many variations in style. The first column refers to the types of heading I would recommend using with working curtains.

The second column refers to the amount of fullness required to make each type of heading look its best. Standard 2.5cm (1in) tape is used mainly under a valance or cornice, and although I have heard people say they use pencil-pleat tape even under a cornice because it hangs better, I must confess I have never thought it make a great deal of difference. A pencil-pleat heading, with its three hook positions, used under a cornice or valance does, however, allow you to adjust the length of your curtains merely by altering the position of the hook. For a superb hang, even under a cornice, I would recommend using hand-sewn pinch pleats. They hang in even folds and the curtains will draw back into a smaller space.

In the third column, the amount of fabric quoted for making-up allowances is the minimum quantity for that style of heading.

A guide to working out fabric quantities for curtains

Type of heading required	Minimum fullness per width of fabric	Minimum making allowances
2.5cm (1in) tape	2 x fullness	25cm (10in)
Pencil pleat	2.5-3 x fullness	25-30cm (10-12in)
Deep pencil pleat	2.5-3 x fullness	25-30cm (10-12in)
Mini pleat	2.5 x fullness	25cm (10in)
Hand-sewn pinch or goblet pleats	2.25-2.5 x fullness	35-45cm (14-18in)
Hand gathered	2.5-3 x fullness	25-30cm (10-12in)
Slot heading	2-3 x fullness	30-50cm (12-20in)
Tab curtains	1.5-2.5 x fullness	according to design

Pencil-pleat tape

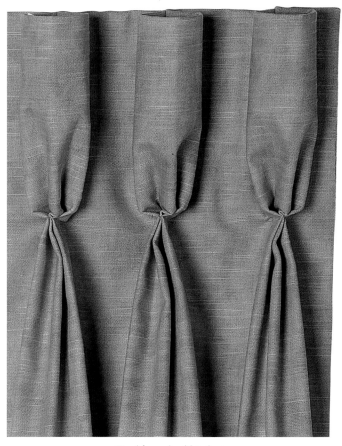

Hand-formed goblet pleats

Standard 2.5cm (1in) tape

28 Calculating fullness and quantities for valances

Valances should always have more fullness than the curtains beneath them. If you use equal amounts of fabric, the valance will look skimpy.

Type of heading	Fullness preferred	Amount for making up allowances
2.5cm (1in) tape	2-2.5 times	Up to 12cm (4¾in)
Pencil-pleat tapes including Velcro-compatible tapes	3-3.5 times	8-12cm (3-4¾in)
Hand-gathered headings	3-3.5 times	8-12cm (3-4¾in)
Slot headings	3 times	8-25cm (3-10in)
Hand-sewn pinch and goblet pleats	2.5-3 times	Minimum 14cm (5½in)

29 Measuring pattern repeats

Unless you are using a plain fabric, you need to know the pattern repeat before you can calculate how much fabric you require.

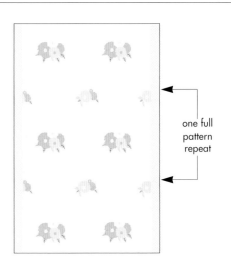

one full
pattern
repeat

The majority of fabrics have a normal pattern repeat that is measured on the selvedge. You can tell if it is a normal repeat by folding the fabric in half widthways, and bringing the two selvedges together. If the pattern matches along the selvedge, this is a normally repeating fabric.

To measure the pattern repeat, measure down from one point to the next identical point on the pattern.

30 Calculating quantities for patterned fabrics

When cutting patterned fabric for curtains each drop is cut to the measured length. The start of the next drop will be at the same point on the pattern as the start of the first drop. There will usually be a piece of waste fabric between drops. The following example will make the method a little clearer.

See Technique 27, Calculating Fullness and Quantities for Curtains, page 34.

Take as an example the measurements of the curtains discussed in Technique 27. If the pattern repeat on the fabric is 60cm (24in), the minimum cut length for each drop is 264cm (103½in) plus 60cm (24in).

264cm (103½in)	÷ 60cm (24in)	= 4.4
minimum cut length	*length of repeat*	*number of repeats*

Round up the number of repeats to the next whole number, in this case, five.

60cm (24in)	x 5	= 300cm (120in)
length of repeat	*number of repeats*	*cut length per drop*

To find the total length of fabric you need to make these curtains, you must multiply the length required for each drop of fabric by the number of widths needed.

300cm (120in)	x 4	= 1200cm (480in)
length of each drop	*number of drops*	*total amount of fabric*

This metreage does not take into account cutting the fabric with the pattern shown to its best advantage. For that reason where there is a 'set' pattern rather than an all-over pattern I always add one full repeat to the total metreage.

1200cm (480in)	+60cm (24in)	=1260cm (504in)
fabric required	*one full repeat*	*fabric required for correct placing of pattern*

31 Calculating quantities for half-drop or dropping patterns

Sometimes the pattern does not match across the fabric. Instead it matches at a point further down, often about halfway between repeats on the other edge.

Always confirm the type of repeat when you are ordering fabric. If you can't do this, the only way to be certain when calculating fabric quantities is to work out the design as though it was a straightforward repeat and add half a repeat for each fabric drop, except for the first drop you cut.

As illustrated, cut the first drop of fabric to your required measurement. Place this drop next to the remainder of the fabric. Make sure the patterns match then mark and cut the second drop accordingly.

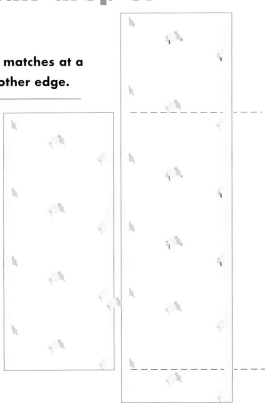

Cutting half widths

The situation is emphasised if you are adding a half width. The illustration below shows how to tackle this problem on a pair of one-and-a-half-width curtains.

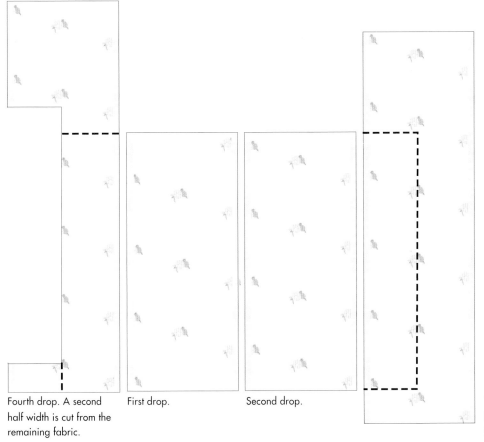

Fourth drop. A second half width is cut from the remaining fabric.

First drop.

Second drop.

Third drop. A half width is cut leaving the remaining fabric intact for the other half width.

Non-matching patterns

Some patterns seem as though they do not match at all. This is usually because the screen used to print them was originally designed for a wider fabric.

In some cases you can match the pattern by moving farther into the fabric, but this is rarely practical as too much of the fabric width is lost. The more usual course is to make sure that the motifs or flowers line up across the width. Make sure there is plenty of fullness in the curtains and hang them so that the joins are concealed. Some fabrics such as panel prints, hand-painted panels and certain woven fabrics are meant to be hung in this way, in fact it is part of their appeal.

32 Translating shapes for valances

This is an absolutely invaluable method for converting a shape from a flat paper template to a gathered valance. You can use this to translate any shape and length of valance.

See Technique 28, Calculating Fullness and Quantities for Valances, page 35.

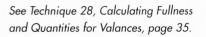

Cut and join the fabric valance strips; each one should include top and bottom seam allowances. Press open the seams and, right-sides facing, fold the strip in half lengthways.

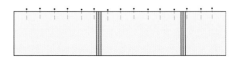

Fold the fabric into quarters, eighths and sixteenths. Mark the top of each fold with a pin. Unfold the fabric, apart from the single fold in the center. Work with the fabric in half, as the valance is symmetrical. Starting at the outer edge, measure from the pin at the top of the valance to the required depth, following the measurements on the template.

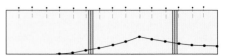

Mark each measurement with a fading marker or tailor's chalk. Move to the next pin and repeat the operation.

When you have measured down from each pin all the way across the fabric, you will have with a series of marks that indicate exactly where to cut the fabric. The width between each mark will, of course, be much wider than on the paper template, but when made up, the marked fabric will reproduce exactly the shape you originally designed. Join all the marks together to produce a cutting line.

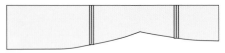

Cut away the excess fabric.

Using the dimensions from your scale drawing, draw and cut out full-size on a piece of brown paper, half the finished shape of your valance, including the returns. If you are unsure as to whether the template is right, you can tape it in position at the window to check that your dimensions are correct.

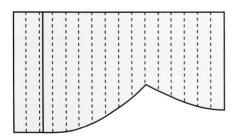

Fold the template into halves, quarters, eighths and sixteenths. If the valance is very wide, or a particularly intricate shape, you might even need to fold it into thirty-seconds.

Draw pencil lines down the fold lines to make them easier to see. This template is the shape of the finished valance, so now you need to add seam allowances. Measure each of the vertical lines and add a minimum of 4cm (1½in) before writing the measurements on each line as shown. This illustration shows a small section of this paper template as an example.

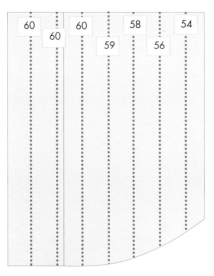

33 Translating shapes from arches and angles for curtains and valances

Having made an exact template of your arch (see Technique 14, Making Templates for Arches, page 24), double check that the arch doesn't taper by putting the template back up to the window in the position where you are going to place the rail. In an ideal world it will also be exactly symmetrical and each curtain can be worked out from the same calculations, but as we all know, windows in buildings old or new are rarely ideal. If the arch is not symmetrical you must work out the shape for each curtain separately.

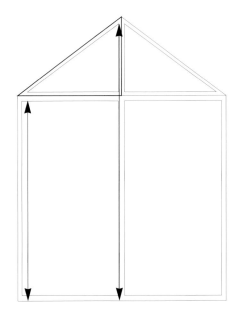

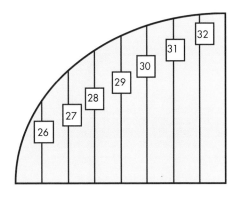

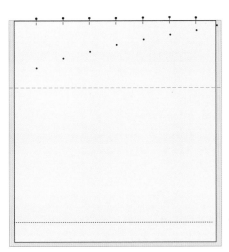

Firstly, take one half of the template and fold it into eighths. Flatten it out and draw lines along the folds. Mark in the measurement of each line (see example above), plus the allowances needed for the turnings at the top of the curtain.

Make up the curtain as usual and place it with the lining face down on the work table. Using the measurement from the floor to the horizontal string at the bottom of the arch (less clearance if required), measure up from the bottom hem and mark a line across the curtain at that height. You can either draw a line with a fading marker pen or use a line of pins.

Measure the width of the curtain and divide it into eighths with pins. Using a metre stick, measure from the horizontal marked line towards the top of the curtain, following the measurements on your template. Connect the dots, pin the layers together and trim away the excess fabric.

Curtains for an angled window are much simpler as they can be made completely by measurements. Measure the longest and shortest points of the angled part of the window.

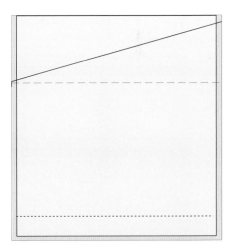

Place a row of pins across the curtain at the shortest measurement. Mark the longest point, add heading allowances to each measurement and mark the cutting line. It is possible to mark the curtain without the horizontal line of pins but there is a tendency for the layers to slip, so I find this method more accurate.

34 Translating double shapes for valances

For a cornice board with a gently curved top you may well be able to make a straight valance and attach it to the curved board with no ill effect on the hang of the fabric. For a valance that has a defined shape at both the top and bottom edges (see Project 34, Cornice with a Shaped Top, page 184) this is not possible; you have to translate the shape on both the top and bottom edges of the valance. The technique is basically the same as that for translating a single shape, you just take it further.

Make a paper template of the valance and fold into eighths and sixteenths. Draw a horizontal line right across the template at a point where it will not interfere with either of the curved edges. On each fold, measure from the center line to the top edge. Add on the amount you require for making-up allowances and write the measurement on each of the upper lines. Repeat the process for the lower section in exactly the same way (see example below).

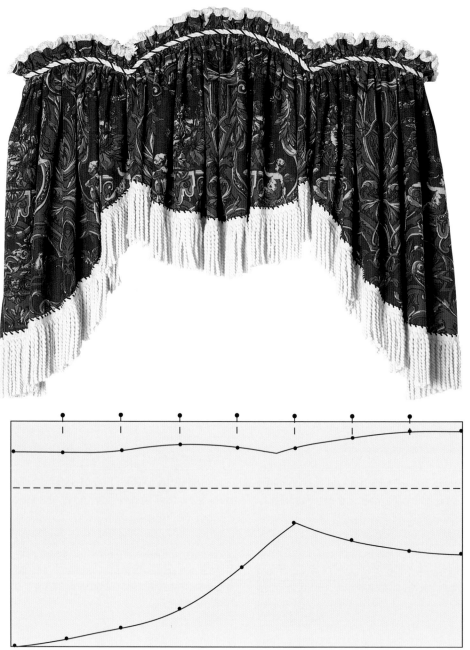

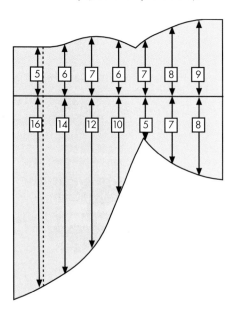

When you have cut and joined the fabric for the valance, divide it into sections with pins as described previously. Mark a horizontal line to correspond with the line on the template on the wrong side of the fabric with tailor's chalk or a fading marker.

On each of the divisions, mark the correct distances from the horizontal line towards the top and the bottom of the fabric with dots. Join the dots together and cut out the fabric for a perfect double-shaped valance.

See Technique 32, Translating Shapes for Valances, page 38.

35 Cutting plain and lining fabrics

Ideally all fabrics are woven and finished with the vertical warp and horizontal weft threads absolutely at right angles to each other, and to the selvedge, but sadly this is rarely the case. For this reason, I almost always cut at right angles to the selvedge for closely woven fabrics and linings, and with the grain of the fabric for obvious weaves.

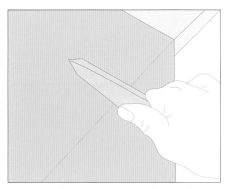

Place the fabric on the table with the selvedge against the long edge of the table and the point where you want to cut level with one end. Clamp the fabric in position. Rub the back of the scissors across the table at the cutting point to give you a good cutting line.
An alternative method is to use a

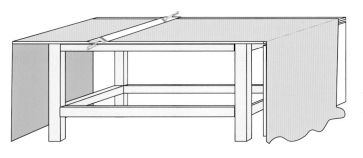

cutting mat, cutting ruler and rotary cutter. With the cutting mat beneath the fabric, clamp the long ruler to each edge of the table and cut against it with the rotary cutter.

If you do not have a large cutting mat, simply fold the fabric into four widthways, lay it on the mat and cut through all the layers together. The cutting wheel can cope with a considerable thickness of fine fabric, though do not attempt to cut bulky fabrics, which tend to stretch and twist, in this way.

If you are working on the floor, ensure that the fabric is as flat as possible and mark a right angle from the selvedge with a large T-square, or as a very inexpensive alternative, use pins and a strip of brown paper or thick wallpaper with a right-angled corner. Hold the fabric in place with covered bricks.

Cutting interlinings

I recommend three types of interlinings: fine domette; medium weight bump and for a heavier weight, I prefer stitched warp. This has no traditional warp threads, instead there are lines of stitching holding the weft threads together that make it somewhat more stable than the normal heavyweight bump, which has a terrible tendency to stretch.

I tend to cut all interlinings using scissors and usually following the weft thread. One trade secret, told to me some years ago, is to always add a couple of centimeters (1in) extra when you are cutting interlining then allow the cut pieces to 'rest', a little like pastry, for at least 12 and preferably 24 hours. The reason is that the interlining is stretched when it is put on the roll and to make it more stable it is best to leave it to regain its own shape. This does help, I promise.

After you have cut the lengths of fabric carefully fold them: if you don't put creases into the curtains you don't have to get them out!

36 Cutting velvets

Panic often sets in at the thought of cutting velvet, but practice this method on some waste fabric first and hopefully it will take away some of the worry.

The most important factor is to use only the 'V' of the scissors, not the points. This part of the scissors, because of its proximity to your hand I suppose, is much more sensitive and, provided you only attempt to cut short stretches, you will find you can actually 'feel' your way across the width following the thread of the fabric. You can also hear yourself cutting across a thread. Sounds odd doesn't it, but it is true.

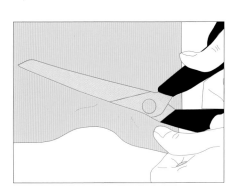

37 Cutting patterned fabrics

Before you start to measure out or cut off the curtain lengths, you must check that the weft threads which run across the fabric are at right angles to the selvedge, and also that the design is printed 'on the straight'. This means that the pattern runs true to the straight grain.

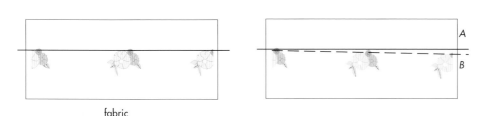

fabric

—— grain line

Above is a perfectly printed fabric, but sadly this rarely occurs. I check the pattern by clamping the sides of the fabric to the table, with the bottom edge hanging slightly over the end of the table. By running the back of the scissor blade across the fabric, pressing against the table edge underneath, you get a crease, which can be pressed out when necessary. This crease gives you a right angle. Check that the pattern falls correctly across this crease and that the weft threads run parallel with it. If you are working on the floor, as many home-sewers do, use a large sheet of card or a T-square and a

fading marker to check the right angle.

If the difference between A (the grain line) and B (the line of the printed pattern, represented by the dotted line), as shown on the diagram above, is greater than 4cm (1½in) I would go back to the suppliers and say that the fabric is not satisfactory. But don't forget that they will not entertain any complaints if you have cut the fabric.

If I can't cut the fabric as I prefer, that is, at right angles to the selvedge, I cut the fabric according to the pattern, following line B in the diagram.

Before cutting, I also unroll all the fabric and check for flaws, again so that the fabric can be returned if it is unsatisfactory. An occasional flaw is inevitable in any cloth so as I come

across them I mark the selvedge with two crossed pins. However, you should note that a manufacturer would consider a roll with up to four quite severe flaws to be perfect. (If you are concerned, it is best to specify the cut lengths you require when ordering from the manufacturer.)

When I have completed all the checks, I measure out all the pieces of fabric I require and mark the cutting points with a single pin on the selvedge nearest to me, being extremely careful to check the pattern match. It is much easier to pin out all the pieces at the same time and it often saves on waste.

Go back to the beginning of the roll and measure again to make absolutely certain that you have placed all your pins correctly.

Now you are ready to cut and for this stage, I like to use a long straight edge of wood or metal and a fading marker or tailor's chalk.

Measure out the first drop, check that the position on the pattern is correct and place the straight edge across the fabric to touch the right position on the pattern on the opposite selvedge. Draw a line. If the pattern occurs several times across the fabric, the line will not necessarily touch the pattern at the same point each time, but it must be correct at the edges where it will match.

38 Cutting sheer fabrics

Pulling a thread across the width of the fabric is the easiest way to mark a cutting line on a sheer, particularly if it is a slippery voile, which refuses to stay in one place while you try to cut a straight line.

With a pin, pick up one thread fairly close to the selvedge. If you are using very fine voile it may be better to pick up two threads. Pull on the thread and snap the end closest to the selvedge. Continue to pull the other end until it breaks. This will leave a gap in the weave of the fabric that you can trace until you find the broken thread. Pick up the thread again and continue pulling until you have a gap right across the curtain to use as a cutting line. If you are really lucky the thread will pull all the way across the width of the fabric without breaking.

39 Cutting on the cross for leading edges

Bound leading edges or contrast leading edges are much more interesting if they are cut on the cross, particularly if the fabric is a check or stripe.

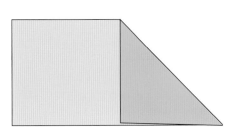

To make the first cutting line, fold the fabric as shown above, unless this does not tie in with the check. Occasionally you may need to adjust the angle of the fold to make the line travel through the check attractively.

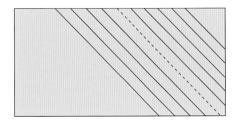

Once you have the first line, carefully measure the widths of fabric you require and mark them out before cutting. An even simpler method uses a cutting mat and rotary cutter.

See Technique 74, Cutting Piping Strips, page 70.

40 Cutting swags and tails

It is easy to glibly mention in passing that a swag should be cut on the cross wherever possible, but what exactly does that mean and what exactly is the reason for doing it?

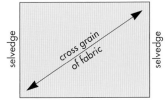

If you hold a piece of fabric and pull it along the weft or warp threads, it will not give or stretch very much. If, however, you pull on the cross, you will find the fabric has a lot more stretch and curves around corners more easily. It is this property that you utilise in your swag.

It is easy to distinguish swags cut on the straight grain of the fabric: instead of forming smooth curves the fabric hangs in small kinks along the folds. The only exception to this rule is velvet, which can be cut on the straight with all the pile running in the same direction. This is because velvet is soft and drapes fairly well on the straight, and because the pile gives different shade variations if it is cut on the cross.

Swags are normally interlined if the curtains are, and often with a lighter weight interlining to cut down bulk in the pleating-up. If the fabric has to be cut on the straight because of the size or the pattern, to help to tempt it into curves cut the interlining, and lining, on the cross.

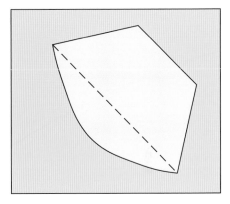

Using the paper template, cut out the main fabric, allowing 2cm (¾in) seam allowance all round. Cut the interlining to the exact size of the template. Cut out the lining, allowing 2cm (¾in) seam allowance at the top and sides, but only 1cm (½in) along the bottom edge. If you need to join fabric, do so before cutting it out. Offset a join so it doesn't run down the center of the swag.

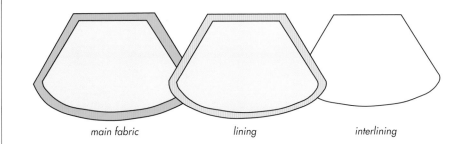

| main fabric | lining | interlining |

Cutting the tail

For an interlined tail, cut the main fabric and lining to the size of the template, adding 2cm (¾in) on all sides. Cut the interlining to the size of the template. If you are not interlining the tail, cut the main fabric and lining to the same size.

Patterns for Swags, page 25 and Technique 18, Making Patterns for Tails, page 27.

41 Joining plain and lining fabrics

Curtains absorb moisture and are baked by the sun or heating. If the selvedge weave is different from the main fabric, it will shrink at a different rate.

When you have cut all the pieces for your curtains, or even as you cut each one, take off the selvedges completely if it is tight or if the weave of the selvedges is closer then the rest of the fabric.

In both cases you are likely to run into problems with shrinkage on the seams and side hems. Do not simply notch the fabric: with plains particularly, the outline of the notches can show on the right side of the curtains and the selvedge between the notches can still shrink and pucker.

Ideally use an overlocker, as it can cut off the fabric and neaten it at the same time. If you do not have one available, use a zigzag stitch with a loose tension or, at the worst, pinking sheers.

With a plain fabric, join the pieces together using a stitch of about 2.8mm (⅛in) in length, a suitable thread and a sharp needle of a thickness to suit the fabric. If you are not sure what to use, consult your machine manual. I use size 10 to 16 needles, size 10 being the thinnest for the finer fabrics and size 16 being ideal for very heavy fabrics or for loose covers.

The amount you take up in the seam varies according to the width of the selvedge, but as a guide I like to take in at least 1cm (½in) of the main part of the fabric, hopefully giving a minimum of 2cm (¾in) from the edge of the piece of fabric.

If the curtains are cut correctly there is no need to pin or tack them together, it is, however, important that you hold the fabrics correctly when you are machining them together, as shown in the illustration below. Place the fabrics together carefully, without pulling either layer. Hold them firmly together both in front and behind the machine and allow the machine to pull the fabric through at its own pace.

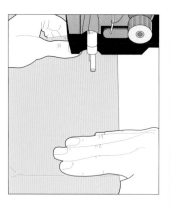

42 Joining velvets

This is another task which fills some people with dread, but like so many furnishing techniques, thinking about it is more worrying than doing it. The most important point in joining velvet is that the pile on both pieces runs in the same direction.

Joining velvet differs from joining other fabrics. Velvet curtains are usually made with the pile facing upwards so if you stroke them from the hem up to the heading, it will feel as though you are smoothing the pile the correct way. If you stroke the curtain in the opposite direction, you can feel the pile standing up. Having the pile running in the right direction adds lustre and richness to the colour. With some inexpensive velvets the colour can vary across the

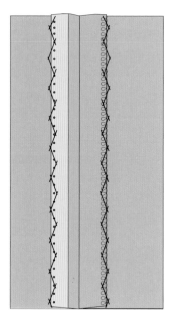

width of the fabric, which causes problems.

If you are joining two widths together, the selvedges will come together in the normal way. If you

are joining a half width to a full width, first overlock the long raw edge of the half width. This overlocked edge is then joined to the selvedge of the full width, giving you a curtain with selvedges on both the outer edges. Machine the widths together with a 2.8mm (⅛in) stitch, sewing in the same direction as the pile lies. You may find that one layer of the velvet will start to 'creep' over the other, in which case you must release the foot pressure a little.

Because of the pile it is not a good idea to press open the seams, unless of course you have a proper velvet pressing pad. Quite frankly, it isn't necessary. Simply run your thumb nail along the join on the wrong side of the curtain, again working with the pile. The selvedges tend to be soft and after a while they often curl. To prevent this use a large herringbone stitch, as shown left, to hold the selvedges in place.

For the side hems on a velvet curtain, turn in the selvedge to give exactly 3cm (1¼in) of pile. The lining then lies up against the edge of the pile, so you are stitching into the selvedge rather than into the pile when attaching the lining.

43 Joining patterned fabrics

A patterned fabric is a little more difficult to join than a plain fabric. The most important factors in making a successful join are holding the fabric correctly to prevent movement and taking care before you start to press the fold line.

See Technique 29, Measuring Pattern Repeats, page 36; and Technique 30, Calculating Quantities for Patterned Fabrics, page 36.

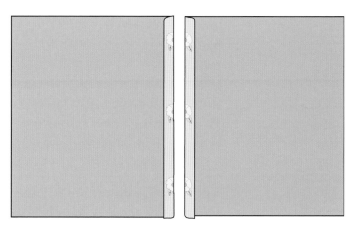

1 Place the two drops of fabric edge to edge, right-sides down. Fold back the selvedges until the patterns match and each edge is folded back by about the same amount. Measure the amount of pattern showing on one edge and press in this amount down the whole length of the fabric.

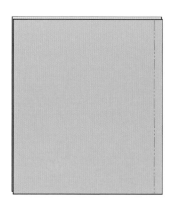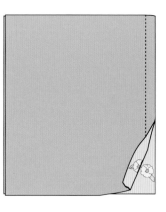

2 Place the two drops face to face with the edges laid flat and the pressed fold line facing you. Carefully line up the pattern.

3 Machine down the fold line in small bursts, lining up the patterns as you sew by lifting the top piece of fabric, making sure the patterns match and stitching another short stretch.

44 Joining sheer fabrics

Joining sheers can raise many problems. Ideally I would always try to make up a plain voile curtain with no vertical joins. You may be able to 'railroad' the voile, that is turn a wide voile on its side and run it horizontally across the window. This doesn't have any detrimental effect on the hang of the sheer at all, though be careful if you are using a patterned voile, as the pattern may look odd sideways.

Plain sheers

Let's start with plains such as voiles, batistes and muslins. The easiest to handle for sewing purposes are those made of cotton, as they are not as slippery. Sadly though, cotton is very unstable and will often shrink or stretch. Nowadays the polyester voiles are so attractive and are, of course, much more stable.

The bottom hem for a plain voile curtain should either be double, which gives a very pleasing result, especially if you make a good deep hem for a long window, or a very small weighted hem. For a double hem you do not necessarily have to insert continuous lead weights, as the weight of the hem helps the voile to hang in neat folds.

See Technique 38,
Cutting Sheer Fabrics, page 42.

I find the most accurate way of making up a voile is to take the cut fabric and pull a thread for the bottom edge of the curtain and another for the top. In this way you only need to measure the whole curtain once at the side hem. Press the hems with a warm, not hot, iron.

If you are using polyester voile, you should also use polyester curtain tape and thread, and I would always suggest replacing the needle at the beginning of each new project. The stitch size (slightly longer than for plain fabric, but not too big), and the tension (fairly loose), are paramount when machining voile. I recommend at least triple fullness for plain voile curtains.

Patterned sheers

One of the main problems with patterned voiles is that the printing process leaves stenter marks (pin holes) on the selvedge. These are made by spiked wheels that help keep the fabric moving through the printing machine.

It is usually almost impossible to pattern match voiles successfully so I use one of two techniques. For the first method I hang widths as individual panels, only connected by the curtain tape. Each width is hemmed at the bottom, though I do not use a large double hem as it tends to look ugly with the pattern showing through. I use a very small hem with lead-weight chain inserted. For the side hems, I turn over a small rolled edge. Sometimes I need to trim off the stenter holes and selvedge from the sides before I get an effective finish. If there is sufficient fullness you can just attach the curtain tape across all of the widths. When you pull up the tape and hang the curtain you will not notice the separate widths.

My second method of joining patterned voile is with either a straight stitch then an overlocker, or a four-thread overlocker with a well-matched polyester thread and a sharp needle. The only problem with this is that overlockers tend to be multi-purpose, designed to cope with all weights of fabric. The teeth that feed the fabric through tend to be rather large and can cause problems with sheers.

To show the design to its best advantage, patterned sheers often look better with less fullness than plains, say two-and-a-half-times fullness.

45 Joining interlinings

To cut down on bulk, interlining is joined in a different way to normal fabric. If the selvedge is at all tight (a common occurrence with interlining) trim it off, either by using an overlocker, which will also neaten the edge, or with scissors. If you use the second option you will then need to neaten the edge with either a zigzag stitch on your machine or at worst, with pinking shears.

Place the two pieces you wish to join on top of each other with an overlap of approximately 1.5cm (⅝in). Stitch down the center of the overlap through both layers. Some people recommend using a zigzag stitch but I have never found any problems using a reasonably large straight stitch. Make sure that the pressure of the machine foot pressing down onto the fabric is not too great, as it will cause the interlining to stretch and distort. If stretching is a problem, ease off the foot pressure or use a walking foot.

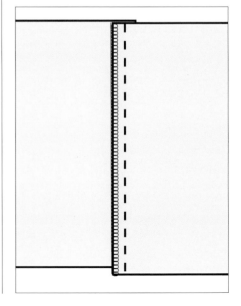

46 Pressing fabrics

Obviously the type of equipment you require for pressing is totally dependent on the size of your workroom and your business.

If you are working from home I would recommend an ironing mat and a good quality domestic steam iron, which quite frankly, you have to throw away at all too frequent intervals if you have to leave it on for long periods every day. Whenever I try to have a domestic iron repaired I am told that it is cheaper to replace it.

At the other end of the scale there are ironing tables with a compressor unit that operates with a kick strip to literally suck the work down onto the table to hold it in position. Alongside this you have a steam unit and a special gantry to hold the steam pipe and the iron itself in the correct position at all times.

For those workrooms in between I can suggest a useful device which costs very little but is invaluable. It consists of a domestic iron to which you will need to attach an extra-long flex. On the wall next to the table you will need an electricity socket and a rack to hold your iron. Above the table, fit a curtain pole or a metal rod attached, preferably to the ceiling, with brackets, this should run the whole length of the ironing area. Slip curtain rings onto the pole. Then, simply take the flex straight up from the iron (laid flat at the furthest end of the ironing table or mat), to the first ring on the rod. Do not pull the flex taut, leave a little room for movement. Attach the flex to the first ring with a short piece of string or wire, then loop it between the other rings, attaching it to each ring, until you get to the last one. From there, take the cable down to the wall plug. When not in use the iron can rest in the wall rack. A small shelf for a water jug is also useful.

Now to the actual pressing of fabrics. The obvious point is to make sure that the iron is at the correct temperature and that it does not spit steam at everything. Be aware of flame-retardant fabrics and thermal or blackout lining, both of which react quite badly to irons that are too warm and can shrink, though this is not particularly apparent at the time. With thermal lining in particular, the problem often doesn't show until it comes to putting the lining into the curtain, so be cautious. With flame-retardant fabrics, especially where the finish has been applied to a fabric you normally press with no adverse effects, the iron can stick, the smell is awful and again, the fabric often shrinks.

Velvet does not need to be pressed during making, merely gently steamed if required when hanging. Most other fabrics cause no problems as long as you proceed with caution.

A little tip that I have often found helpful was given to me by an electrician many years ago. If the sole plate of your iron becomes sticky or even discolored, which may mark more delicate fabrics, firstly turn it to the highest temperature possible. Take an old tea towel or towel, completely wet it then squeeze it out as much as possible. Place this over the sharp edge of a table or shelf; this must be plastic or metal, not beautiful wood or your best dining table. Rub the sole plate of the iron very hard against the sharp edge. All the rubbish from the sole plate will come off onto the edge so keep moving the towel until there is no more discoloration. It works beautifully with no cost or fumes and you don't scratch the sole plate as you would using an abrasive, which just allows more rubbish to accumulate at an even quicker rate.

47 Making an ironing mat

For those working at home, either making up soft furnishings just for themselves and family or as a small business, space is usually at a premium. If you have the space for a worktable but not a separate ironing table there are two solutions. One is to make up an ironing mat and the second is to upholster the whole of your working table. I have very mixed feelings about the second alternative as I find it slows up my work by dragging on the fabric as I try to manoeuvre it, though for actual pressing it is ideal.

An ironing mat is a useful compromise, especially if you don't have a worktable at all, as it enables you to work anywhere, even on the floor. The size of my mat is 137 x 76cm (approximately 54 x 30in), but of course it can be any size you want.

I use a central layer of wool underfelt in my ironing mat, which is available from good carpet shops. I then make a separate outer cover (like a bag) which has one side of absorbent cotton and the other side of a metalised cotton, like the fabric used to make ironing board covers. I fasten the cover with Velcro so that I can remove it for cleaning.

The reason I use the two different materials for the cover is because if I have a badly creased 'tough' cotton it will need plenty of steam, so I iron on the metalised side, which helps to bounce the heat and moisture back into the fabric. For delicate fabrics, which spots of moisture may mark, I use a dry iron and the absorbent cotton side of the mat.

48 Making lead-weight bags

Lead weights are an absolute must to help curtains to hang well. I rarely use lead weight in the form of a chain or tape as it disfigures the bottom hem, though I do use a lightweight version for sheers. Instead I make small bags of lining fabric to hold the weights. The bags help to position and attach the weights correctly and to prevent the outline of the weight showing through after cleaning.

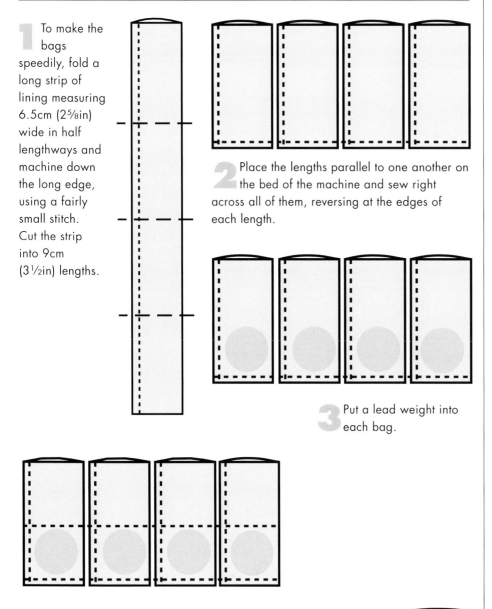

1 To make the bags speedily, fold a long strip of lining measuring 6.5cm (2⅝in) wide in half lengthways and machine down the long edge, using a fairly small stitch. Cut the strip into 9cm (3½in) lengths.

2 Place the lengths parallel to one another on the bed of the machine and sew right across all of them, reversing at the edges of each length.

3 Put a lead weight into each bag.

4 Machine across the strips again, this time above the lead weights to hold them in position. Clip the connecting threads and the bags are ready to use.

5 For interlined curtains you only require small lead weight bags, like the one shown here. They can be made using the same method, but the strip should be cut into shorter pieces of 4cm (1½in).

49 True mitres

To make a true mitre the fabric should be cut away at the corner and the seam allowance stitched to keep it in position. Without this step the bulk in the corner tends to move over time. The disadvantage of this type of mitre is that as the fabric is cut away, it is impossible to let down the curtains without altering the side hems as well.

1 Press in 6cm (2½in) for the side hems or mark a line with a fading marker. Also mark a double bottom hem of 6cm (2½in) then 10cm (4in).

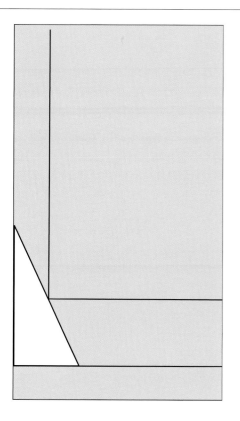

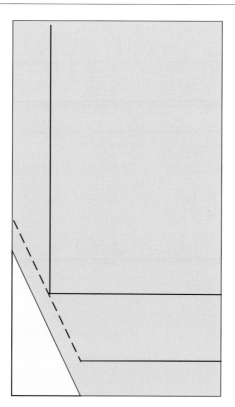

2 Place a 60° set square on the corner, as shown.

3 Mark a line (the dotted line in the illustration) along the edge of the set square then remove it. Add 2cm (¾in) seam allowance and cut away the excess fabric.

4 Turn over the seam allowance along the angle and herringbone stitch it into position.

See Technique 53, Herringbone Stitch, page 53.

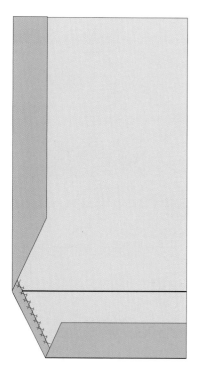

5 Turn over 6cm (2½in) along the side hem and herringbone stitch it in place. Turn up the double bottom hem and slip stitch or herringbone it in place. Ladder stitch the mitre closed.

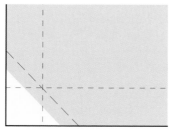

6 For the corner of a Roman blind you can use a true mitre of 45°. Firstly press in the side and bottom hem, as shown by the dotted line. In the case of a Roman blind without a bottom weight bar this will be 5cm (2in). Fold a line that bisects the bottom and side hem fold lines where they join. This line should be at 45° to the outer edges of the blind. Add a 2cm (¾in) seam allowance and cut away the excess fabric.

7 Fold in the seam allowance and herringbone stitch it in position.

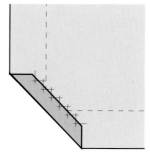

8 Herringbone the side and bottom hems of the blind to prevent the edges from rolling.

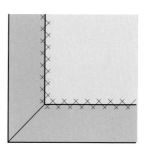

50 Folded mitres

This mitred corner is one I have used for many years. It has an advantage over the normal type of folded corner as the bulk is held in place and, in the long term, will not form a lump of fabric in the corner of the curtain, particularly after cleaning or washing.

See Project 1, The Classic Curtain, page 96.

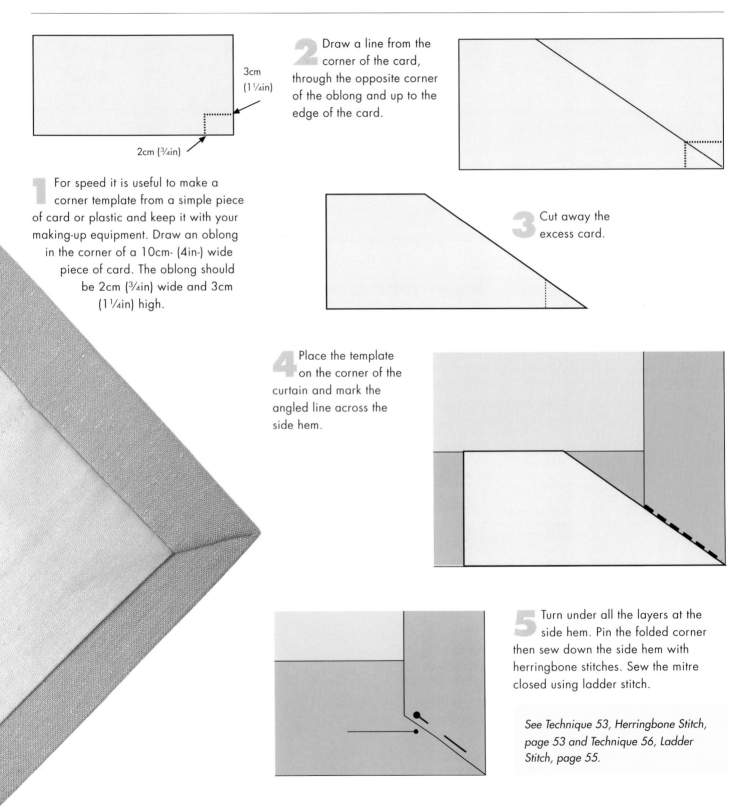

3cm (1¼in)

2cm (¾in)

1 For speed it is useful to make a corner template from a simple piece of card or plastic and keep it with your making-up equipment. Draw an oblong in the corner of a 10cm- (4in-) wide piece of card. The oblong should be 2cm (¾in) wide and 3cm (1¼in) high.

2 Draw a line from the corner of the card, through the opposite corner of the oblong and up to the edge of the card.

3 Cut away the excess card.

4 Place the template on the corner of the curtain and mark the angled line across the side hem.

5 Turn under all the layers at the side hem. Pin the folded corner then sew down the side hem with herringbone stitches. Sew the mitre closed using ladder stitch.

See Technique 53, Herringbone Stitch, page 53 and Technique 56, Ladder Stitch, page 55.

51 Interlined mitres

When making interlined curtains it is very important that you cut out the excess bulk in the corners of the hems, although again this will make it very difficult if the curtain has to be lengthened at a later stage.

See Project 2, The Classic Interlined Curtain, page 102.

1 Mark two lines on the interlining with a fading marker: line A is 6cm (2½in) from the side of the curtain, line B is 16cm (6¼in) from the bottom of the curtain. Place a 60° set square on the interlining, with its long-side edge up to the edge of the curtain and its diagonal edge bisecting the lines as shown. The 10cm (4in) mark on the set square should touch line B.

Draw a line on the interlining, along the diagonal of the set square.

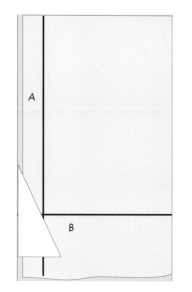

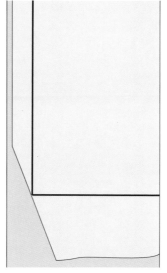

2 Cut away the interlining to the line you have just marked. Add a 2cm (¾in) seam allowance and trim away the main fabric.

3 Trim off some of the interlining 6cm (2½in) up from the bottom of the curtain. Don't cut all the way across, just far enough to clear the mitre.

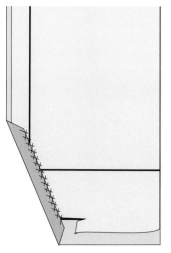

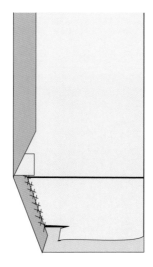

4 Fold the fabric seam allowance over the interlining at the corner and use small herringbone stitches to secure it.

See Technique 53, Herringbone Stitch, page 53.

5 Place the lead weight in position. In due course, when the interlining is completely in position across the curtain, the bottom hem will be folded up, the hem herringboned and the corners completed using ladder stitch.

52 Velvet mitres

The corners for velvet curtains are treated differently to ordinary mitres in order to cut away the maximum bulk.

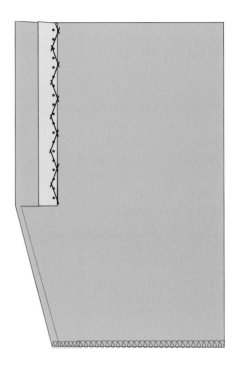

1 On the side hem place a pin at the point where the you will fold up the bottom hem. With velvet you only need a single 10cm (4in) hem, which is overlocked. Again this is to cut down on bulk. However, for extra-long curtains you can use a deeper hem if preferred. Cut into the side hem from the selvedge leaving approximately 1cm (½in) of side hem uncut.

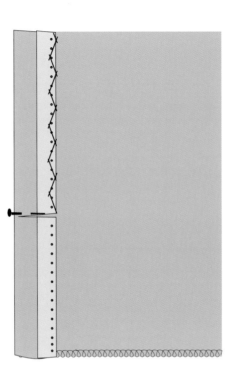

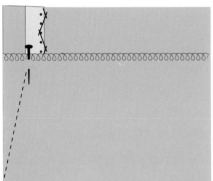

2 Turn up the hem to its finished position and place a pin on the overlocked edge,1cm (½in) in from the selvedge edge.

3 Flatten out the hem as shown and cut from the pin to the end of the cut in the side hem.

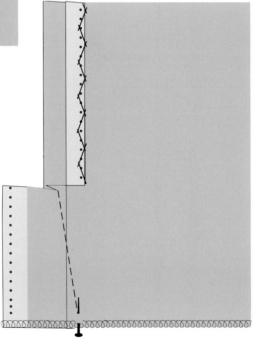

4 Turn over a small seam allowance on the cut edge of the mitre.

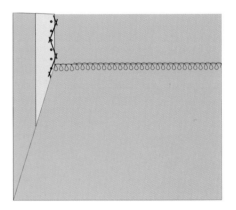

5 Fold up the hem using herringbone stitches to secure it and ladder stitch along the mitre.

See Technique 53, Herringbone Stitch, page 53 and Technique 56, Ladder Stitch, page 55.

53 Herringbone stitch

Herringbone stitch is most useful for side hems, bottom hems (when using interlining) and true mitres as it prevents the hem rolling. The top part of the stitch picks up a little of the main fabric of the curtain and will be very slightly visible as a slight indentation on the curtain face. To prevent the hem rolling, the lower part of the stitch should be caught through all the layers and will also show slightly.

If the fabric is sturdy and there won't be too much pulling on the side hems (that is, if the curtains are hung on a corded curtain rail), the stitch on these hems could be caught through all the layers on alternate stitches, which will speed up the process. If you are right handed this stitch is started from the left-hand side and vice versa if you are left handed.

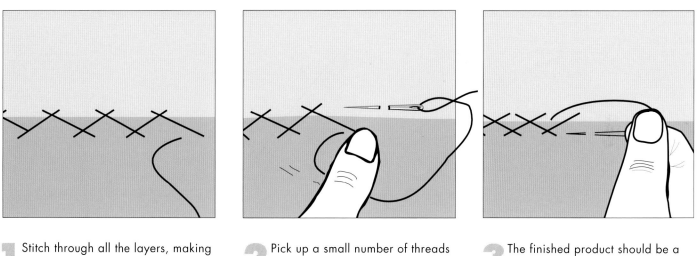

1 Stitch through all the layers, making certain that as little thread shows on the main fabric as possible.

2 Pick up a small number of threads above the hem.

3 The finished product should be a neat row of criss-cross stitches, which should not be too tight or they will show on the front of the curtain.

54 Slip stitch

Slip stitch can be used for hems at the bottom of a curtain. Make the stitches well and they will be neat at the back and almost invisible on the front of the curtain.

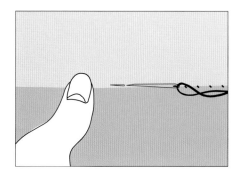
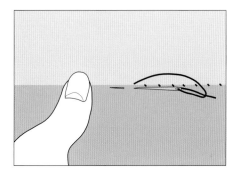
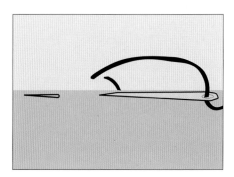

1 Catch only a small amount of the fabric from the back of the main part of the curtain.

2 Run the needle through the hem then catch a small amount of main fabric. The stitch should be very tiny.

3 For a neater finish, place the point of the needle slightly to the right of where the thread emerges.

55 Laying-in stitch

Laying-in stitch is used to anchor the main fabric of a curtain to the interlining and the lining. These stitches are vital to the long life and good looks of the curtain, so take time to make them well.

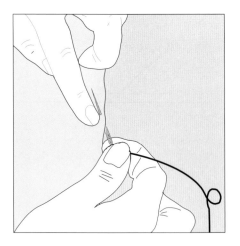

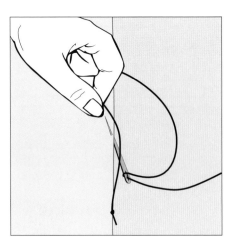

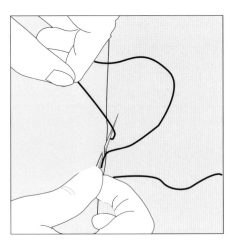

1 Start with a knot and an overstitch on the interlining.

2 For the first stitch, pick up a little of the main fabric, then a little of the folded edge of the interlining or lining.

3 Wrap the thread that comes directly from the last stitch twice around the needle, as for a French knot. You may find this easier if you raise the point of the needle slightly.

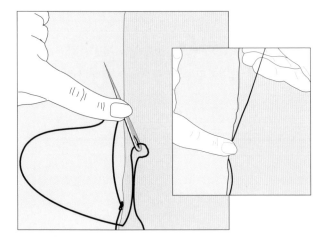

4 Press your finger over the point where the needle emerges from the fabric and continue pressing until you have pulled all the thread through. If you release the pressure before you have pulled all of the thread through, the thread will knot and you will have problems.

5 Remembering that these lines of stitches are to help prevent movement, they should be loose enough to prevent them pulling on the face fabric, but not sloppy, and approximately 5cm (2in) in length.

Some people recommend just a large sloppy stitch rather than my 'French knot' approach, but in my experience just using a large stitch does not prevent movement. This technique helps to lock the layers of fabrics together.

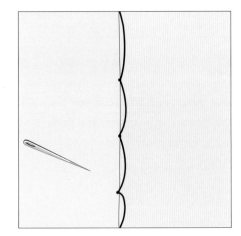

56 Ladder stitch

This stitch is used for sewing together the two sides of a mitre. Do not pull the stitches up too tightly or they will cause the mitre to pucker.

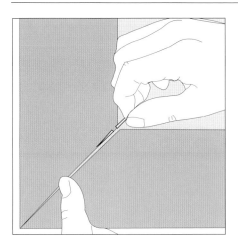
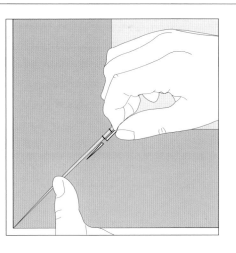
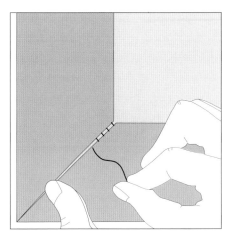

1 Run the needle and thread inside the folded edge of the mitre.

2 At the point at which the needle emerges from the fold, bring the needle straight across to the opposite fold and repeat the process.

3 After a few stitches, the threads should make a 'ladder'. They should be parallel and at right angles to the folded edges you are sewing together. Pull gently to close the seam.

57 Stab stitch

Stab stitch is often used when the thickness of the fabric prevents the item from being stitched by machine, as in pinch or goblet pleats, or where you don't wish to see any stitches but want to connect fabrics together.

1 Simply stab the needle through the layers of fabric from one side to another. On the surface of the fabric, allow just a very small stitch to be visible. As the needle passes into the fabric make sure it is at quite an extreme angle, so that the actual length of the stitch is contained between the layers where it isn't visible.

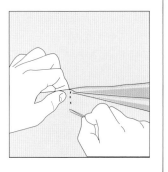

This stitch is also invaluable when you want to attach main and lining fabrics together on a Roman blind and where machined lines would spoil the fabric design.

58 Lining-in stitch

Lining-in stitch is used when you want to attach a lining by hand. This could be on a Roman blind, a curtain or a swag. It

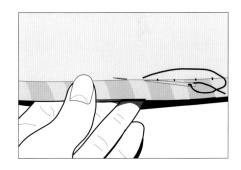

provides a neat, strong stitch very similar to slip stitch, except that the needle is run between the two layers of the main fabric forming the hem before catching the very edge of the lining.

59 Applying standard tapes

There are many different types of curtain tapes and each will give your curtains a different look. Shown here are samples of the most popular types, plus all you need to know to apply them perfectly.

If you have not had much practice at curtain making, turn over the top of the curtain and press the fold to make sure the heading remains level while you are applying the tape. The amount of fabric I turn over varies although there are guidelines which will apply in most cases.

With standard 2.5cm (1in) curtain tape I usually allow a 2cm (¾in) heading above the tape and 1.5cm (⅝in) beneath the tape (to conceal the raw edges). Therefore, I turn over 3.5cm (1⅜in) at the top of the curtain and place the tape so that 2cm (¾in) of fabric shows above it.

With most deep tapes, I turn over 5cm (2in) if there is sufficient fabric and place the tape 1cm (½in) down from the top of the curtain, which allows 4cm (1½in) beneath the tape. In both cases, if I needed to lengthen the curtains just a little, I could remove the tape and replace it close to the top of the curtain with a very small heading. The following example uses 2.5cm (1in) curtain tape, but the principle is the same for all standard tapes.

Standard tape

Mini pencil-pleat tape

Pencil-pleat tape

Deep pencil-pleat tape

1 Lay the curtain tape in the correct position on the curtain with approximately 2cm (¾in) of tape hanging over the edge of the curtain.

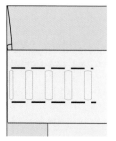

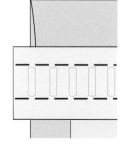

2 Before starting to sew on the tape, turn under the 2cm (¾in) of tape so that it lays within the fold of the heading.

3 If you are confident on the machine, stitch across the top of the curtain, checking with a small ruler as you go to maintain the correct heading. If you are less certain, pin the tape in position before machining. Before you reach the opposite end of the tape, pause, trim off the excess tape allowing 2cm (¾in) to tuck under the fold as in step 2. Sew to the end and reverse to secure.

4 The cords should be left free at the outer edges of the curtain. If you have used a half width, the cords would be left loose at the half-width edge of the curtain, which will be at the outer edge.

Starting at the bottom corner of the tape, sew up to the top machine line before turning and stitching down the end of the tape again. If the tapes are to be secured at this end, stitch and reverse many times over the cords themselves. If you prefer, you can knot the cords on the underside of the tape before stitching; personally I think this creates unnecessary bulk.

5 At the opposite end of the tape leave the cords free but still machine the end of the tape. Stitch along the bottom edge of the tape, checking at frequently that the fabric on the front of the curtain is not twisting. If you are making up a pair of curtains, make sure that you machine the tape with the cords protruding at the outside edge in both cases.

60 Applying decorative tapes

In general decorative tapes are attached in a similar way to the more normal tapes. However some tapes can have slight differences and it is important to discover all the information before you start to sew. Some tapes are intended to have a heading above them while others, particularly some of the box-pleat type tapes, will only work correctly if they have no heading at all.

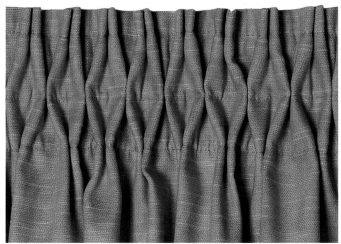

Smocking tape

The most common mistake concerns the number of machine lines and their position. Smocked-type tapes, particularly, need at least one extra row of machining (three rows in all) to hold the fabric to the tape. Without it the tape does not pull up correctly.

61 Drawing-up tapes

This job can be time consuming and hard work. However, if you pull the cords out until you have enough to tie the ends around a table leg or a door handle, whatever is convenient, this leaves both your hands free making the task much less strenuous.

Pull the cords up until the pleats are as tight as you can make them. Check that all the pleats are vertical. The cords rarely pull up to be exactly the same length, so pull on the looser cord to level up the pleats. Let the pleats out until they are half the length of your rail plus the return and the overlap. I also add a little extra, 5-10 cm (2-4in) per width, especially if the curtain track is not corded or fitted with a tension pulley. If you don't make this extra allowance you will find that the curtains jump apart in the center of the window.

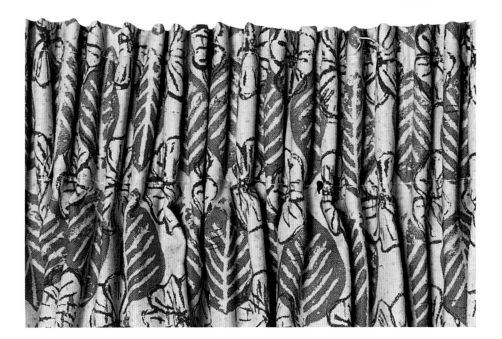

62 Tying curtain cords

Many people spend time making-up their curtains beautifully, carefully applying the curtain tape and drawing up the cords neatly, then they knot the ends of the cords and cut them off short.

However, when curtains are cleaned, the heading has to be smoothed out flat to clean it properly. So, if the cords have been chopped off, when the heading is flattened the cords disappear along the tape and the only way to re-form the heading properly is to sew on new tape. This means that these curtains can never be properly cleaned without having to unpick all the curtain tape and apply new tape afterwards. What a waste of time and effort.

However, what do you do with the cords? You certainly don't want to leave them loose. Shown on these pages is is a neat way of tying the cords, which means that you don't have yards of cord trailing down the sides of your curtains, yet when it comes to cleaning, the cords are still there.

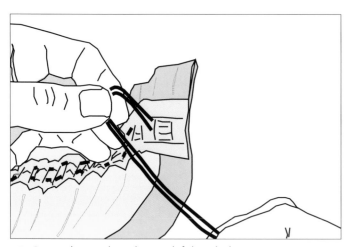

1 Grasp the cords with your left hand about 4-5cm (1½-2in) from the tape.

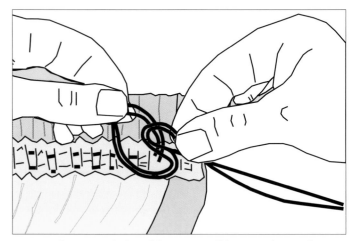

2 With your right hand form a small loop and pass this behind the main loop.

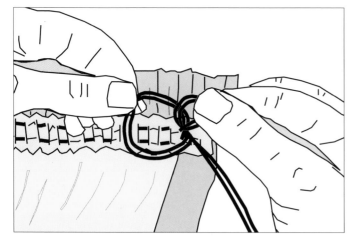

3 Bring this small loop through the large loop from back to front, grasp it firmly and pull until taut, making the large loop disappear.

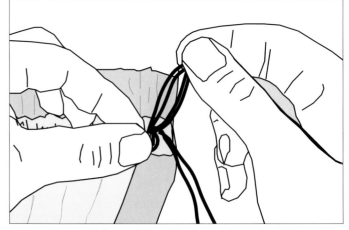

4 With your left hand, hold the base of the slip knot you have made to prevent it from coming loose.

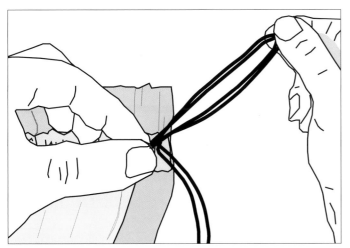

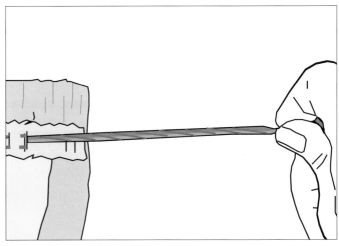

5 By pulling on one side of the loop in your right hand you will slowly pull the remaining cord through, until all the cords are equal in length. If you pull on the wrong cord it will merely tighten the slip knot.

6 Twirl the cords together between your fingers until they form a tight twist.

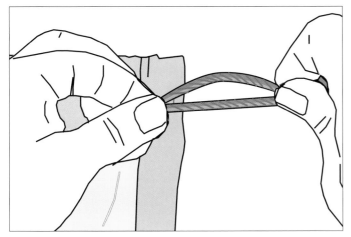

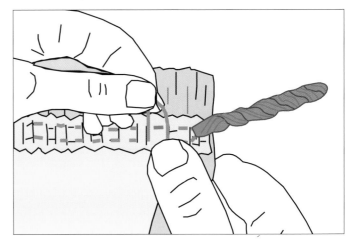

7 Fold the twist in half, holding the ends nearest the tape securely. Let go of the end of the twist held in the right hand and you will find the cords curl themselves together neatly.

8 Pull a section of the cord in the tape free until you can pass the twist underneath it.

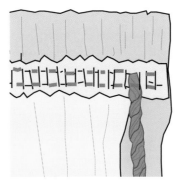

9 Pass the twist under the cord, which will then hold the twist together neatly and out of sight.

10 Even out the pleats and fit the hooks to complete the valance or curtain ready for hanging.

63 Forming pinch pleats

The curtain is pleated up to the exact finished measurements, which involves some mathematics, so have a calculator handy. Working out the amount of fabric is easier if you understand how the pleats are formed. If we look at the reverse of the curtain after pleating up you can see that the total width of the curtain is made up of spaces and ends. The extra fabric is taken up in the pleats.

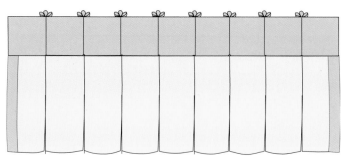

Each pleat starts life as a flap of fabric, lining and buckram. A pleat can use as little as 13cm (5in) if the fabric is fairly thin and up to about 16cm (6¼in) if the fabric is thicker. The spaces should be from 10-14cm (4-5½in and the ends about 10cm (4in). If the curtains are on a pole with no

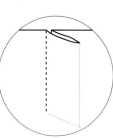

cording, I usually make the end at the leading edge of the curtain, where the two curtains meet, only 6cm (2½in). Remember if you use very large pleats and very small spaces the curtain will not stack back at the side of the window very well. It is wise not to place a pleat on the return to the wall, so if necessary make this end longer.

The total amount of fabric to be taken up in the pleats is calculated by taking the total pleated-up width of the curtain (or finished width) from the full width of the flat curtain. If we have a curtain which when flat measures 222cm (87¼in) and we need it to be drawn up to 115cm (45¼in) the calculation is as follows.

222cm (87¼in)	to be pleated down to 115cm (45¼in)	
the finished width of the curtain	the length of the track the curtain has to cover, including overlaps, returns and springback	

222cm (87¼in)	– 115cm (45¼in)	= 107cm (42in)
full width of flat curtain	total pleated-up width	amount taken up in pleats

The ends will measure 10cm (4in) each.

115cm (45¼in)	–20cm (8in)	= 95cm (37in)
Pleated up width of curtain	total of two ends	amount left in spaces

Before we can progress any further with the calculations, we need to know how many pleats we will be using. An ideal pleat size for a full-length curtain of a reasonably substantial fabric is 15cm (6in).

To calculate the number of pleats.

107cm (41in)	÷15cm (6in)	= 7.13 pleats
amount to be taken up in pleats	ideal sized pleat	approx. number of pleats

We require a whole number of pleats, so therefore we cannot have our pleats at exactly 15cm (6in). So, round the number of pleats either up or down, depending on whether you would like the pleats to be slightly larger or smaller than 15cm (6in). I would prefer them to be smaller in this case, as we have barely sufficient fullness.

107cm (41in)	÷8	=13.37cm (5¼in)
amount to be taken up in pleats	exact number of pleats	size of pleats

In other words we will use eight pleats of 13.37cm (5¼in). From the diagram you can see that there is always one less space than there are pleats (not including the ends), therefore for this curtain we will have seven spaces. We have already calculated that we will have 95cm (37in) for the spaces.

95cm (37in)	÷7	=13.57cm (5¼in)
amount to be taken up in spaces	number of spaces	size of spaces

Before you start to pin out the pleats it is best to make a quick calculation as a double check.

Eight pleats at 13.37cm (5¼in) each	= 106.96cm (42in)	
Seven spaces at 13.57cm (5¼in) each	= 94.99cm (36¾in)	
Two ends at 10cm (4in) each	= 20.00cm (8in)	
Total	= 221.95cm (86¾in)	

These calculations show a curtain with minimal fullness, giving us very small pleats, which are almost the same size as the spaces. For a more luxurious look you would use a curtain of two and a half widths which could give us a finished width of say 282cm (111in). To illustrate the difference let's work out the calculations for a curtain of this measurement.

282cm (111in) *finished width of curtain*	to be pleated down to 115cm (45¼in) *the pleated up width of the curtain*	

282cm (110in) *finished width curtain*	–115cm (45¼in) *pleated up width of curtain*	=167cm (65¾in) *amount to be of taken up in pleats*

As in the previous calculation the two ends will be 10cm each.

115cm (45¼in) *pleated up width of curtain*	–20cm (8in) *total of two ends*	=95cm (37¼in) *amount in spaces*

Ideal pleat size is 15cm (6in).

167cm (65¾in) *amount to be taken up in pleats*	÷15cm (6in) *approx. pleat size*	=11.13 *number of pleats*

Round the pleats up or down to a whole number, in this case eleven or twelve. I will choose a large pleat.

167cm (65¾in) *amount to be taken up in pleats*	÷ 11 *number of pleats*	=15.18cm (6in) *size of pleats*

To calculate the size of the spaces (there is always one less space than pleat).

95cm (37¼in) *amount to be taken up in spaces*	÷10 *number of spaces*	=9.5cm (3¾in) *size of space*

Again, to double check.

Eleven pleats at 15.18cm (6in)	= 166.98cm (66in)
Ten spaces at 9.5cm (3¾in)	= 95cm (37½in)
Two ends at 10cm (4in)	= 20cm (8in)
Total	= 281.98cm (111½in)

Pinning out the positions of the pleats

1 The next stage is to pin out the pleats on the front of the curtain. A really helpful hint is to insert a pin at an angle in each of the spaces, as shown. This helps to prevent mistakes in stitching a space instead of a pleat.

2 Bring together the two pins indicating the first pleat and make a crease at the front of the fold.

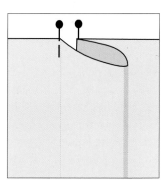

3 Remove the pin on the underside and turn the top pin, pinning through the top layer of fabric only, so that the point of the pin is at the top of the curtain.

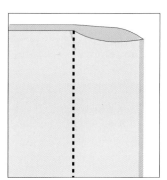

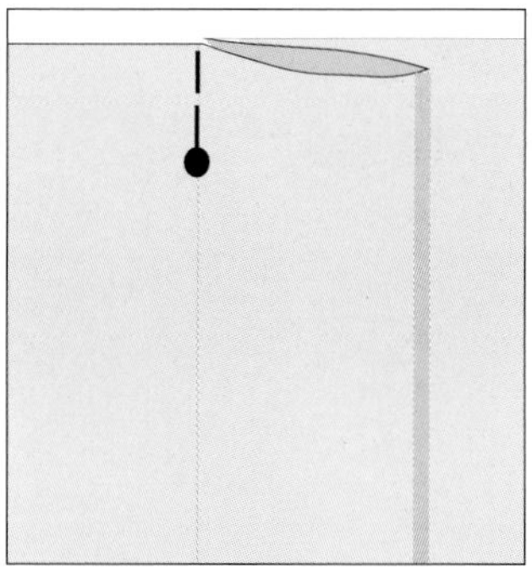

4 Machine from the pin down to the bottom edge of the buckram.

5 Because of the bulk involved, the machine foot may push the fabric, resulting in the tops of the pleats being uneven. To prevent this, place the needle in the fabric about 1cm (½in) from the top of the pleat. Reverse up to the top of the pleat before

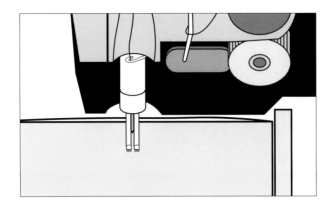

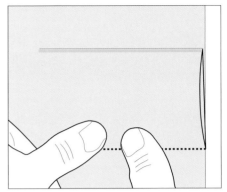

stitching to the bottom of the buckram. Reverse for three or four stitches to secure.

To form a perfect pleat, it is important that the machine line is parallel to the folded edge of the pleat. This can be done in a number of ways but I have always found it simplest to place a piece of brightly colored freezer or masking tape on the machine bed at the correct distance from the needle. Instead of watching the needle itself, just keep the folded edge of the pleat up to the tape. To save mistakes due to lost pins, complete all these fabric 'flaps' first, and then check that the pleated-up measurement is correct. Now you have to form the actual triple pleats.

6 Fold the pleat to one side and press the line of machining quite firmly with your thumbs. Fold the pleat to the opposite side and press again.

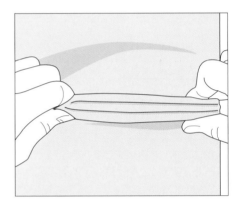

9 Bring all three pleats together so that they are of equal size; the triple pleat is now formed. Hold it firmly and place it under the machine foot.

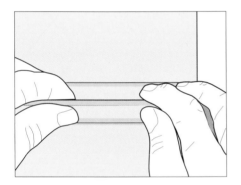

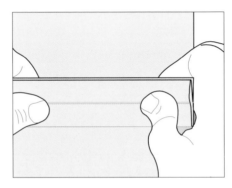

7 With the curtain flat on the table, take the center of the pleat between the thumb and forefinger of each hand. Press it gently towards the machine line. This should result in a pleat being formed either side of the one you are holding.

8 Fold the center pleat towards each side pleat in turn and press with your thumbs to crease the buckram and the fabric.

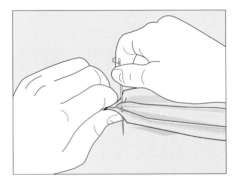

11 If the fabric is bulky or marks easily, the pleat will have to be stab stitched. Start at the front; threads don't go over the pleat, but through the fabric so that they aren't visible.

See Technique 57, Stab Stitch, page 55.

10 If the fabric is thin, it is possible to machine across the bottom of all three pleats, reversing well to secure at each side. It is not necessary to use a zip or piping foot to get in really close to the bottom edge of the buckram as this results in a rather severe, characterless pleat. Use a normal foot and place the edge of the foot up against the edge of the buckram.

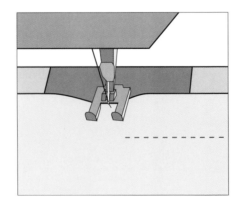

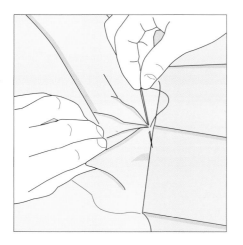

12 For neatness, take the needle and thread to the back of the curtain and finish with overstitches.

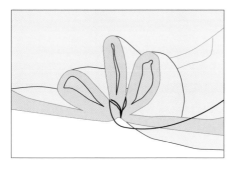

13 Finally, carefully stitch the top of the pleat into position, as shown, to secure it.

64 Forming goblet pleats

Goblet pleats are calculated, pinned and made in exactly the same way as pinch pleats until the last stage, where the pleats are stitched by hand to secure the tops. Goblet pleats look their best if you use buckram of at least 12.5cm (5in) in depth.

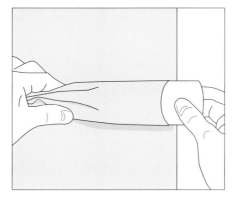

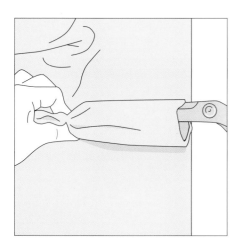

1 After stitching along the base of the pleat, use your fingers or scissors to push the pleats out to form a goblet shape. The base of the goblet should retain the triple pleats.

See Technique 63, Forming Pinch Pleats, page 60.

2 Insert a coiled piece of buckram, cut to the depth of the pleat, into the goblet. This adds body and helps to retain the shape. Once inserted, the strip, which should be approximately 35cm (14in) in length, should be uncoiled a little within the heading so that it spreads to fill the goblet.

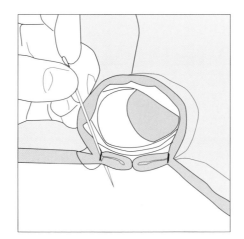

3 Stitch the top of the pleat at the back, as shown, to help to retain the goblet shape.

65 Forming box pleats

This style of heading is only really used for valances. If your fabric has a random, all-over pattern, simply pin one or two pleats in position until you have the effect you require. With a stripe or a geometric design, pin the pleats according to the fabric design. This will give you approximate sizes for the width of the pleats and also show you how much space to leave between them. Never make the spaces wider than the pleats, as it tends to make the valance look rather skimpy. Before you can proceed any further you will need to calculate the exact sizes of the pleats, gaps, spaces and returns.

By initially folding the fabric I have decided that the pleats should be approximately 10cm (4in) wide with a gap of about 1cm (½in) between them. This means that the spaces will be 11cm wide. Now the exact measurements must be calculated.

For this example, I will use a cornice board which is 210cm (84in) long plus 15cm (6in) returns, giving us a total width of 240cm (90in).

See Technique 63, Forming Pinch Pleats, page 60

Working on a similar principal to the pinch pleats, work out the end, space and pleat sizes. The following diagram may make it a little easier.

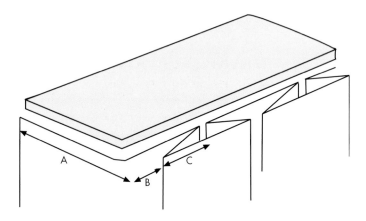

The end is made up of A, the depth of the cornice board, and B, the distance from the corner of the board to the first pleat (which is usually 1cm), plus C, half the width of a pleat.

15cm (6in)	+ 1cm (½in)	+ 5cm (2in)	=21cm (8½in)
A	B	C	the end

Therefore we need two ends at 21cm (8½in) each.

As the whole width of the board as 230cm (90in), the remaining width to be divided into spaces is:

240cm (90in)	- 42cm (17in)	=198cm (73in)
total width of the board including returns	width of the two ends	remaining width of the board

The number of spaces is calculated as follows.

198cm (73in)	÷ 11cm (4in)	= 18 spaces
remaining width of board	approx. width of space	number of spaces

If this calculation had not resulted in a whole number of spaces, you would have to round the number either up or down, then divide the remaining width of the board by this figure to give you the exact size of each space.

The actual amount of fabric taken up by each pleat is exactly double the amount you see on the front of the valance. Therefore, as I would like the pleats to be 10cm (4in) finished width:

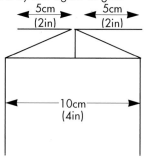

10cm (4in)	x 2	= 20cm (8in)
width of pleat	extra fabric required per pleat	total fabric required per pleat

As there is always one more pleat than space I will be using 19 pleats at 20cm (8in) each.

The total width of fabric needed is as follows:

2 ends at 21cm (8½in) each	= 42cm (17in)
18 spaces at 11cm (41½in) each	= 198cm (81in)
19 pleats at 20cm (8in) each	= 380cm (152in)
2 seam allowances at 2cm (¾in) each	= 4cm (1½in)
Total width of fabric needed	= 624cm (251.5in)

See Project 3, The Classic Valance, page 106.

Cut the valance to the exact calculated width and make it up in the usual way, until you reach the stage where you form the pleats. If you are worried about the accuracy of your calculations and making up, cut the valance generously and form the pleats. Then, trim the ends to size and close them with ladder stitch.

Stitching pleats

Before sewing in the pleats, I usually turn the top edge over so that at a later stage I can attach Velcro by hand with a heading above it if required. The amount turned over will vary according to your design. If the valance is to be attached to a cornice board that is top-fixed to the ceiling and therefore has no clearance above it, turn over only a small amount and attach the Velcro right at the top of the valance. In both cases the Velcro will cover the raw edges. If you are attaching a top band the pleats should be sewn in position leaving the raw edges at the top of the valance.

See Technique 69, Making Top Bands, page 67.

Fold each pleat by bringing the two pins marking it together. Once folded, remove the pin from the back of the pleat and place the valance under the sewing machine. Machine from the top edge of the fabric down the back of the pleat. As with pinch pleats, it is critical that the stitching line is parallel to the folded front edge of the pleat, which is

See Technique 63, Forming Pinch Pleats, page 60

a much simpler task if you place a strip of freezer or masking tape on the bed of the machine. Instead of watching the needle, just make sure that as you are machining that you keep the folded edge of the pleat up to the tape.

The distance you machine down the pleat varies according to the fabric and how gentle or tailored you want the finished box pleat. As a general rule, I machine approximately one-third of the way down the pleat for a gentle box pleat and two-thirds for a more tailored pleat.

66 Making hand-gathered headings

Easy to make, this style of heading can be used for curtains, valances and blinds. I would always recommend at least two-and-a-half-times fullness for this heading.

Cut a piece of Velcro, or if you are using sew-on hooks, strong herringbone tape, of the correct dimension for the width of the heading you want to achieve. Divide the piece into eighths with pins, or for very large items you could divide it into sixteenths or even thirty-seconds.

Make up the curtain in the usual way until you get to the stage of forming the heading.

See Project 1, The Classic Curtain, page 96, and Project 3, The Classic Valance, page 106.

See Technique 28, Calculating Fullness and Quantities for Valances, page 35.

1 Turn under the raw top edge of the valance to give the depth of heading you require, allowing an extra 1.5cm (⅝in) on the turning to lie under the Velcro. Divide the top of the valance in the same way as the

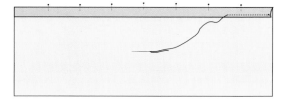

Velcro, although obviously the distance between the pins will be greater.

Thread a long needle with a double length of strong thread, making sure it is approximately 15cm (6in) longer than the piece of Velcro. Run a gathering stitch along the valance where the Velcro will be attached. Always start with a knot and a double overstitch. The length of the stitch will vary according to the type of fabric and the fullness you have allowed, but it is better to use a reasonably small stitch as this will help to prevent the gathers from moving around too much.

See Technique 59, Applying Standard Tapes, page 56.

2 As you progress across the valance, you will have to pull up the gathers as you will not have sufficient thread to keep the whole valance flat. This process is really much faster and easier than you perhaps imagine. When you have reached the opposite end, adjust the valance so that it fits the Velcro exactly and secure the end of the thread by oversewing two or three times.

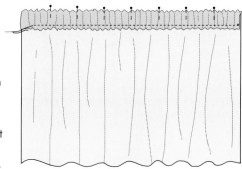

67 Applying Velcro or tape for hand-gathered headings

Use the same method for either Velcro or tape, depending on how you are going to hang your curtain or valance.

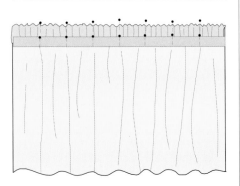

Position the Velcro on the heading and, by adjusting the gathers as necessary, make sure the pins in the Velcro and the gathered fabric line up. Use the pins from the Velcro to pin the layers together. Machine along the top of the Velcro, very close to the edge.

This machine line will, of course, show on the front of the valance, but you can camouflage it by hand-sewing a cord or other trim in over it. If the trim you are using is quite narrow, it is best to hand-stitch the lower edge of the Velcro rather than machining it.

See Technique 69, Making Top Bands, page 67.

Alternatively, if you are using top bands, do not turn over the raw edges before you start your row of gathering stitches.

68 Making slot headings

In most cases, a slot heading is made up of a slot, or pocket, a heading and a turning, which allows the raw edges to be contained within the slot. The measurements of each will vary according to the type of pole you are using and the heading you want for your particular design of valance or curtain. It is always tricky to get these dimensions correct: I would recommend making a small sample from a similar thickness of fabric, as a common mistake is to make the slot wide enough to fit the pole, but without sufficient ease to allow for pushing up the fabric.

See Project 1, The Classic Curtain, page 96 and Project 3, The Classic Valance, page 106.

Make up the valance or curtain in the usual way until you get to the stage where you form the heading. The next step is to form the slot.

1 I find it easiest at this stage to draw a small diagram to help calculate exactly how the heading is going to work and what measurements are involved.

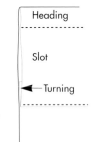

Measure the valance or curtain from top to bottom using a metre stick and mark your cutting line with a fading marker or tailor's chalk. Pin the fabric and lining together and trim off the excess. To avoid the problem of the rod being caught on loose threads as it is inserted, overlock or zigzag stitch the raw edges together.

3 Machine along the bottom edge of the slot, as close to the folded edge as possible. Machine a second line to form the top of the slot at the marked distance from the top of the valance or curtain to form the heading.

2 For this stage I use an iron and an ironing mat, which gives me a greater work area.

See Technique 47, Making an Ironing Mat, page 47.

If you do not have an ironing mat, use an ironing board. A small metal ruler is also invaluable. At the top of the valance turn over the depth you require, turning both the main fabric and the lining together. It is important that the slot is lined, as this allows the pole to be inserted without catching on the seam allowances. Turn under the raw edge so that it will be contained within the slot. Press the folded edges. Pin the fabric in place along the bottom edge. Mark the line that will form the top of the slot using a marker or chalk.

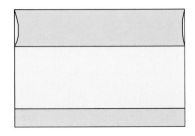

4 To complete the valance or curtain, thread the completed item onto the pole and attach this to its brackets.

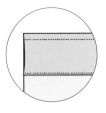

69 Making top bands

Top bands are a very useful way of attaching a gathered or pleated valance to a cornice board. They are not bulky and make it easy to take the valance down for cleaning.

See Technique 11, Making Pelmet Boards, page 22 and Project 3, The Classic Valance, page 106.

Make up the valance in the usual way until you reach the stage of forming the heading. Trim off the fabric at the required depth of the valance plus 2cm (¾in).

If you are using a top band, cut a piece of fabric 16cm (6¼in) wide by the length of the cornice board, plus seam allowances.

200cm (78in) *length of cornice board*	+ 4cm (1½in) *2cm (¾in) at each end seam allowances*	= 204cm (79½in) *length of top strip*

For the returns, cut two pieces, again 16cm (6¼in) wide by the width of the return plus seam allowances.

15cm (6in) *width of return*	+ 4cm (1½in) *2cm (¾in) at each end seam allowances*	= 19cm (7½in) *total length of strips for returns*

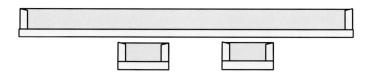

1 Once you have cut out the pieces, press in a 2cm (¾in) seam allowance on three sides of all three pieces.

2 Right sides facing, place the pieces on top of the valance, with the raw edges of the strips aligned with the raw edge of the top of the valance. Pin in position before machining with a 2cm (¾in) seam allowance. Where you cross between the long and the short strips, reverse over the join three or four times for strength.

3 Clip down almost to the machine line to allow the valance to lie correctly at the corner of the return.

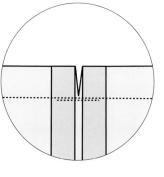

5 Machine loop Velcro to the underside of all three fabric strips.

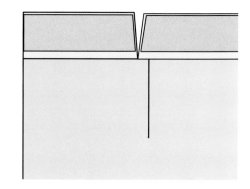

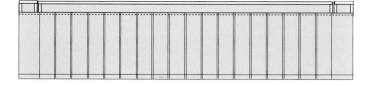

4 Press the strips with all the seam allowances pointing upwards. If necessary, trim back the seam where there is too much bulk. Fold the strips in half, enclosing all the raw edges, being especially careful to include the seam allowances at the joins between the long and short strips. Stitch the strips to the back of the valance by hand or machine, although I usually find it quicker to do this by hand as the fabric often twists on the machine, and I hate having to redo anything!

6 To enable the strip to fit correctly at the corner, machine pieces of hook Velcro to the top of each of the return strips as shown.

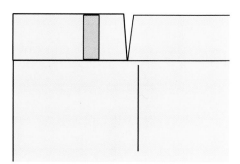

70 Headings for arches and angles

Depending on the type of fitting you are using at the top of the curtains for an arch, angle or slant-topped window, you can have a number of different headings. In all cases, the top of the curtain will have to be static, the curtains held back by tiebacks, holdbacks or Italian stringing.

Tape headings

You can use normal curtain tapes, though the top of the curtain will have to be anchored at the highest point to prevent it sliding down the track. If the track has Velcro attached, you can use Velcro-compatible tapes.

Pinch or goblet pleats

Pinch or goblet pleats can be a little trickier. I find it best to make an actual paper template, as in the long run this saves time.

See Technique 63, Forming Pinch Pleats, page 60.

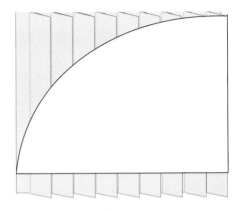

1 Take a piece of paper the full width of your curtain and at least 10cm (4in) deeper than the arched part of the window, to allow for errors. Work out the amount you will be using in each space, pleat and end. Mark and fold the paper as though it was the curtain itself, with all the pleats folded towards the center of the arch or angle.

See Technique 14, Making Templates for Arches, page 24.

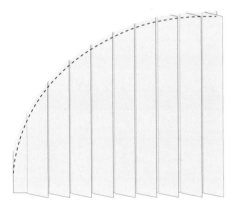

2 Place the template of half of the arch on the pleated paper and draw around the curved edge. Add a seam allowance of 2cm (¾in) and cut away the excess paper.

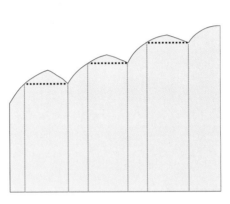

3 Flatten out the paper, which should now look like this illustration. Cut away the tops of the pleats, as marked by the dotted lines.

5 Cut a facing, neaten it along the lower edge and, right-sides facing and raw edges aligned, place it against the top edge of the curtain. Machine the facing to the curtain, taking a 2cm (¾in) seam allowance. Notch the corners and curves and turn the facing to the back. You can hand-stitch the lower edge of the facing to the curtain if you want to. If you are using Velcro, machine it onto the facing, in small

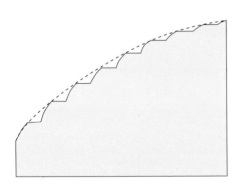

4 The resulting template is now ready to be placed on the curtain. Carefully draw round the top edge with a fading marker or tailor's chalk, then cut away the excess fabric.

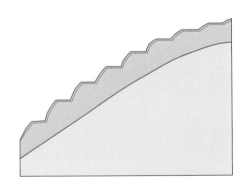

sections in the areas defined as spaces, before the facing is attached to the curtain.

Stitch the pleats. These will be very soft pleats but, because the curtain is static, this will not cause problems. If you prefer, you can attach buckram to the facing before you attach that to the curtain. For angle or slant windows, use exactly the same technique, though the spaces will be diagonal instead of curved.

71 Attaching standard hooks

These are the most commonly used type of hook and are simple to attach. However, do look at the pictures, as it is surprising how often they are attached wrongly.

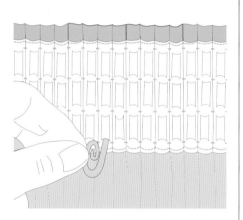

1 Place the longer part of the curtain hook in the bottom of the appropriate hook pocket.

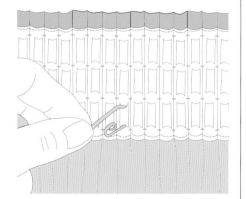

2 Turn the hook until the longer part is pointing straight down, so that it is in the correct position to place in the glider on the curtain track or the ring on the pole.

72 Attaching pin-on hooks

In Europe, pin-on hooks are only used with buckram to make hand-pleated headings.

See Technique 63, Forming Pinch Pleats, page 60 and Technique 64, Forming Goblet Pleats, page 63.

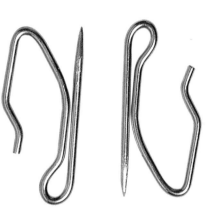

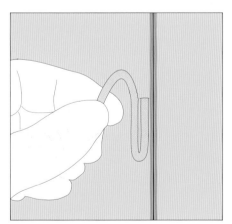

The hook has a pointed end that is pushed into as many layers of the curtain and buckram as possible to secure the hook well, without it showing on the front of the curtain. However, you must be careful not to insert it in the stitching line itself, as it acts brilliantly as an unpicker. Insert it slightly to one side of the stitching line.

73 Attaching sew-on hooks

I use these traditional sew-on hooks in several very specific situations: where the fabric is too flimsy to 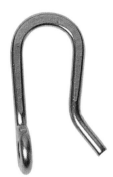 support a pin-on hook; on the leading edge of a pinch-pleated curtain on a hand-drawn track or pole. For really special curtains it doesn't seem quite right to use rather flimsy pin-on hooks, so to complete a top class curtain I use sew-on hooks. I also use them in any tricky situation where you have to attach a hook.

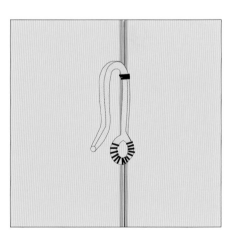

Stitch the hook onto as many layers of the curtain as possible, without the stitches showing on the front of the curtain. Stitch around the 'eye' and under the top part of the hook.

74 Cutting piping strips

Piping strips are usually cut at 5cm (2in) wide for reasonably fine cord, but wider if you are using jumbo cord. Smooth polyester cord is preferable as it never shows through the fabric and it does not shrink if you wash the item. The piping strips should be cut on the cross for all fabrics except velvet, which is usually cut on the straight. It is important that the strips are cut accurately as it makes the cushion or other item you are piping much quicker and simpler to sew, just like putting together a good jigsaw.

One method of cutting the fabric strips is to find the cross grain of the fabric, then mark out the strips with a ruler and marker. However, a cutting mat and rotary cutter are the easiest, quickest and most accurate tools for cutting fabric, not just for piping, but for gathering and pleating strips and linings. For straightforward strips, simply fold the fabric, usually into four, and lay it on the mat. Use the cutting ruler, lined up with the marks on the mat that show above and below the fabric, to make sure that the first cut is square. Cut through the layers, cutting away from the body with an even pressure, and be sure to press firmly to ensure a good clean cut.

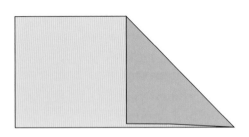

1 For piping strips on the bias, or cross, fold the fabric at 90° to the selvedge or, better still, following the grain of the fabric, which may not necessarily be at exactly that angle.

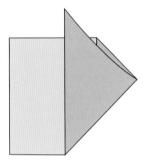

2 To make the fabric a suitable size for the mat, fold it again as shown. This particular method of folding will let you cut a number of long piping strips.

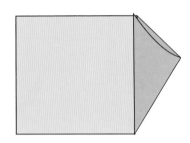

3 For small amounts of piping, make the second fold as illustrated above, to cut shorter strips.

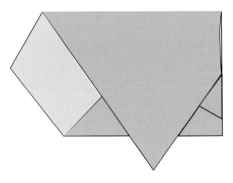

4 Keeping the folded edges together, swing the fabric around until the folded edges are vertical. Then fold the top points towards you, with the left-hand point against the folded edges.

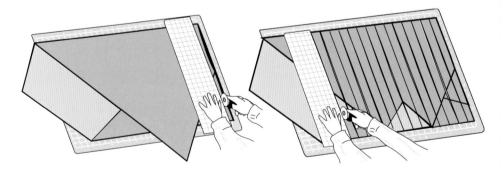

5 Place the fabric on the mat, with the folded edge along a vertical line. Pressing hard on the ruler to prevent it moving, use the rotary cutter to trim off the folded edges, so that the cut edge aligns with the next line on the mat. Use the markings on the mat and those on the cutting ruler to cut piping strips of the appropriate width.

6 If the fabric obscures your view of the markings on the mat, fold it further so it is confined within the markings, and continue to cut across it. It is an advantage to use a larger cutting mat, as you can cut more strips without moving the fabric.

75 Joining piping strips

Joining the fabric strips for piping perfectly is the first, and an essential step, in making neat, smooth piping. Make sure you have got this right before going any further. I think it is much easier to stitch the cord in position at the same time as sewing it on to the cushion. Try it and, with a little practice, I know you will find it easier. It also saves trying to hide the previous line of machining.

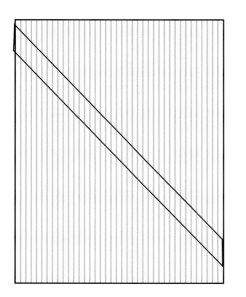

1 If the strips of piping fabric are not long enough to go right around the cushion, you will have to join them. Joining the strips is easier if both ends are cut to follow the grain of the fabric. This illustration shows how the grain of the fabric runs on the piping strips, and also why usually the ends of the piping strips are diagonal, following the straight grain.

2 If the ends of the piping strips do not match, they will have to be cut to match before you can join them together.

3 These strips could now be joined together but, if you are uncertain if they are cut correctly, fray out the edge of the fabric. As you can see in the inset illustration, if you trim the frayed edge back to the solid fabric, you will have a strip with an end that follows the grain of the fabric. If all the piping strips are frayed and cut in this way, it will guarantee that they are cut at the same angle, which in turn will ensure a smooth, flat seam when the strips are joined.

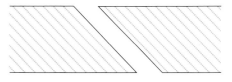

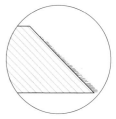

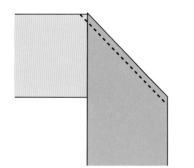

4 Keeping the two angled edges together, bring one over the other as shown. Most new students attempt to join the strips along the dotted line.

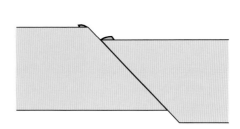

5 Unfortunately, this will result in an uneven strip of piping fabric.

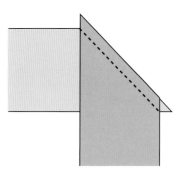

6 If, however, you move the piping strips until they are offset by the depth of the seam, and line up as shown, you will obtain a perfectly smooth strip of piping.

76 Piping with square ends

There are two types of starting and stopping ends in piping, a joining end and a square end. Both have their uses and both are illustrated on these pages. When the end of the piping will be visible or will be butted up to a seam, you need to finish it neatly or the raw ends will show. This neat end is called a square end. The method shown below is for starting piping with a square end, but the same principle applies for finishing with a square end. Stop machining a few centimeters (a couple of inches) before the point where the piping will end, trim and fold the cord and fabric as in steps 1 and 2 and machine to the end.

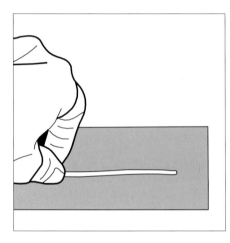

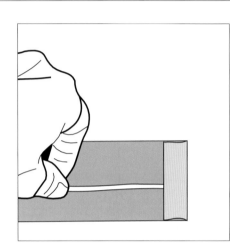

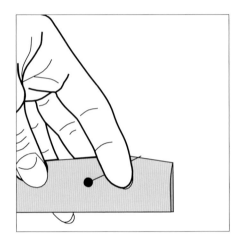

1 Place a smooth piping cord onto a strip of piping fabric long enough for the project. Trim the end of the piping strip so that it is square.

2 Fold the edge of the fabric over the end of the cord; 1-2cm (½–¾in) will be sufficient.

3 Fold the strip of fabric in half, covering the cord, to make the piping strip. Place a pin through the cord and fabric, as it is easy to pull the cord out of the fabric.

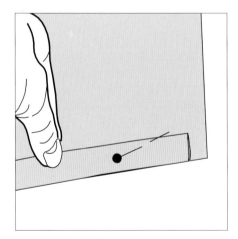

4 Place the piping strip 2cm (¾in) in from the edge of the fabric.

5 Machine the piping to the main fabric using a zip foot, or a piping foot if you prefer. Do not stitch too close to the cord; you will only give yourself the problem of hiding that stitching line later. You will have to remove the pin to machine, but it is best to replace it as soon as possible.

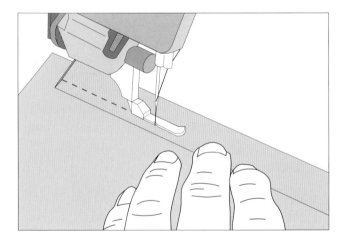

77 Piping with joining ends

When you are piping an item such as a cushion, you will need to join the two ends of the piping, so you must make the piping strips with a joining end.

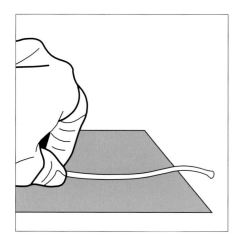

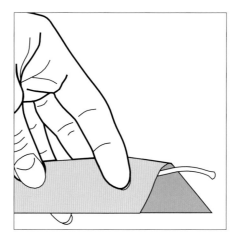

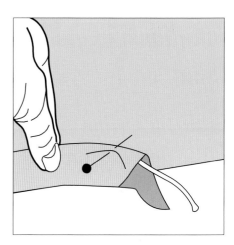

1 Leave the end of the fabric strip as an angle. Fold the fabric in half over the cord and place the two together onto the fabric.

2 Ensure that a little of the cord is protruding from the end of the piping strip.

3 Put a pin through the fabric and the cord to prevent the cord from slipping out.

4 Remember, having attached the piping, you will have to join the ends of the piping strips together. For ease of working make sure you don't start the piping too close to a corner.

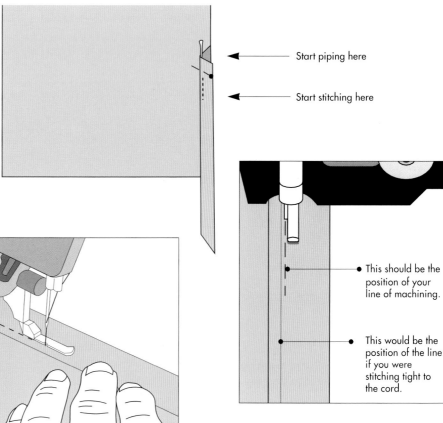

← Start piping here

← Start stitching here

● This should be the position of your line of machining.

● This would be the position of the line if you were stitching tight to the cord.

5 Leaving the first 5cm (2in) of the cord and fabric free to allow us to join the ends together more easily, machine using a 3mm (⅛in) stitch.

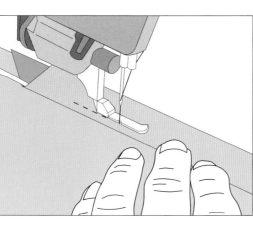

6 Don't sew too close to the cord.

78 Joining piping

When you have piped right round an item such as a cushion, you have to join the ends. This technique may look fiddly but, if you follow the steps carefully, you can make a perfect join.

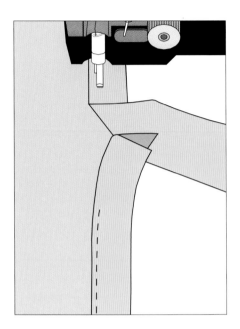

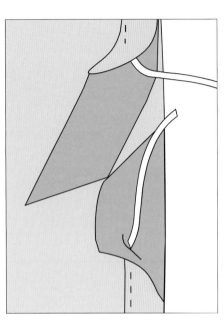

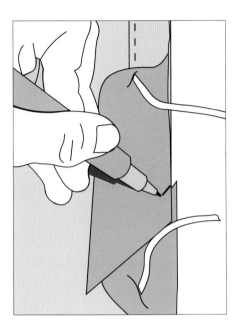

1 Finish machining about 8cm (3in) before you reach the start of the previous line of machining.

2 Remove the fabric from the machine and lay the two ends of the piping strip flat.

3 Make a mark where the two ends of the piping fabric overlap.

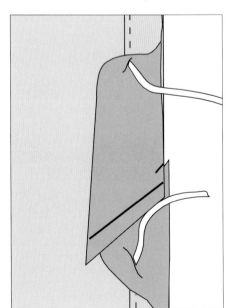

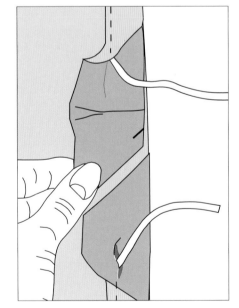

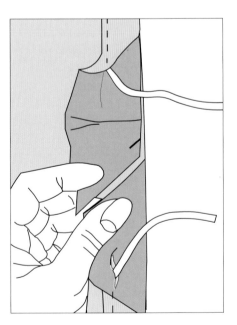

4 Allow just 1cm (½in) and draw another line, exactly following the angle of the cut end. Both the cut end and the new line should be parallel to the grain of the fabric.

5 Trim the piping fabric to the drawn line. The two ends should look as shown.

6 Bring the two ends of the piping fabric together.

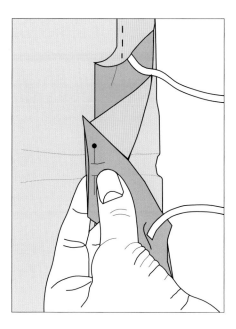

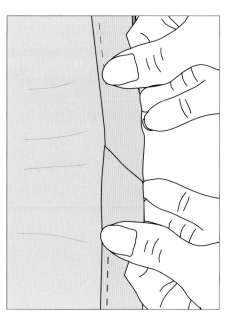

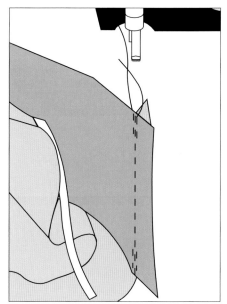

7 Right sides facing, pin the ends together with just one pin in the center. Take up almost all the 1cm (½in) seam allowance on stretchy fabrics and just over 0.5cm (¼in) on stiff fabrics. Fold the fabric back over the cord and lay it in position on the edge of the cushion.

8 The piping may seem tight, but pull it gently and the gathering should disappear. If it doesn't, take less fabric in the seam. If the piping fits without pulling, take more in the seam. This fit is important: as you machine the piping it stretches a little, so if it fits exactly now, you will get a bump when it is machined.

9 Machine the two ends together, taking the correct seam allowance as indicated by the position of the pin.

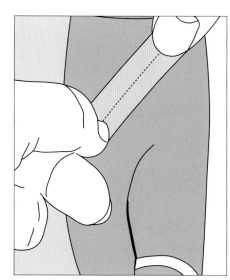

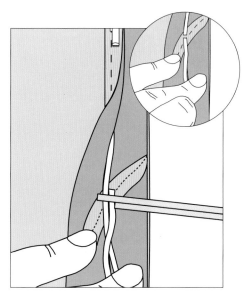

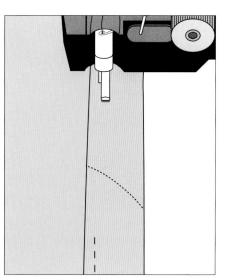

10 Use your thumbnails or a small metal ruler to open and flatten the seam. Place the main fabric back under the machine, where you stopped machining. Put the needle down.

11 Pull the main fabric and piping fabric taut and cut both cords where the piping fabric is joined. When the fabrics are pulled taut, the ends of the cord will just butt together.

12 Pull all the layers taut and check that the cord is in position before stitching across the join.

79 Piping square corners

This is a neat way of making perfect piped corners. It is not at all difficult, but do take the time to measure and mark carefully.

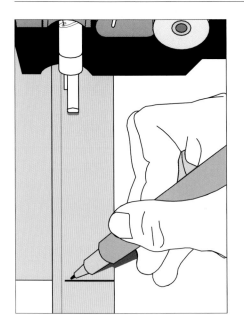

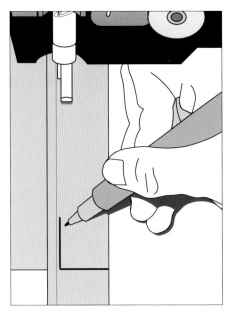

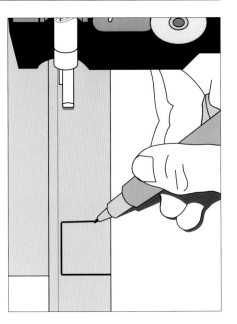

1 Before you get to the corner, stop machining with the needle in the fabric. Mark a line across the piping strip, level with the lower edge of the main fabric.

2 Draw a second line at right angles to the first line. This line should be on the potential machining line, not too close to the cord. It should be the same length as the first line.

3 Draw a third line at right angles to the second one to form a square.

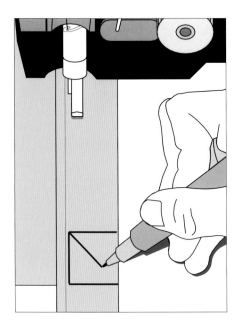

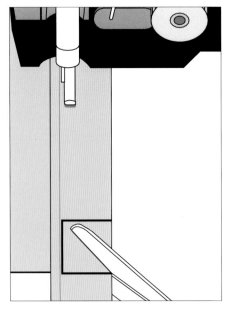

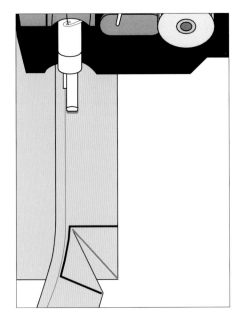

4 Draw a diagonal line as illustrated – this will be your cutting line.

5 Cut exactly along the diagonal line, making sure you cut through the piping fabric only.

6 Make sure that the cut finishes precisely at the corner of the marked square.

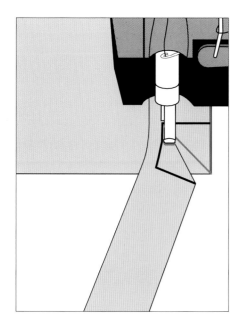

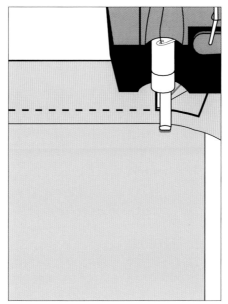

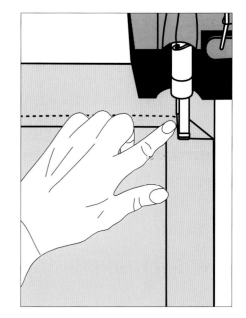

7 Sew up to the marked corner and stop with the needle in the fabric.

8 With the needle still down, raise the machine foot and turn the main fabric 90° anti-clockwise.

9 Swing the piping strip round and line up all the edges. Before you machine, press the strip flat, so that the foot stitches at the correct distance from the cord. There will be some fullness at the corner as at this stage the piping is on the inside: on the finished piece the piping will be on the outside. Lower the machine foot and continue to the next corner, where you repeat the process.

The secret of good piping is to make sure you do not pull on the cord or the fabric. Merely lay the cord and fabric strip onto the main fabric, hold the layers together firmly and allow the machine to stitch at its own pace: you are only preventing the layers moving one over the other.

80 Piping curves

In this instance, it is best to mark a stitching line on the main fabric with a fading marker before you begin. If the main fabric is even slightly stretchy on the cross, it is best not to cut out the curve. Simply leave the fabric as a whole piece, complete your piping then trim away the fabric. The fabric may stretch slightly as you sew the piping to the curves and this method helps to stabilise it.

1 To check you are sewing exactly on the line, lift the piping strip after each stretch of sewing. Care taken at this stage will ensure an exact fit.

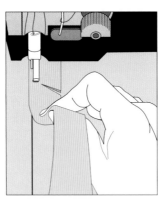

2 To enable the piping strip to lie smoothly on the curves, particularly on tight curves, notch it well before stitching. Be careful to only cut the piping fabric.

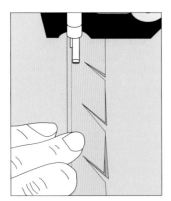

3 If the finished product is to have lining attached by hand, make sure that you stitch as tight to the cord as possible at this stage. If you are attaching another piece of fabric by machine, do not stitch so close to the cord.

See Technique 77, Piping with Joining Ends, page 73.

81 Piping with flanged cord

Attaching flanged cord to fabric is not the easiest of tasks. The most difficult types of cord to use are those which are too soft, too hard, have a light-colored flange rather than a color which matches the cord itself, and those which are attached to the flange with a straight stitch rather than a triangle stitch. The first three of these are self explanatory, the last can be shown in the following illustrations.

Flange attached with a straight stitch: this type is often more difficult to apply as it has a tendency to roll.

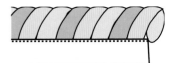

Flange attached with a triangle stitch: this type seems to lie much flatter.

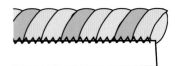

It is important to use a narrow, one-sided zip foot on your machine, as opposed to a welting or piping foot, if you want to show as little of the flange as possible. Of course you can help matters by choosing a cord with a flange which matches the cord well. Use the cord in the same way as you use fabric-covered piping and don't forget to notch the flange at the corners.

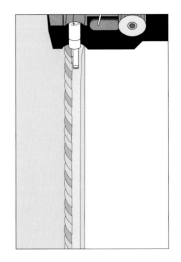

When assembling a cushion piped with flanged cord, firstly stitch the pieces together from the side of the cushion where the line of machining from attaching the cord shows. However, you will not get close enough to the cord with this line of machining, so then turn the cushion over and machine as close as possible to the cord on the other side.

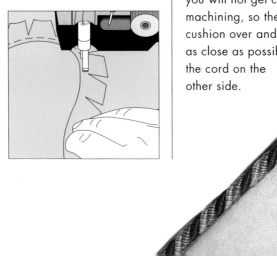

82 Joining flanged cord

This is a fiddly process but it is worth the effort as your join will be almost invisible. Use the same technique for joining both multi-colored and plain cords.

1 Stitch the cord to the cushion, leaving a 2cm (¾in) gap between the two ends of the cord.

See Technique 81, Piping with Flanged Cord, page 78.

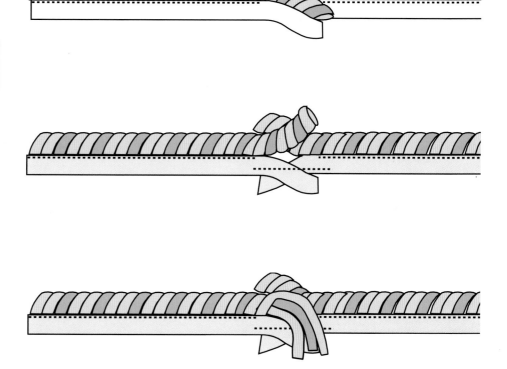

2 Undo the cord from the flanging as far back as the stitching. Cross over the loose ends of the flanges and machine across them to hold them out of the way.

3 On the left-hand side, untwist the cord a little and flatten the strands as shown.

4 Untwist the cord on the right side of the join and flatten the strands out so that the right-hand strands lie over the left-hand ones. If you are using a multi-coloured cord, it is not always possible to finish the operation with all the coloured strands in the correct sequence.

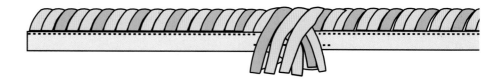

5 Machine across all the strands to secure them. If you are using a domestic machine, you may have to stitch the ends by hand. Trim off any excess cord.

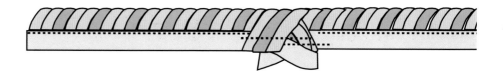

83 Inserting a zip between two pieces of fabric

This technique is illustrated on a round cushion, but the same method applies for any two pieces of fabric. If you are putting a zip into a cushion, it should measure approximately 8cm (3in) less than one side of the cushion.

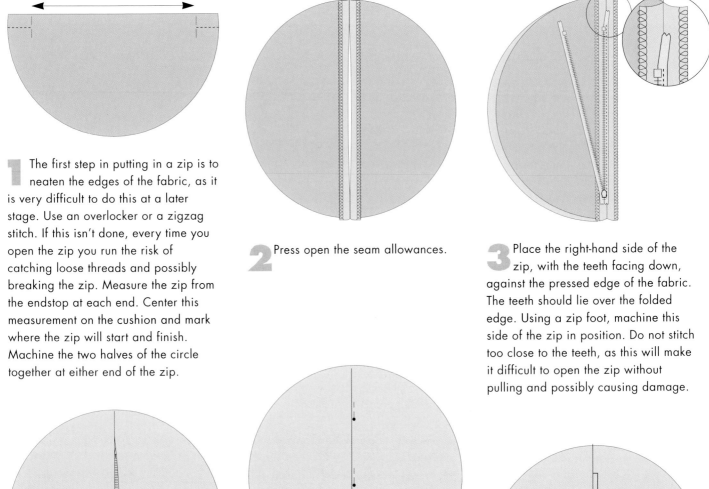

1 The first step in putting in a zip is to neaten the edges of the fabric, as it is very difficult to do this at a later stage. Use an overlocker or a zigzag stitch. If this isn't done, every time you open the zip you run the risk of catching loose threads and possibly breaking the zip. Measure the zip from the endstop at each end. Center this measurement on the cushion and mark where the zip will start and finish. Machine the two halves of the circle together at either end of the zip.

2 Press open the seam allowances.

3 Place the right-hand side of the zip, with the teeth facing down, against the pressed edge of the fabric. The teeth should lie over the folded edge. Using a zip foot, machine this side of the zip in position. Do not stitch too close to the teeth, as this will make it difficult to open the zip without pulling and possibly causing damage.

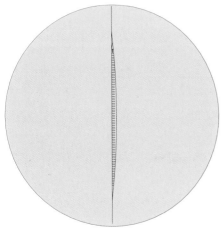

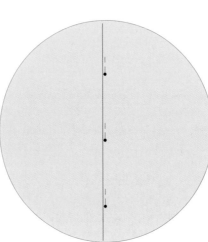

4 Do the zip up and turn the cushion over to the right side.

5 Pin the second side of the zip to the second side of the fabric. The pressed edges of the fabric should butt closely together. Machine the second side of the zip to the fabric with a zip foot. Start at the top and machine from the folded edge to about 2mm (⅛in) beyond the teeth; machine down the zip then back across to the folded edge.

6 As well as attaching the second side of the zip to the fabric, this second line of machining creates a flap that covers the zip.

84 Inserting a zip in a piped seam

This has been illustrated on a piped cushion, but the same technique can be used on any two pieces of fabric where one piece is piped. If your zip is made of nylon and is not the correct length, it is simple to stitch over the teeth a few times and then cut off the part of the zip that is not required.

See Technique 83, Inserting a Zip Between Two Pieces of Fabric, page 80.

1 Neaten the edges of the fabric. Mark where the ends of the zip teeth will lie with large pins. Then, right-sides facing, put the two sides of the cushion together.

2 Machine from the corners of the cushion to the pins, sewing as close as possible to the piping cord. Reverse to finish.

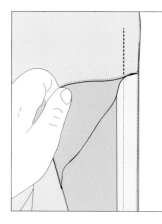

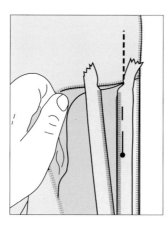

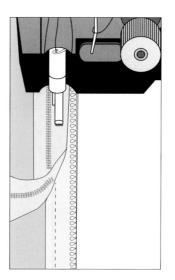

5 Close the zip and machine the pinned side in position as close to the teeth as possible, lifting the zip frequently to make sure you are lining it up correctly. If you try to sew longer stretches, the zip will move and a line of machining will show.

3 Fold back the section of the cushion that is not piped to enable you to place the zip.

4 Open up the zip and place it face down onto the piping, with the teeth of the right-hand side of the zip sitting in the center of the piping cord. Pin the top of the zip in place.

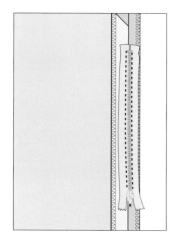

6 Turn the cushion over. Line the zip up with the inner edge of the overlocking line and stitch the second side to the fabric, as close to the teeth as possible, though not so tight that you can't move the slider easily.

7 Turn the cushion through to the right side. If you prefer, you can leave the zip as it is at this stage, or you can make a flap of fabric to cover the zip, which is useful if your zip is not a very good colour

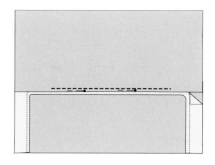

match. Pin the fabric over the zip: with some fabrics it is easier if you press the fabric over first. One row of stitching, as shown, will then make a flap. If you try to stitch the ends you will probably start to make it look quite ugly, so I think it is better to leave well alone.

85 Inserting a zip in the center of a border

This technique is used in making box cushions. The two strips of fabric either side of the zip should measure half the depth of the main border, plus 2cm (¾in) seam allowance on each long edge. This gives a 2cm (¾in) allowance on the edge joined to the zip, and a 2cm (¾in) allowance for joining the zip border to the main part of the cushion. The strips should be 4cm (1½in) longer than the zip.

See Technique 83, Inserting a Zip Between Two Pieces of Fabric, page 80.

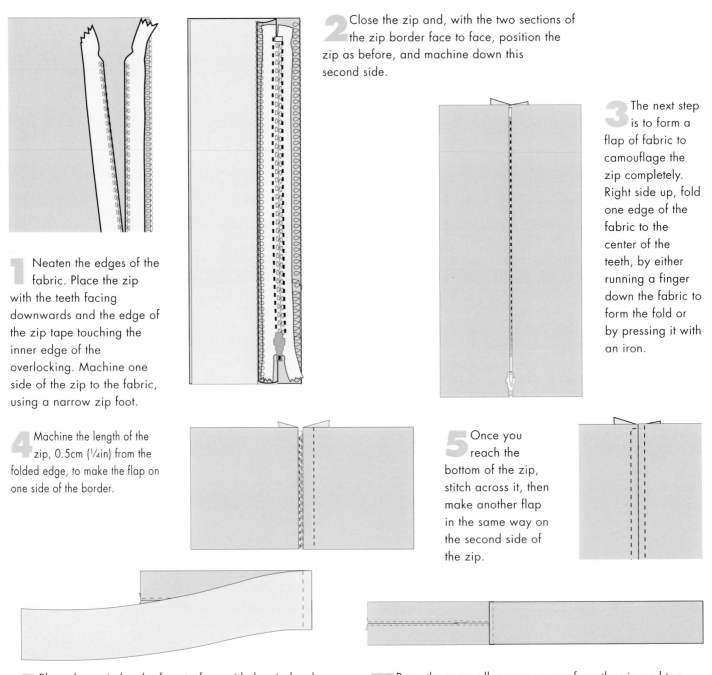

1 Neaten the edges of the fabric. Place the zip with the teeth facing downwards and the edge of the zip tape touching the inner edge of the overlocking. Machine one side of the zip to the fabric, using a narrow zip foot.

2 Close the zip and, with the two sections of the zip border face to face, position the zip as before, and machine down this second side.

3 The next step is to form a flap of fabric to camouflage the zip completely. Right side up, fold one edge of the fabric to the center of the teeth, by either running a finger down the fabric to form the fold or by pressing it with an iron.

4 Machine the length of the zip, 0.5cm (¼in) from the folded edge, to make the flap on one side of the border.

5 Once you reach the bottom of the zip, stitch across it, then make another flap in the same way on the second side of the zip.

6 Place the main border face to face with the zip border and machine them together, taking up a 2cm (¾in) seam allowance at each end. You will be stitching very close to the end of the zip.

7 Press the seam allowances away from the zip and top-stitch the seam for extra strength.

86 Making frilled edging

A frill is a versatile and easy-to-make edging that can be used on a multitude of soft furnishing projects. It must be in proportion to the item and the fabric must be fairly stiff or the frill will hang limply.

1 Cut a strip of fabric twice the depth you want the frill to be, plus 6cm (2½in). Fold the strip in half and press it if you prefer a crisp edge. If this is the first time you have used this method, it is best to stitch the raw edges together with a row of very large machine stitches to keep everything aligned while you are gathering. With practice you can miss this stage out.

2 Taking a 3cm (1¼in) seam allowance, place the strip under the machine, with the raw edges to the right. The extra allowance makes it easier to push the gathers under the machine foot. Place the needle down into the fabric, then raise the foot so that you can push the first group of folds under it. This is done by moistening your fingers and placing them flat on the fabric at either side of the needle. Gently push and you will find that a number of small gathers form.

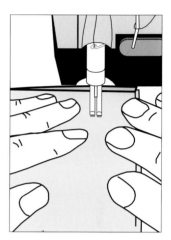

3 Once you have pushed the first group of gathers under the foot, repeat the action once or twice more, depending on the thickness of the fabric.

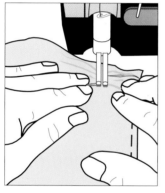

4 You don't have to actually form gathers. Make sure your fingers are flat on the fabric, push and the gathers will form themselves. Using the left hand only, hold the gathers in place and lower the machine foot with the other hand – you will not be able to machine with the foot raised. If the machine makes a strange noise and knots up, you have probably forgotten to lower the foot.

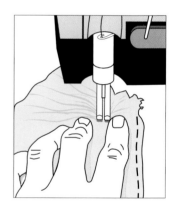

5 Sew to the front of the group of gathers, making sure you push the fabric on each side of the needle as the machine stitches. Initially this may seem difficult, but relaxing your shoulders and practice will make it easier. If you do not continue to push, the gathers will be flattened out by the machine and you will end up with a very uneven frill. Continue to gather the fabric, though you do not have to raise the foot again, simply push a group of gathers up to it, then machine over them.

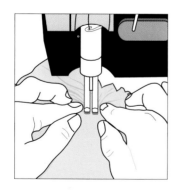

Whenever I show this method to students, their first query is how they judge the amount of fabric they will need. The answer is to allow two-and-a-half to three times fullness, depending on the thickness of the fabric. Gather a sample section of the frill. Measure this piece and if the gathers are too tight and you are not getting a sufficient length of frill, pull to release the gathers. Gather up the fabric again, but this time do not push as hard when you are forming the gathers.

You should always end up with a slightly longer strip of frill than you actually need. This may be required when you are attaching it to a cushion, particularly on the corners. Using this method of gathering, you may waste a small amount of fabric, but this will be more than compensated for by the time you save, let alone the lack of aggravation from sore fingers and broken gathering threads if you do it by hand.

See Technique 92, Inserting Edgings Around a Corner, page 85.

87 Making bound-edge frilled edging

This is a pretty variation on a plain frilled edging and it is only very slightly more complicated to make.

See Technique 86, Making Frilled Edging, page 83.

Cut and join two pieces of fabric, one a minimum of 2cm (¾in) wider than the other. Machine the two strips together and press open the seam. Press the fabric strip in half and gather in the normal way.

88 Making double-frilled edging

For this technique the thickness of the fabric is critical. A fine quality chintz is the perfect weight to use.

See Technique 86, Making Frilled Edging, page 83.

Cut two strips of fabric, one 2-3cm (¾-1¼in) wider than the other. Fold each strip in half widthways and lay the narrower one on top of the wider one. Machine the strips together, close to the raw edges, with a very large stitch to hold the layers together while you are working on them.

The technique for gathering is exactly the same as for making a normal frill. You will not be able to push the gathers quite so close together, however, because of the bulk of fabric involved.

89 Making pleated edging

If you want to achieve a stunning pleated edging, make the pleats fairly small. Large pleats tend to make your work look amateurish. Fold the strips of fabric and machine the long raw edges together. Allow three times fullness.

See Technique 86, Making Frilled Edging, page 83.

1 Place the strip under the machine and form the first pleat by folding the fabric, with the fold pointing away from the needle and towards you. Machine until you just catch the back of the pleat. Do not stitch any further or there will not be enough space to form the next pleat.

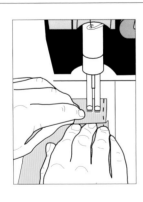

2 Place a piece of tape on the machine bed where you push to form the next pleat; from the front of the last pleat, this will be twice the width of the finished pleat. Form the next pleat, pushing the fabric under the new pleat until it touches the last one. A small pointed tool such as scissors or an unpicker can help make this easier.

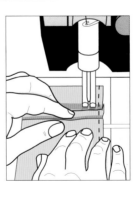

3 Machine until you catch the back of the new pleat, then start to form the next pleat. Continue the process until you have sufficient pleated edging.

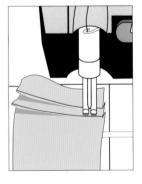

90 Making ruched edging

This is an attractive alternative edging, made from strips of fabric approximately 9cm (3½in) wide. As with the normal pleated edging, you will need to allow three times fullness.

See Technique 89, Making Pleated Edging, page 84.

1 Insert a length of thin cord or a narrow strip of selvedge into the fold of the fabric strip and pin it in place. Pleat up the strip of fabric. The cord makes it a little more difficult, but if you use your left hand to help to form the pleats, it makes the process a little easier.

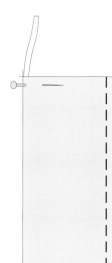

2 After you have pleated up about 25cm (10in) of the fabric strip, stop the machine with the needle down in the fabric. Gently pull on the cord, while holding the end of the fabric securely with your left hand, to ruche the edge. Continue to pleat up and ruche 25cm (10in) sections in this way. The cord remains inside the edging.

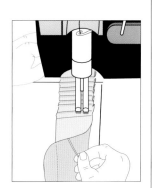

91 Inserting edgings

If you are attaching an edging to a piped piece of fabric, it is important to do it the right way or it will look untidy.

Place the piped fabric right-side down on top of the edging. Following the line of machining attaching the piping to the fabric, stitch the piped fabric to the edging. Every few centimeters (couple of inches), raise the top fabric and line up the layers, making sure that the new stitching line covers the line of machining on the edging. As there is a 3cm (1¼in) seam allowance on the edging, you will have to trim away excess once the edge is attached. Do not sew tightly against the piping, but merely on top of the previous line of stitching.

92 Inserting edgings around a corner

Nothing looks worse than frills or pleats that are stretched and flattened at the corners. The following technique will give you a perfect corner.

See Technique 91, Inserting Edgings, page 85.

Approximately 1cm (½in) before you reach the corner, stop the machine with the needle down in the fabric. Raise the foot and gently close together the pleats or gathers, pushing in as much fabric as you can. Take care not to push the folds on top of one another, as this will create even more bulk and may break the needle.

Machine to the corner, place the needle in the fabric and turn the cushion through 90°. Again, ease in extra fabric for the first 1cm (½in) of this side of the cushion.

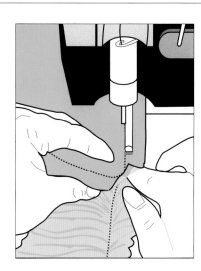

A good corner

A bad corner

93 Joining edgings

A neat join will reduce bulk and stop the edging sticking out, as well as looking good.

See Technique 91, Inserting Edgings, page 85.

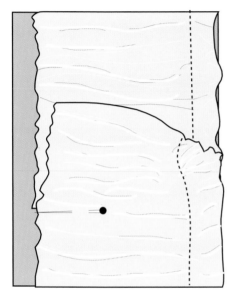

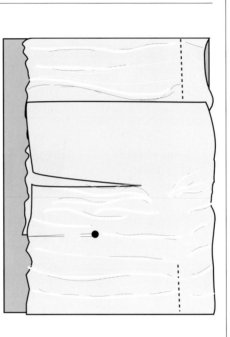

1 Where the two parts of the frill or pleats overlap, place a pin on the upper piece of edging. From this point to the end of the edging, pull on the gathers to break the gathering thread, giving you a flattened area for joining the two pieces.

2 Leave a 2cm (¾in) seam allowance from the pin and trim away the excess fabric.

3 Pull to release the gathers on the underneath section of the edging to flatten it. Completely unfold the two pieces of edging and, right sides facing, join them together, taking just a 1cm (½in) seam allowance. Flatten the seam and fold the frill in half again. You will have excess fabric in the edging around the seam, which you can then tuck by hand to fit the main fabric. From the edging side, machine these gathers or pleats in position.

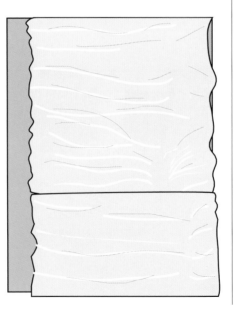

94 Joining ruched edging

Joining ruched fabric is very similar to joining a frilled or pleated edge.

See Technique 93, Joining Edgings, page 86.

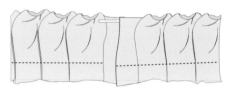

1 Lay one end of the ruche over the other and join in the usual way.

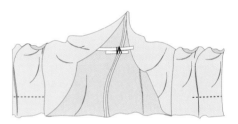

2 Before reforming the pleating, lay the two ends of the cord together. The cord must fit the frill snugly. Then stitch the ends of the cord together. This is essential to maintain the ruched edge.

95 Attaching fan-edge, bullion and cushion ruche trimmings

In general, I prefer purchased trims such as fan-edge and bullion to be attached by hand using a small backstitch. Cushion ruche can be attached by machine in a cushion seam or by hand if being used as a surface trim. Occasionally some others can be machined; for instance, a very stable, mainly cotton fringe to a bedspread. Sometimes trims are glued to fabric-covered cornices, though this is something I avoid at all costs as I am still not convinced that it doesn't fall off in the long term. I have occasionally been asked to repair such work and there is nothing worse than stitching a trim that has been previously glued.

For attaching trims to stiffened or bulky fabrics, and especially fabric-covered cornices, I usually use a small, slender circular needle, which helps to give a much flatter finish. Do not attempt to use the enormous upholstery needles you find in household repair kits.

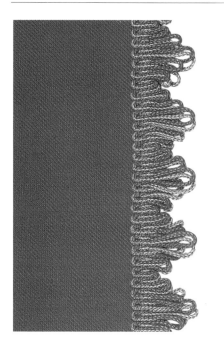

Fan-edge

This can be used to great effect on the leading edge of a curtain. It can either be stitched on so that the actual 'fan' protrudes from the edge of the curtain, or set back from the edge, leaving 2-3cm (¾-1¼in) of the curtain edge showing. I usually use two rows of stitching through the braided section to attach it or it tends to curl in use.

You can also use it on cornices, cushions, tiebacks and valances. However, be particularly careful using it on the lower edge of valances, as it can look a little feeble and not quite in proportion.

Bullion

This can be found in varying depths and weights, so be careful to choose one that is appropriate for your project. On a cautious note, if you are using this type of fringe for a valance, make sure that it is not an upholstery bullion, which has a rather stiff and bulky top. Because of the fullness involved in a valance the fringe will cause it to hang very strangely, rather than in the beautiful folds the correct weight of trim encourages.

Cushion ruche

When used in cushions, this trim is undoubtedly best machined in position on one side of the cushion in just the same way as piping. I overlock the fabric edges first, as it is difficult to do this once the ruche is attached. Do not remove the thread which holds the outer edge of the ruche together until you have completed the cushion: it prevents the loops from catching in the machine and from being caught up in the seam allowance.

To join the ends of cushion ruche on the cushion, simply butt them up to one another and machine across them.

96 Making ribbon mitres

The best type of ribbon to use with furnishing fabrics is petersham, which is available in various widths and a wonderful range of colors. It is undoubtedly the easiest way of adding a contrast border, as there is no need to turn in raw edges and the mitres are too simple to be true.

I don't find any need to pin the ribbon onto the fabric, in fact, I find if I do it tends to move. Using a fading marker, draw a line on the fabric where you want the outer edge of the ribbon to lie. Starting in the top right-hand corner of the fabric, place the ribbon in position and machine down the right-hand edge. Make sure you do not stretch the fabric or the ribbon, and stitch as close to the edge as possible. Stop stitching before you reach the corner, then fold the mitre as shown.

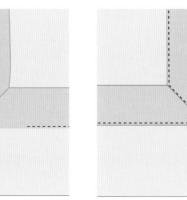

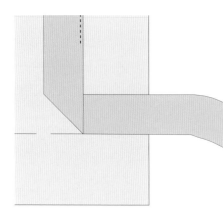

1 Fold the ribbon under as shown, making sure that the lower point is exactly on the line. Because petersham ribbon has ribbed lines, it is easy to make certain that the angle is 45°.

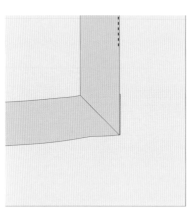

2 Bring the ribbon tail back on itself to the left, under the piece you have already stitched to the blind.

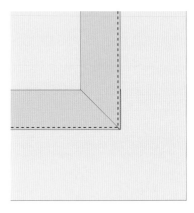

3 Line up all the edges to look as shown and stitch around the corner. Continue stitching until you are approximately 10cm (4in) from the second corner.

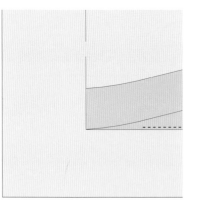

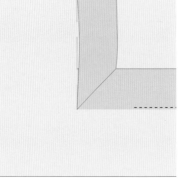

4 To make this mitre match the first one, fold the ribbon back on itself exactly on the marked line. Fold the ribbon up from the corner at 45°. Machine around the corner. Continue in this way to complete the border. Start a second line of machining, close to the inner edge of the ribbon, at the point where you started the first line.

5 At the corner, stitch down the mitre. With the needle down, turn the work so that you can stitch back in exactly the same stitch holes.

97 Making Maltese crosses

Maltese crosses are usually used to trim traditional soft furnishings, such as swags and tails. They can also be used instead of rosettes for a more tailored look, which is emphasised if the cross is not padded. Make crosses in a complementary or contrasting fabric to the main item, either can look stunning.

I have given dimensions for a Maltese cross below, but you can, of course, make them larger than this. However, the fabric must be stiff enough to support itself or the cross will droop and look absolutely dreadful. Attach the Maltese crosses to the main item with a few small hand stitches or, if you want to be able to remove them easily for cleaning, with small squares of Velcro.

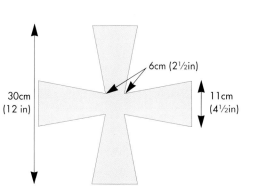

1 Cut out a paper or card template, as shown. Add 1cm (½in) seam allowance all round and cut out two pieces of fabric for each cross.

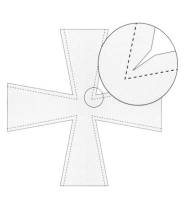

2 Machine round the edges as shown. Cut a notch in the corners before turning the cross through to the right side and pressing it.

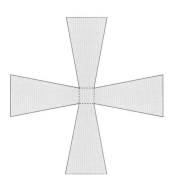

3 If you want a padded look, machine a square in the center of the cross and lightly fill the arms of the cross with wadding. If you prefer a crisper look, miss out this stage.

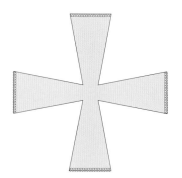
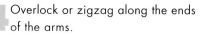

4 Overlock or zigzag along the ends of the arms.

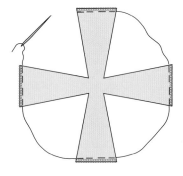

5 Using large stitches, four to each arm, and a strong thread, sew across the end of each arm of the cross.

6 Pull the threads tight to gather the ends to the center of the cross. Sew through the center of the cross, connecting all the layers of fabric. Cover a 29mm (1¼in) self-cover button and stitch it to the center of the cross.

98 Making ruche rosettes

Ruche rosettes look wonderful in the middle of cushions or attached to the ends of bolsters. They can be bought ready-made, but if, however, a rosette to match your cushion is not available, it is possible to make one from cushion ruche or brush fringe.

The ruche has a number of lines of stitching along the lower edge. Sometimes, if they are very tight, it makes it impossible to curl the ruche. To make the rosette and to prevent the ends from fraying, I machine another line of small

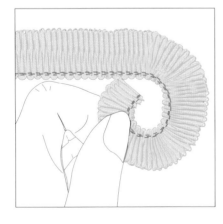

stitches as close to the bottom edge of the ruche as possible. Reverse a number of times at each end to finish. The manufacturer's stitching lines can then be cut off if necessary. Curl the ruche round as shown. Continue turning until a good shape is formed, then secure with hand stitches and strong thread. Attach the rosette by hand. For a large rosette, like the one shown, you will need 60cm (24in) of fringe and for a small rosette, 10cm (4in).

99 Making inserted borders

This type of contrast band is mainly used on valances of all types, dressing-table frills and bed hangings. It is important to choose a weight of fabric for the contrast band that is similar in weight to the main fabric or the border will not hang properly.

See Project 3, The Classic Valance, page 106.

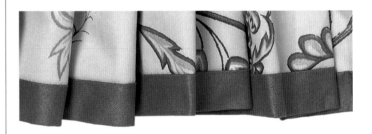

Cut the strips very accurately, allowing the required amount for the front of the band, plus 3cm (1¼in) at the back of the valance, plus 2cm (¾in) seam allowance on each long edge. So, if you want the strip to measure 4cm (1½in) on the front of the valance cut it as follows: 4cm (1½in) + 3cm (1¼in) + 2cm (¾in) + 2cm (¾in) =11cm (4¼in).
Join the contrast band to the main fabric taking a 2cm (¾in) seam allowance. To make absolutely certain the that band will be level, place a piece of tape on the machine bed 2cm (¾in) from the needle, and make sure the edges of the fabrics are kept against the tape while you machine.

Attach the lining to the other side of the border strip. Press open the seams and measure with a small ruler to make sure that there is the correct amount of contrast showing on the front of the valance. Press the edge.

100 Making curved borders

Adding a contrast band to the base of a curved valance is a little trickier than adding one to a straight valance.

See Project 3, The Classic Valance, page 106.

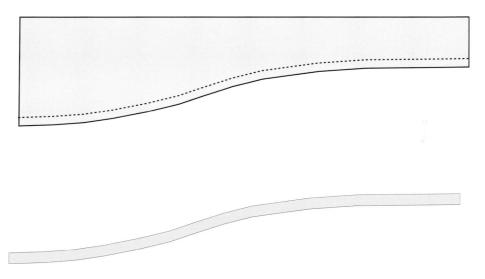

1 For the valance itself, I make a brown paper or thick polythene template, which includes the seam allowances, then cut out the main fabric and lining. Using the same template, a small ruler and a pencil, I draw a line on the paper which should be the final width of the contrast band, plus a 1cm (½in) seam allowance for the top edge of the band, plus 2cm (¾in) for the bottom edge.

2 Cut this strip from the paper template and use it to cut out the contrast fabric. The drawback of this method is that it can be very wasteful of fabric, but the finished product will look professional. Take the strip to your ironing table and place it right side down. Press 1cm (½in) at the top edge of the band to the back. You cannot get a smooth curve if you take the normal seam allowance of 2cm (¾in). Be careful not to stretch the strip at all.

Pin the contrast band right side up to the right side of the lower edge of the valance, aligning the raw edges along the bottom of the valance. Machine very close to the top edge of the band.

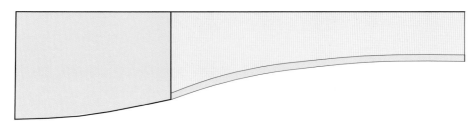

3 Repeat the process with the lining. If the valance is very shaped the lining might show, so you can line the whole valance with the contrast fabric, though this could look messy from outside the window. Alternatively, line the outer widths (which are hanging over the curtains and are rarely seen from outside) with the contrast fabric and use a contrast band and lining for the remainder of the valance, as shown above.

Right sides facing, put the front and back of the valance together and machine along the bottom and side hems.

With some fabrics, you may find it best to trim the bottom seam allowance back to 1cm (½in). Notch the curves well and press, making sure you slightly roll the bottom hem so that the seam does not show on the front of the valance.

91

101 Making contrast leading edges

These do add an extra-special touch to a curtain. They can be made in a contrast color or in a pattern if the curtain is plain, and vice versa. At its simplest, a contrast leading edge can be machined on if the fabrics are of equal weight.

See Project 1, The Classic Curtain, page 96.

1 Add the contrast leading edge to the curtain once you have cut and pattern-matched all the lengths, but before you start making up the curtain. Decide how wide you want the contrast to be and cut a strip to this width plus 4cm (1½in) seam allowances, by the length of the main fabric plus 2cm (¾in). Prepare the contrast band by turning up the bottom edge 2cm (¾in) and folding the band in half.

2 Right-sides facing and raw edges aligned, place the band against the edge of the curtain with its lower, folded edge against the fold line for the bottom hem. Machine from the hem towards the top of the curtain taking a 2cm (¾in) seam allowance.

3 Turn to the reverse of the curtain and gently press the contrast band with the seam towards the main fabric. To improve the hang of the leading edge, I would suggest using a herringbone stitch to hold the band's seam allowance flat. Press in the 2cm (¾in) seam allowance on the side hem below the contrast band.

4 Fold up and slip stitch the bottom hem, then ladder stitch the corner.

5 Place the lining in position and attach it by hand to the back of the contrast leading edge, making sure you hide the line of machine stitching.

See Technique 76, Piping with Square Ends, page 72.

6 For a truly beautiful finish, add interlining and complementary piping to the contrast leading edge, as shown in the picture opposite. Fold in the end of the piping fabric, place in the cord and machine to the edge of the curtain.

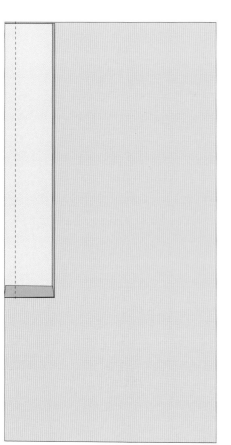

7 Cut a strip of interlining 2cm (¾in) shorter than the contrast band. Turn the lower edge of the band over the interlining and machine the two fabrics to the edge of the curtain, making sure you cover the stitching line from the piping. On the seam allowance, trim the interlining back to the machining line to cut down on bulk.

8 Turn the curtain over and gently press the contrast band only, with the seams towards the main fabric. Press under the 2cm (¾in) seam allowance on the side hem below the contrast leading edge. Fold the interlining and the contrast band to the back of the curtain and secure them with herringbone stitches. Finish the bottom hem and attach the lining as previously described.

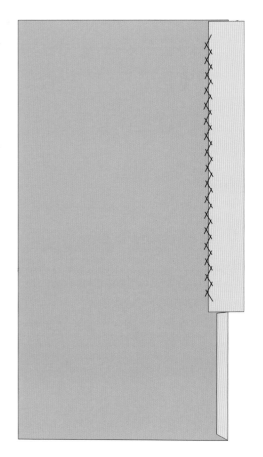

102 Making mitred borders

Mitred borders have many uses in soft furnishings, whether functional, as on the corners of a bed valance, or decorative, as on a cushion. They can be used on wallhangings, loose covers, fitted bedspreads; in fact a-million-and-one items. I always found the method itself very laborious until I developed the following technique, which for ease I will illustrate on a cushion.

2 Cut the strips with sufficient length for each corner angle; check this by folding the end of the strip over at 45°. Place one strip against the center section, raw edges aligned. Machine very precisely between the two marks, reversing at each end to secure.

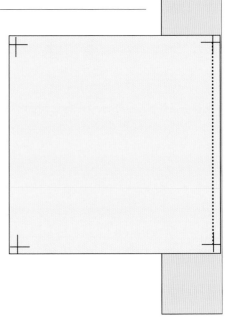

1 Very accurately mark a point 2cm (¾in) in from each corner on the wrong side of the center part of the cushion.

3 Fold back both the corners, as shown, before attaching the second strip.

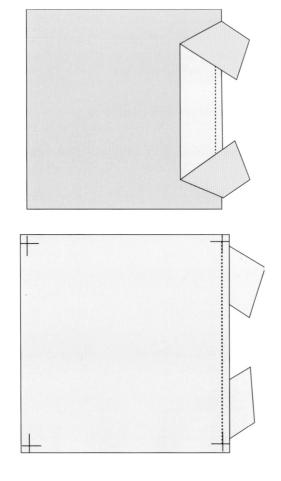

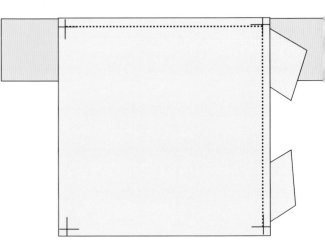

4 Attach the second strip in exactly the same way as the first one, making sure that you do not catch the first strip in the line of machining.

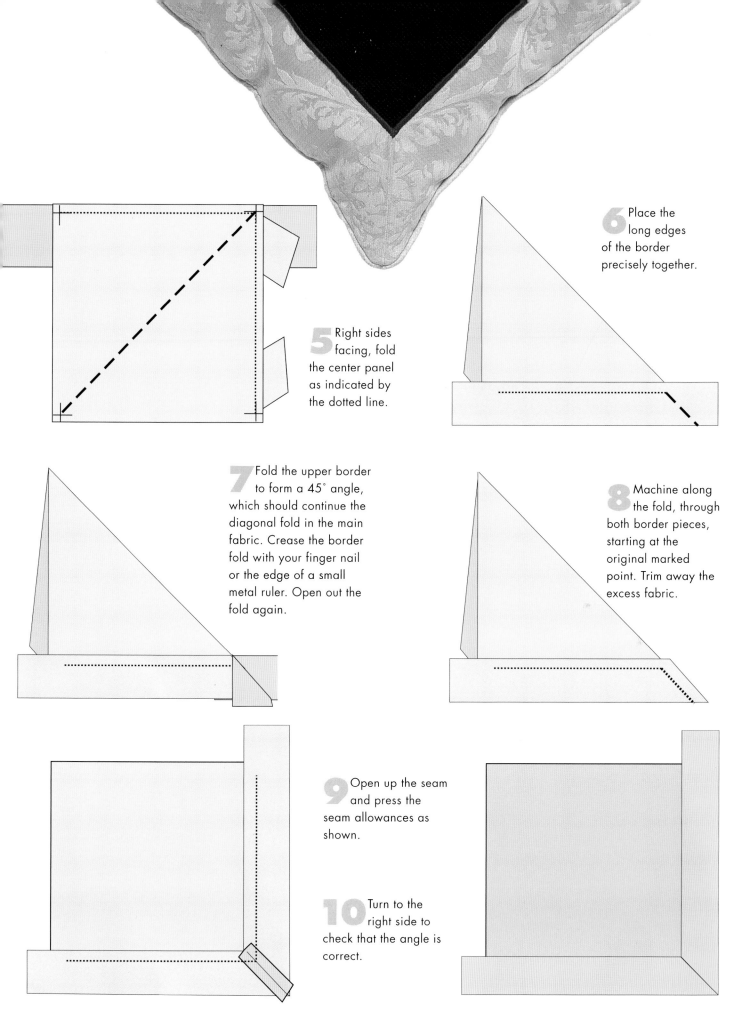

5 Right sides facing, fold the center panel as indicated by the dotted line.

6 Place the long edges of the border precisely together.

7 Fold the upper border to form a 45° angle, which should continue the diagonal fold in the main fabric. Crease the border fold with your finger nail or the edge of a small metal ruler. Open out the fold again.

8 Machine along the fold, through both border pieces, starting at the original marked point. Trim away the excess fabric.

9 Open up the seam and press the seam allowances as shown.

10 Turn to the right side to check that the angle is correct.

PROJECT 1

The classic curtain

All curtains are simply variations on this project, so learn to make it well and you will be able to tackle anything. Don't be put off by the size of curtains; there is a lot of fabric involved, but don't forget that the largest curtain in the world only has two side hems and one bottom hem. As long as you are methodical, all will be well. Whenever you are making a soft-furnishing item, and particularly curtains, measure off the lengths you need and then measure again before you cut into expensive fabric. If you get a seam wrong you can unpick it and usually it won't show, but you can't lengthen a wrongly cut drop without putting a really ugly join right across it.

Materials

Fabric

Lining

Tape or buckram

Machine thread

Hand-sewing thread

Curtain hooks

Lead weights, plus strips of lining for weight bags

Equipment

Long pins

Long fine needles

Clamps or bricks

Measuring tape

Small ruler

Iron and ironing mat

Scissors

Vanishing marker

1 See Techniques 19-20, Hook Positions for Curtain Tracks and Hook Positions for Curtain Poles, pages 28-29.

2 See Technique 22, Measuring for Curtains, page 30.

3 See Technique 27, Calculating Fullness and Quantities for Curtains, page 34.

4 See Technique 29, Measuring Pattern Repeats, page 36.

5 See Technique 30, Calculating Quantities for Patterned Fabrics, page 36.

6 See Techniques 35-37, Cutting Plain and Lining Fabrics, Cutting Velvets, Cutting Patterned Fabrics, pages 41-42.

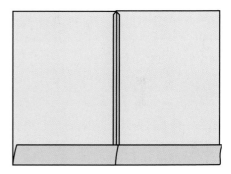

7 Cut off the first curtain drop and fold it carefully. I rarely iron a completed curtain, it is unnecessary hard work and is not terribly effective as the curtain tends to crease up as it is moved off the ironing board. The curtain, however, needs to be carefully looked after at all stages, not just left in a bundle.

Fold the fabric vertically to a quarter of its width, then fold the top of the curtain to the bottom, but insert a piece of tubing or a rolled-up magazine in the fold to prevent it from creasing. The reason for doing this is that when a curtain is hanging, the vertical creases will usually hang into the folds, but any horizontal creases across the folds are painfully obvious and will have to be removed by steaming or pressing on site. An alternative to this method is to purchase a mobile wardrobe rail, which the curtains can be hung over at all stages, and then they can be wheeled to any part of the workroom. Specialist companies make mobile racks specifically for this, though these tend to be expensive.

If the fabric is plain or striped, cut a small notch in the bottom edge of each drop. Sometimes there will be color variations if a length of fabric is turned upside down, so the notches make it easier to join the drops in the same direction.

8 See Technique 101, Making Contrast Leading Edges, page 92.

9 See Techniques 41-43, Joining Plain and Lining Fabrics, Joining Velvets, Joining Patterned Fabrics, pages 44-45.

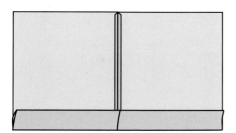

11 Turn up a further 10cm (4in), gently pressing the fold, making an almost double hem to add weight, and provide fabric to use if ever the curtains need to be let down. Pin to hold the hem in place.

10 Having added a contrast leading edge, if required, and joined the curtain drops, we are now ready to turn up the bottom hem. Lay the curtain across your table with an ironing mat underneath, or lay it over an ironing board, but be careful not to pull the board over with the weight of the curtain. Using a 15cm (6in) ruler, carefully turn up 9cm (3½in) along the bottom edge of the curtain gently pressing the fold as you go; do not use a 'steam roller' action. If you are turning up the hem according to the pattern, choose an appropriate point and turn up the remainder of the hem to that same point. If the pattern varies across the width, or if by turning up the fabric to show exactly the right amount of each pattern the hem becomes twisted, work from seam to seam using the pattern at one point only on each width of fabric. Any serious pattern problems should have been sorted out before you started cutting.

Techniques 46-47, Pressing Fabrics and Making an Ironing Mat, page 47.

12 Press in the side hems. The measurement of these can vary because of the way the fabric has been printed, but it is usually 7.5cm (2⅞in). If a printed fabric has a very wide selvedge, make sure that at least 3.5cm (1⅜in) of the printed fabric shows on the side hem. Trim off part of the selvedge if it is too wide.

A recurring problem is fabric with borders printed too close to the selvedge. In this case, in turning in the correct amount for the side hem you have to fold in part of the border, or the amount of fabric available to turn in is too narrow for the side hem to hang correctly. The only solution to this problem that I have been reasonably happy with is to cut off the border from the outer edge of the curtain (or some of the plain fabric if the design has a border down one side only) and stitch it to the leading edge. I then use this to form the side hem. This means that you get a seam on the leading edge, which you must roll to the back of the curtain. Occasionally you can take the seam round the back of the curtain until it lies just under the lining.

Sadly, until fabric designers take this matter into consideration, this is the best solution to the problem.

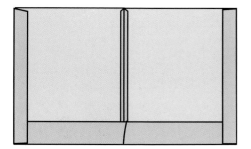

13 See Technique 50, Folded Mitres, page 50.

14 See Technique 48, Making Lead Weight Bags, page 48.

15 Having mitred the bottom corners of the curtain, unfold the side and bottom hems to place the lead weight bags as shown. Machine across the top of each bag to secure it, then re-fold the hems. The bottom hem can be stitched in place using blind hem stitch on a sewing machine or by hand, using slip stitch. The side hems can be stitched by hand using herringbone stitch or machine blind hem stitch into a single layer of fabric.

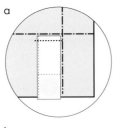

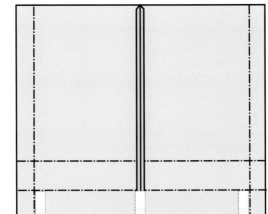

16 To make-up and attach the lining, lay the curtain face down on the table, with the bottom hem to the bottom edge of the table and the side hem to the side edge of the table. Place a clamp at the lower corner and gently smooth the side hem flat, without pulling or stretching it. Place another clamp at the top of the curtain. For an extra long curtain, it is advisable to put a third clamp in the center. Measure the whole width of the curtain from side to side. This measurement is the basis of the calculation you must do to work out how much lining fabric you will need.

See Techniques 53-54, Herringbone Stitch and Slip Stitch, page 53.

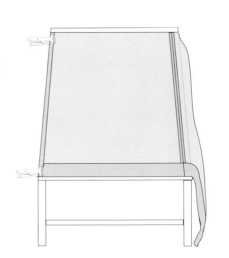

Take as an example one curtain made of two widths of 122cm- (48in-) wide fabric. You would also use 122cm- (48in-) wide lining. The total width of the curtain should be approximately 222cm (87¼in), depending on the amount taken in for pattern matching etc.

222cm (87¼in)	– 6cm (2½in)	+ 10cm (4in) = 226cm (88¾in)
Width of curtain	*sides 3cm (1¼in) narrower than curtain width*	*5cm (2in) of lining turned under each side*

You do not always have the luxury of 5cm (2in) for the side turnings on the lining, but it is difficult to get a smooth line with a turning of less than 2cm (¾in).

I do not like to make the lining so that it fits the curtain exactly. Somehow, during the process some lining always seems to disappear, so I add on 1cm (½in) per width. This excess can always be made into a tiny tuck in the lining when sewing on the curtain tape, but it is difficult to find extra fabric if the lining is a little too tight.

Therefore the width I would cut my lining would be;

226cm (88¾in)	+ 2cm (¾in)	= 228cm (89½in)
width of lining	*1cm (½in) for each width of lining*	*cut width of lining*

17 Cut the necessary drops of lining, join them together and press open the seams. Press up 4cm (1½in) then a further 8cm (3in) for the bottom hem. You do not normally allow any extra for shrinkage because lining looks very unsightly if it is let down, as the machining line shows very badly. The second turn is 8cm (3in), as opposed to the 10cm (4in), of the main fabric, because when the fabric and lining are put together, the bottom of the lining hem should be 2cm (¾in) up from the bottom edge of the curtain. Lining can be very unpredictable so you make this allowance in case it stretches or drops. Also, if light shines through the curtain, it looks so much better if the top of the lining hem and the top of the main fabric hem are level. Machine the bottom hem. If you think the linings may have to be altered at a later date, it is worth sewing them by hand or at least blind-hemming them to minimise the stitching line. Gently press the hem. If the lining was folded in half and wrapped on a board, you will also need to press out the fold lines.

See Technique 41, Joining Plain and Lining Fabrics, page 44.

While making this project you will end up with a lot of fabric on the floor at various times. Treat it carefully and avoid creasing it.

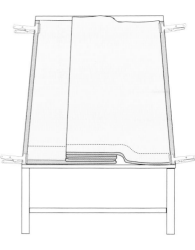

18 Press under the side hems of the lining by the calculated amount. Wrong-sides facing, lay the lining onto the curtain, with one pressed side of the lining against one clamped side of the main fabric. Remove the clamp at the bottom of the main fabric and place the corner of the lining 2cm (¾in) up from the bottom hem and 3cm (1¼in) in from the side hem. The corner of the lining should sit exactly on the fold of the folded mitre in the main fabric.

Pin the corner in position, replace the clamp and gently lay the lining in position along the side hem of the main fabric without stretching or pulling it. Holding the lining and fabric firmly, adjust the top clamp to hold both the fabrics. Measure along the side hem to check that there is exactly 3cm (1¼in) of main fabric showing and pin the layers together very close to the edge of the lining: the stitching will then help to conceal the pin holes.

19 Repeat the process on the other side hem, folding the excess fabric in the center of the table to prevent creasing. If you do not have a table available, try to recreate the same situation on the floor using covered bricks instead of clamps. Clamping and folding the fabrics in this way allows you to stitch both side hems without moving, and thereby creasing, the fabric any further.

Use slip stitch to attach the lining to the curtain. This is so much sturdier than a machined hem and the fabric is much less likely to twist. Should the lining or the main fabric shrink in cleaning, this row of hand-sewing can be undone, leaving a complete curtain intact. It is then a simple matter to re-attach the lining.

See Technique 54, Slip Stitch, page 53.

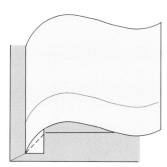

20 At the bottom corner, lift the lining and make three oversew stitches to strengthen the end of the seam. To prevent the folded-under lining from hanging down, fold the lining into a triangle, as shown by the dotted line, and secure it with a few stitches.

21 The next stage is to take the final cutting measurement. Take as an example a curtain with a hook drop measurement of 239cm (94in). When you were working out your fabric quantities, you added 25cm (10in) to this measurement to allow for the hem and heading, but now you must make a more exact calculation so that your curtain fits the window exactly.

When you are working out a final cutting measurement you must first take a piece of the right tape, place the curtain hook in the correct hook pocket and measure from the top of the hook to the top of the tape. In this example we will use a standard 2.5cm (1in) tape. The hook actually comes to the top of this tape when the curtain is hung.

2.5cm (1in) tape can be placed right to the top of the curtain, as it is rarely used without some form of top treatment. However, I prefer to use a 2cm (¾in) heading above the tape, as this gives me the opportunity to let down the curtains if necessary, by removing the tape, turning over 1.5cm (⅝in), and re-applying the tape to the top of the curtain. This is a much simpler task than letting down the hems.

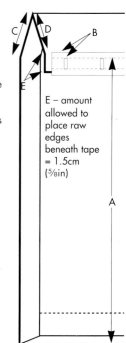

A – floor to hook = 239cm (93½in)

B – from top of hook to the top of tape. On standard tape this does not apply as hook comes to top of tape.

C – from top of tape to top of curtain = 2cm (¾in)

D – from top of curtain back down to tape = 2cm (¾in)

E – amount allowed to place raw edges beneath tape = 1.5cm (⅝in)

floor level

To work out the final cutting measurement you need to add together measurements A to E shown in the illustration on the right.
239cm (94in) + 0 + 2cm (¾in) + 2cm (¾in) + 1.5cm (⅝in) = 244.5cm (96¼in)
– 0.5cm (¼in) for clearance from the carpet = 244cm (96in)
A + B + C + D + E = final cutting measurement

Following the same sequence every time will help prevent costly mistakes.

For a pencil-pleat heading there are up to six hook positions, depending on the type of tape and hook used. Therefore, you have to put a hook into the tape in the position you intend to place it in the completed curtain, and then measure from the top of the hook to the top of the tape. With most decorative tapes, I allow a heading of 1cm (½in) above the tape and 4cm (1½in) for beneath the tape, if I have sufficient fabric. To be on the safe side, you should show a calculation for this type of tape with a distance of 4.5cm (1¾in) from the hook to the top of the tape as an example.

239cm (94in) + 4.5cm (1¾in) + 1cm (⅜in) + 1cm (⅜in) + 4cm (1½in) = 249.5cm (98in)
less 0.5cm (¾in) clearance = 249cm (97¾in)
A + B + C + D + E= final cutting measurement

22 Pinch pleats are another matter. If the curtain is not interlined, I favor this method, where the fabric, lining and buckram are folded over to the back of the curtain.

Use the following calculation for the final cutting measurement.
The hook drop measurement of the curtain is 239cm (94in).
239cm (94in) + (A) 4.5 (1¾in) = 243.5cm (95¾in)
Add the depth of the buckram (this distance can vary according to the depth of buckram you choose).
243.5 (95¾in) + (B) 15cm (6in) = 258.5cm (101¾in)
Add a fabric allowance to turn under the buckram.
258.5 (101¾in) + 1cm (½in) = 259.5cm (102¼in)
Finally, take off an allowance for clearing the carpet or floor.
259.5 (102¼in) - 0.5cm (¼in) = 259 cm (102in). The distance from the top of the hook to the top of the curtain may vary according to the track or pole used.

24 Pin the two layers together beneath the line of marks, with the pinheads towards the right. Trim off the excess fabric and lining before completing the top of the curtain.

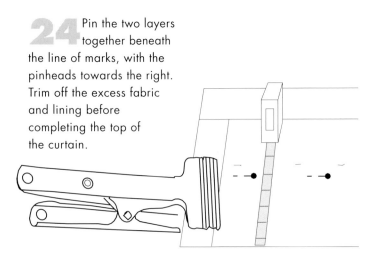

23 In a workroom, cutting the curtain to the final measurement would be done either on a special 'tabling' table, where the bottom hem is clamped in place and a bar with a motorised cutting machine is run across the curtain at the appropriate length, or on a vertical tabler. For those without this type of sophisticated equipment (and there are many of us), leave the curtain edge that will be hung at the center of the window clamped to the table. Unclamp the other side and gently pull the fabric and lining, leaving a flat section of curtain on the table ready for cutting.

Smooth the fabric and the lining using a metre (yard) stick. Measure from bottom to top as shown. Mark the final measurement on the lining with a fading marker or fine pencil. Move the tape approximately 8cm (3in) across the curtain and mark again. Continue measuring and marking at 8cm (3in) intervals across the curtain. If the curtain is too long for your table, measure up to 200cm (78in) (or whatever fits your table), put a mark and a pin. Continue all the way across the curtain, then return to the first side and measure from the pin up to the required measurement.

25 See Techniques 59-60, Applying Standard Tapes, Applying Decorative Tapes, pages 56-57; Techniques 63-64, Forming Pinch Pleats, Forming Goblet Pleats, pages 60-63; Technique 66, Making Hand-gathered Headings, page 65; Technique 68, Making Slot Headings, page 66.

26 See Techniques 61-62, Drawing Up Tapes and Tying Curtain Cords, pages 57-58.

27 I find the following method the best way of attaching buckram to a lined curtain. Neaten the cut top edge of the curtain with zigzag stitch, catching both the main fabric and lining in the stitches. Place the buckram in position on the lining side of the curtain 1cm (½in) down from the neatened edge.

28 Turn 1cm (½in) of fabric and lining over the buckram and machine through all layers, 0.5cm (¼in) from the fold. Turn it all to the back of the curtain.

Technique 63-64, Forming Pinch Pleats, Forming Goblet Pleats, pages 60-63.

29 Pin through all the layers to hold them in position. The next step is to calculate the pleats. Adding the extra thickness of fabric and lining helps to make good, full pleats, although some people prefer to insert the buckram between the fabric and the lining, which is a good technique to use for machine bag-lined curtains. Another method is to hand-sew across the top of the curtain with the buckram retained between the fabric and the lining.

30 See Techniques 71-73, Attaching Standard Hooks, Attaching Pin-on Hooks, Attaching Sew-on Hooks, page 69.

31 Now that the curtain is complete it is time to hang it. Always start to hang curtains from the center of the rail, working towards the outer edges. This allows for the easy addition and removal of gliders. If the curtains have a half width, this section should always be hung towards the outer edge of the window.

32 Curtains do not automatically hang in neat folds. Professionals always dress the curtains, giving that finishing touch for perfect curtains. The dressing bands are strips of fabric about 10cm (4in) wide, by whatever length is required to wrap around the whole curtain, holding it securely without being so tight that the curtains are creased.

Starting from the edge nearest the center of the window, use the distance between your thumb and forefinger to create folds, placing one hand at the front of the curtain and one at the back. This is normally carried out at the top of a stepladder, as you need to be as close to the top of the curtain as possible. Continue across the full width of the curtain and secure with a dressing band and two pins.

Standing level with the center of the curtain, run your hands down the folds you have already created to extend them further down the curtain and again, hold them in place with a dressing band. Repeat the same exercise at the bottom of the curtain. Leave the bands in place for about three days, in a warm room, to literally set the folds in place.

The method varies slightly for pinch pleats, as the folds must correspond with the pleats. If the curtains are very long, or the fabric is particularly springy, you may need more bands.

PROJECT 2

The classic interlined curtain

Interlined curtains are a must if you have a cold and draughty house; they really will help to keep the heat in. Interlining also gives curtains a luxurious look as its added weight helps them to hang beautifully. It is especially good with fabrics like silk or stiff chintz, which do not normally hang well as they are too papery or too stiff.

Materials

As for The Classic Curtain, page 96, with the addition of interlining

1cm (½in) iron-on bonding tape, if making a pinch-pleat heading

Equipment

As for The Classic Curtain, page 96, with the addition of a 60˚ set square

1 See Techniques 19-20, Hook Positions for Curtain Tracks and Hook Positions for Curtain Poles, pages 28-29.

2 See Technique 22, Measuring for Curtains, page 30.

3 See Technique 27, Calculating Fullness and Quantities for Curtains, page 34.

4 See Technique 29, Measuring Pattern Repeats, page 36.

5 See Technique 30, Calculating Quantities for Patterned Fabrics, page 36.

6 See Techniques 35-37, Cutting Plain and Lining Fabrics, Cutting Velvets, Cutting Patterned Fabrics, pages 41-42.

7 See Techniques 41-43, Joining Plain and Lining Fabrics, Joining Velvets, Joining Patterned Fabrics, pages 44-45.

8 See Technique 45, Joining Interlinings, page 46.

9 Cut and join the main fabric as for *The Classic Curtain*. Press open the seams and right-side down, lay the curtain on the table. Place the leading edge, which will hang in the center of the window, to the side edge of the table, where you can work on it easily, and the bottom hem to the bottom edge of the table. Draw a line all the way across the curtain 6cm (2½in) up from the bottom edge. Use tailor's chalk, a fading marker or a very soft lead pencil, according to the fabric you are using.

Lay the interlining in position with the lower edge approximately 2cm (¾in) up from the bottom edge of the main fabric. This is the only time in this project that you do not have to be precise and it is for a very good reason. Interlining is not a particularly easy fabric to work with and if you try and pull it in any way, it will do its best to regain its shape. So it is best to lay the interlining in position without stretching it and then trim it back to the 6cm (2½in) line of the bottom hem at a later stage.

The side edge of the interlining should be slightly set in from the side edge of the main fabric, to allow for folding over the two fabrics together. Draw a line on the interlining 16cm (6¼in) up from the bottom hem. Then, on the one side edge only, draw a line 6cm (2½in) in from the vertical edge as shown, (this should only be on the lower part of the curtain).

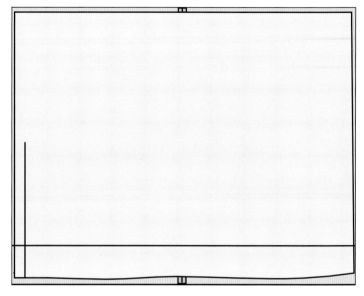

See Project 1, The Classic Curtain, page 96.

10 See Technique 51, Interlined Mitres, page 51.

11 Turn in 6cm (2½in) along the side edge. Herringbone the side hem in position. Place a weight bag at the corner of the curtain and use overstitch into the interlining to hold it in place.

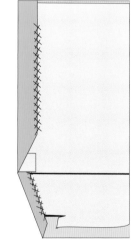

See Technique 53, Herringbone Stitch, page 53 and Technique 48, Making Lead Weight Bags, page 48.

12 The next step is to fold back the interlining in order to form rows of laying-in stitches to hold the interlining and main fabric together right across the curtain. To help prevent the interlining from moving while you are stitching, place a row of pins on the first stitching line and along the first part of the bottom hem.

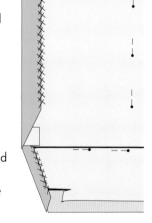

See Technique 55, Laying-in Stitch, page 54.

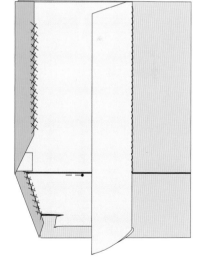

13 Make the rows about 40cm (16in) apart, or to put it another way, on every seam and twice on each width of fabric. Work gradually across the curtain, it will get easier with practice. When you come to the second side hem, trim off any excess interlining and complete the corner and side hem in exactly the same way as the other side of the curtain.

103

14 Do not take any of the herringbone or laying-in stitches right to the very top of the curtain or they may be cut when you trim the top of the curtain to the final cutting measurement. If you are making a hand-pleated heading, you need to leave enough space to insert the buckram under the side hems.

15 Turn the curtain so that the bottom hem is against the longest side of the table and you can work on it easily. Trim back the interlining on the bottom edge of the curtain to the original 6cm (2½in) line.

16 Fold the main fabric over the bottom of the interlining. Fold up the hem again on the 10cm (4in) line. If you have been very accurate with the measurements, the corners should fit exactly. Use a small neat ladder stitch to complete the corner, then herringbone stitch across the bottom hem. Make sure you go through all the layers on the bottom part of the stitch.

See Technique 56, Ladder Stitch, page 55 and Technique 53, Herringbone Stitch, page 53.

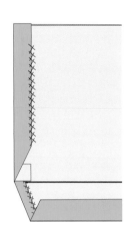

17 For a hand-pleated heading, measure the curtain bottom to top then draw a line, on the interlining at the final cutting measurement.

See Project 1, The Classic Curtain, page 96.

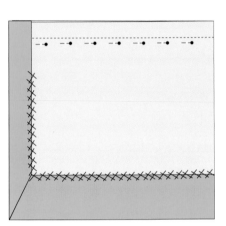

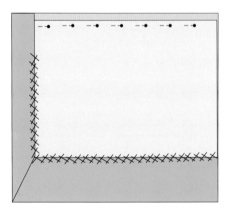

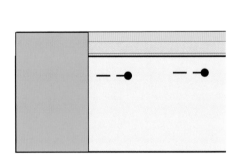

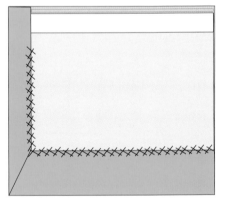

18 Pin the layers together and trim away any excess interlining. If you want a tape heading, rather than a hand-pleated one, again you will need to measure the curtain before you attach the lining and cut back the interlining level with the top edge of the curtain. If you turn it over with the lining and main fabric, it will form a bulky heading and make the pleats uneven.

19 To insert buckram, trim back the main fabric to the final cutting measurement, plus 2cm (¾in). To hold the buckram in position, use a strip of iron-on bonding fabric along the top of the curtain. Place the strip glue-side down onto the fabric and iron with a reasonably hot iron. Allow it to cool a little before removing the paper backing.

20 Insert the buckram between the interlining and the main fabric, with its upper edge level with the top of the interlining and its side edge tucked under the side hem. Turn the main fabric, with its iron-on bonding fabric attached, over the buckram and iron it as before to bond the fabric to the buckram.

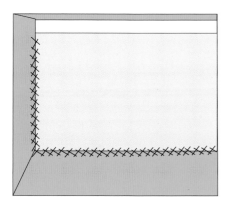

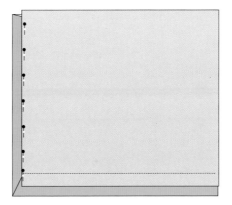

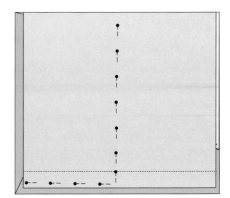

21 Cut away a little of the interlining at the top of the side hem and neatly fold the fabric over the interlining, so that the top of the side seam is at a slight angle.

22 Cut and join your lining drops, press open the seams and make a bottom hem. Clamp the leading edge of the curtain to the edge of the table. Make sure you do not pull or stretch the curtain. Turn under 5cm (2in) of lining before placing it on the side edge, starting at the bottom hem.

23 Position the corner of the lining so that it is 2cm (¾in) up from the bottom hem and 3cm (1¼in) in from the side of the curtain. Put clamps or covered bricks at each end of the curtain to prevent the layers from moving. Use slip stitch to attach the lining to the curtain down the side edge. Then, place a row of pins from the top to the bottom of the curtain to enable you to fold back the lining easily.

See Technique 54, Slip Stitch, page 53.

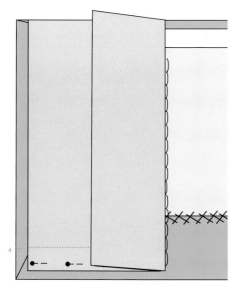

25 At the top edge of the curtain, turn under the raw edges of the lining to show 0.5cm (¼in) of the main curtain. Slip stitch across the top edge and along the angles at the top of the side seams. Pinch or goblet pleats can now be calculated and sewn. Because of the bulk, you may find it difficult to stitch the bottom of the pleats on your machine so they would be better done by hand. Because interlined curtains are so heavy, I would always recommend that you use sew-on rather than pin-on hooks. Tape headings can be completed as normal. Turn over the lining and fabric at the top of the curtain and machine the tape in position. Use a standard metal hook, again for strength.

26 Interlined curtains must be dressed in the same way as ordinary curtains to allow the folds to hang well.

See Project 1, The Classic Curtain, page 96.

24 Use a laying-in stitch to attach the lining to the interlining, finishing just below the buckram for hand-sewn pleats or below the position of the tape for a gathered heading. Continue across the curtain, stitching in the same positions as described in step 14. Complete the second side hem in the same way as the first one.

See Technique 55, Laying-in Stitch, page 54.

See Techniques 63-64, Forming Pinch Pleats, Forming Goblet Pleats, pages 60-63; Techniques 59-60, Applying Standard Tapes, Applying Decorative Tapes, pages 56-57 and Techniques 71-73, Attaching Standard Hooks, Attaching Pin-on Hooks, Attaching Sew-on Hooks, page 69.

PROJECT 3

The classic valance

A simple, soft valance is an easy project to tackle and as it is not as big as a pair of curtains, so there is no need to worry about dealing with large quantities of fabric. The variations on a valance are almost endless, so do experiment with fabrics, headings, trims and borders.

Materials can include

Brown paper or lining paper for making templates

Main fabric

Contrast fabric

Lining

Interlining (if used in accompanying curtains)

Tape or buckram

Machine thread

Hand-sewing thread

Curtain hooks

Adhesive-backed hook Velcro

Sew-on loop Velcro

Piping cord

Equipment

Long pins

Long fine needles

Clamps or bricks

Measuring tape

Small ruler

Iron and ironing sheet

Scissors

Vanishing marker

Cornice board or valance track

1 See Technique 11, Making Cornice Boards, page 22.

2 See Technique 21, Hook Positions for Cornice Boards, page 29.

3 See Technique 26, Measuring for Valances or Cornices, page 33.

4 See Technique 28, Calculating Fullness and Quantities for Valances, page 35.

5 See Technique 29, Measuring Pattern Repeats, page 36.

6 See Technique 30, Quantities for Patterned Fabrics, page 36.

7 See Technique 32, Translating Shapes for Valances, page 38.

8 See Techniques 35-37, Cutting Plain and Lining Fabrics, Cutting Velvets, Cutting Patterned Fabrics, pages 41-42.

9 See Techniques 41-43, Joining Plain and Lining Fabrics, Joining Velvets, Joining Patterned Fabrics, pages 44-45.

10 See Technique 47, Pressing Fabrics, page 47.

Cut strips of the main fabric to the right measurements, then join them together and press open the seams. Repeat the same process with the lining. It will be almost impossible to place the joins of the lining exactly on top of the joins of the main fabric, as widths of linings and fabrics vary so dramatically, but get them as close as possible.

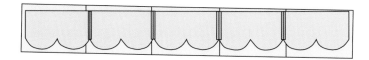

11 One of the most common problems that occurs when stitching the fabric and lining together along the bottom edge is that they twist. For this reason, I always add approximately 6cm (2½in) extra to the minimum cut length on each strip of lining. Once you have joined all the main fabric and lining strips together, place the lining face up on the table. Place the main fabric face down onto the lining and smooth them out so that the two fabrics are completely flat. You usually find that the two fabrics do not align exactly when put together.

Lining a Valance
There are three basic ways to line a valance.
Method One
This method is used for a straight-edged valance that has no inserted trimming on the bottom edge, but the main fabric, or a contrast fabric, shows as a border on the reverse.

13 If you are adding a contrast border, it needs to be attached before attaching the lining. Otherwise, cut the main fabric 3cm (1¼in) longer than the lining. Machine the fabric and lining together along the lower edge, taking a 2cm (¾in) seam allowance.
Line up the notches to ensure the two layers are kept aligned.

See Technique 99, Making Inserted Borders, page 90.

16 Open the valance out then fold it again so that the right sides are facing. Do not press the fabric. Machine the outer edges, stitching from the bottom to the top on each side. Trim off the lower corners to cut down on bulk. Press the end seams open as best you can before turning the whole valance right-side out. Press the side seams so that the lining does not show on the front of the valance. A purchased trim can be applied by hand.

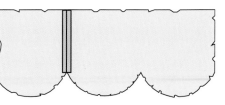

12 Pin the layers together and trim away the excess lining. At intervals along all edges make small notches of varying shapes. (These should be no more than 1cm (½in) in depth). These notches will be your guide in making sure that the fabrics don't move or stretch. They allow the two parts to be separated and put back together with ease if you wish to insert a frill or piping, and also allow accurate placement when putting the two fabrics together to complete the valance. I would use this technique with a shaped or a straight valance.

14 Press open the seam.

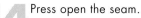

15 Wrong sides facing, fold the valance in half withways so that 3cm (1¼in) of the main fabric shows on the reverse side of the valance. Gently press along the bottom edge.

Method Two
This method of lining a valance is used mainly when an inserted trim, such as a frill, or an applied trim, such as a bullion, is being added to the lower edge of the valance.

17 If you are using an inserted trim such as a frilled or pleated edging, attach it to the main fabric before you attach the lining. Join the fabric and the lining together, with the trimming sandwiched between them. Start from one end and machine along the lower edge, then up one side edge. Work on the main fabric side of the valance.

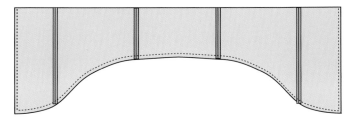

18 Go back to the starting point of the machining and machine up the other side edge to the top of the valance. This pattern of machining ensures that the corners will hang correctly. Trim away the bulk at the corners. Press the seams open as much as possible before turning the valance right-side out. Then, press all the seams so that the lining doesn't show on the right side.

If the whole thing appears a little bulky you can take up a smaller seam allowance, or trim the allowance to 1cm (½in). I usually leave the seam allowance at 2cm (¾in), particularly if I am applying a trimming instead of inserting one, as the extra fabric gives a good firm base for the trimming.

See Technique 91, Inserting Edgings, page 85.

19 The same guidelines also apply to a valance with a curved edge, though you must take great care if the lower edge is deeply curved or the lining may show at the front. A deep bullion or tassel fringe that will hide the lining is preferable to a small fringe or fan edge on a valance with a curved edge, unless a decorative contrast lining or self-lining is used, or a curved border added. However, some people do not like to see a change of lining (between the curtain and the valance) from outside the window. To get round this, you could contrast line the outer sections of the valance only, which will be hidden by the curtains at all times, and apply a curved border to the middle section.

See Technique 100, Making Curved Borders, page 91.

Method Three
The third method of attaching lining is used for an interlined valance only.

20 For speed, interlining is often attached by machine along with the lining. To do this, you lay the main fabric face up, with the interlining beneath it and the lining right-side down on top of it. Machine the edges as described in Method Two.

For a really top-quality job, however, the interlining would be laid on the main fabric and laying-in stitches used to connect the layers. The side and bottom edges of the main fabric would then be folded over the interlining and secured with herringbone stitches, as for a curtain. The lining would be attached by hand using slip stitch.

See Technique 55, Laying-in Stitch, page 54, Technique 53, Herringbone Stitch, page 53, Technique 54, Slip Stitch, page 53 and Project 1, The Classic Curtain, page 96.

Once you have reached this stage there are an almost infinite number of varieties of heading and trimming that can be used to complete the valance.

21 See Techniques 59-60, Applying Standard Tapes, Applying Decorative Tapes, pages 56-57; Techniques 63-66, Forming Pinch Pleats, Forming Goblet Pleats, Forming Box Pleats, Making Hand-gathered Headings, pages 60-65; Technique 68, Making Slot Headings, page 66.

22 See Techniques 61-62, Drawing Up Tapes and Tying Curtain Cords, pages 57-58; Technique 67, Applying Velcro or Tape for Hand-gathered Headings, page 66; Technique 69, Making Top Bands, page 67.

23 See Techniques 71-73, Attaching Standard Hooks, Attaching Pin-on Hooks, Attaching Sew-on Hooks, page 69.

PROJECT 4

The classic cornice

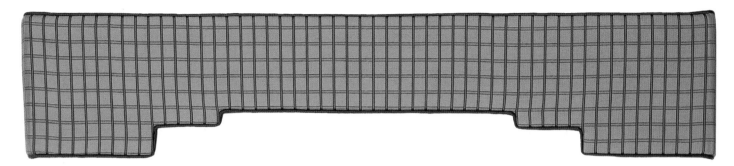

A cornice can turn a simple window treatment into something grand. It is also useful if you have a problem window: one that is too low or is on a slope. A cornice can be set above the window to give an illusion of height, or at an angle to correct a slope. Cornices can be made to almost any shape, but tight curves and angles should be avoided at first as they can be tricky to handle.

Materials

Fabric

Interlining

Lining

Velcro, either 2cm (¾in) or 5cm (2in) wide, depending on the size of the cornice

0.5cm (¼in) thick plywood; use marine ply if the cornice is to be in a damp situation

Hand-sewing thread

PVA glue

Four strips of thin, strong fabric for fabric hinges, 8cm (3in) wide by the depth of the cornice board

Brown paper, thick polythene or thick wallpaper to make a template

Equipment

Circular needle

Pins

Scissors

Staple gun and 0.5cm (¼in) staples

Hammer

Jigsaw

If the jigsaw cannot cut mitred edges, you will need a plane or a sander as well

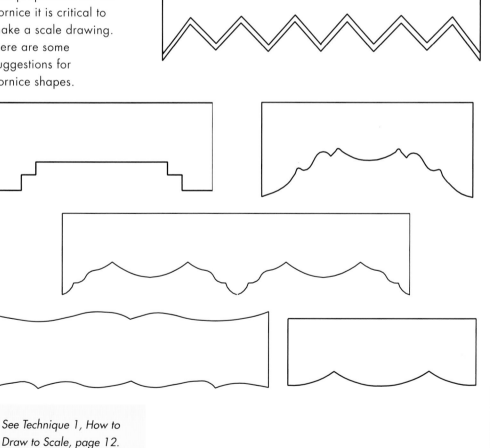

To achieve the right shape and proportions for the cornice it is critical to make a scale drawing. Here are some suggestions for cornice shapes.

See Technique 1, How to Draw to Scale, page 12.

1 See Technique 16, Making Templates for Cornices, page 25.

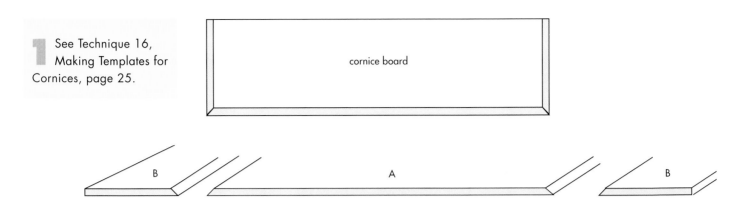

cornice board

B   A   B

2 Draw out the shape you want your cornice to be full-size on brown paper and cut round it to make a template. Place your template on the wood and cut around it using a jigsaw. Alternatively, ask your local timber merchant to do this for you. The front piece (A) should be the width of the cornice board, plus the thickness of the wood at each end. The returns (B) should be the depth of the return, plus the thickness of the wood on one edge. This thickness allows for the mitres, which can be made using a plane or an electric jigsaw that has the facility for cutting angles, or with a plane or a sander.

3 Please note that intricate shapes can be tricky to cut, as it is difficult to turn the blade and still keep to the shape. If the design has tight inward curves or points there are two ways to cut away the excess wood. Cut across the wood, almost at the bottom of each point, then cut into the points from two directions.

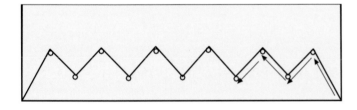

4 Alternatively, with a drill bit of the same diameter as the cutting blade, drill holes at the points large enough to turn the jigsaw in. This enables you to always cut in the same direction, which I find easier, especially on a deeper cornice.

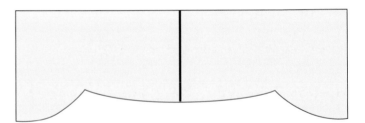

5 Draw a vertical line down the center of the back of the cornice, using a tape measure and a set square.

6 See Technique 26, Measuring for Valances or Cornices, page 33.

7 See Technique 29, Measuring Pattern Repeats, page 36.

8 See Technique 30, Calculating Quantities for Patterned Fabrics, page 36.

9 See Techniques 35-37, Cutting Plain and Lining Fabrics, Cutting Velvets, Cutting Patterned Fabrics, pages 41-42.

10 See Techniques 41-43, Joining Plain and Lining Fabrics, Joining Velvets, Joining Patterned Fabrics, pages 44-45.

11 See Technique 45, Joining Interlinings, page 46.

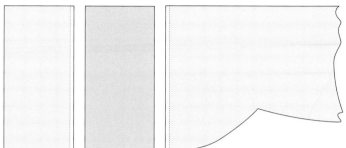

12 For plain fabric, cut pieces approximately 4cm (1½in) larger all round than the largest dimension of the wood you are going to cover. Join the pieces in the normal way, cutting off any bulky selvedges and pressing open the seams. For patterned fabric, cut and pattern match the pieces. If you have to join widths of fabric together to achieve the dimensions you need, offset the joins as shown.

Treat the lining in exactly the same way as plain main fabric. The interlining should be cut to the same size and joined if necessary. Where possible, I turn the interlining on its side to get round the problems of joins and bulk.

13 Use the strips of thin strong fabric to make fabric hinges. Apply glue to one fabric strip. The amount will vary according to the absorbency of the fabric, but be careful not to let it dry out before it is placed on the wood. Place the strip, glue side up, on the table, then place the front and a return of the cornice onto the glued fabric so that they almost touch, with the mitred inside edges of the cornice facing upwards. Allow to dry a little.

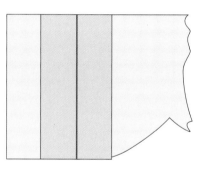

14 Glue a second strip to the inside of the cornice, making sure the fabric goes down into the mitre. Before the glue sets completely, gently bend the return to check that there is enough movement to allow it to form a right angle with the front of the cornice. Repeat the procedure at the other end of the cornice. Allow the glue to dry.

15 Starting from one end of the front of the cornice, cover approximately 30cm (12in) of the cornice with glue.

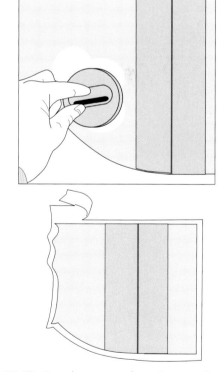

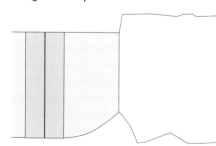

16 Smooth the interlining over the glue without stretching it. Continue gluing sections and smoothing on interlining until the front of the cornice is covered.

17 Only glue the front of the wood, there is no need to put glue on the edges.

18 Turn the cornice face-down and trim the interlining, leaving about 1cm (½in) showing around the edge. You may find it easier to mark a line, then cut the interlining.

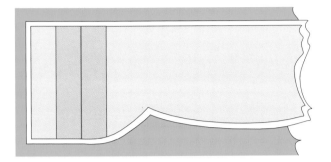

19 Mark the center of the cornice fabric on the wrong side, at both the top and bottom edge. Place the fabric face-down on the table, with the wood face-down on top of it, lining up the marks on the fabric with the mark at the center of the cornice board.

20 To hold the fabric in position while you mark the piping line, pin it to the interlining around the edge of the board. Also, place one staple, very loosely, to hold the fabric to the back of the return. This helps to keep the fabric taut.

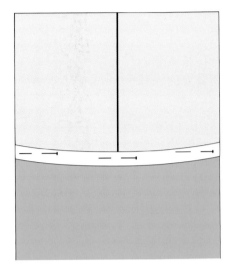

21 Turn the cornice right side up and, one edge at a time, fold the fabric over the edge of the wood. Using a fading marker or well-sharpened tailor's chalk, whichever is most appropriate for the fabric, mark a piping line on the fabric. This should lie in the center of the thickness of the wood, as the piping should not sit on the front of the cornice.

22 When the fabric has been removed from the wood it is sometimes difficult to be precise as to where to make a point on the shape or where to finish the piping for the returns. The pins in these illustrations mark the points where I would normally place indicating pins, so that I can be sure of exactly where to pipe. It is only when you try to make a shaped cornice without these pins that you realise what a useful idea this is.

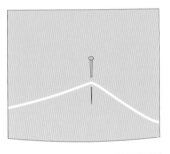

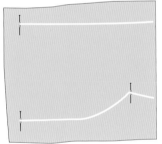

23 Attach the piping to the top and bottom edges, making sure you machine on the marked line. When you come to the points marked with pins, cut a notch, as shown, and sew exactly to the notch before you turn the corner. Make sure that there is sufficient piping to go into the corner itself. There is a tendency to pull the piping to get round the corner as quickly as possible. Believe me, this doesn't work.

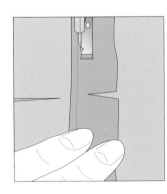

See Technique 76, Piping With Square Ends, page 72 and Technique 80, Piping Curves, page 78.

24 As you come out of the corner, again don't pull on the piping fabric or cord. Ease it in a little rather than stretching it. Don't cut away the excess fabric before attaching the piping, as there is a tendency for the curved edges to stretch.

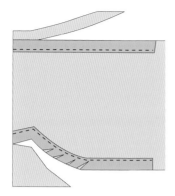

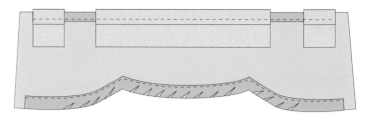

25 Trim away the main fabric, leaving a 2cm (³⁄₄in) seam allowance all round.

26 If you are fixing the cornice to the top of the cornice board, attach sew-on loop Velcro to each part of the top bands. Use 5cm (2in) Velcro if the cornice is heavy, otherwise, 2cm (³⁄₄in) Velcro is fine. Lay the top bands on the right side of the main fabric, with the Velcro pieces face-up. Machine in position.

See Technique 69, Making Top Bands, page 67.

27 Right-sides facing, lay the cornice fabric on the lining and machine all the layers together along the top edge. Leave 1cm (¹⁄₂in) open at each end of the cornice so that it is easier to trim away any excess bulk.

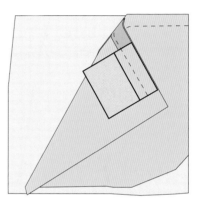

28 Cut the lining back to match the fabric. If the main fabric is fairly stiff and there are a lot of curves, this is a good time to make notches in the main fabric. Test the fabric to see if it requires notching by folding it over the edge of the board. If it puckers and does not sit smoothly round the curves, then you should notch the seam allowances where necessary.

29 This is how the fabrics should look at this stage.

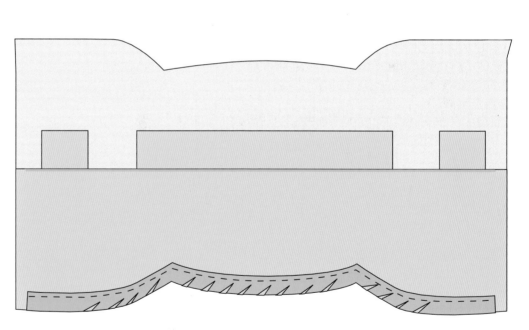

30 If you are fixing the cornice to the front of the cornice board, machine sew-on loop Velcro to the very top edge of the lining. The lining can still be joined by machine to the top edge of the cornice fabric.

31 For cornices with shaped tops, machine sew-on loop Velcro to the lining in the right position, but do not machine the fabric and lining together along the top edge. The fabric is stapled to the wood and the lining attached by hand around the edges. Staple through the Velcro into the wood in a few places. If you don't use staples, the lining and Velcro seem to stretch away from the cornice.

See Project 34, Cornice with a Shaped Top, page 184.

32 The next step is to attach the fabric to the wood. Align the center of the main fabric with the center of the wood. Anchor the main fabric to the back of the wood with a staple through the seam allowances at the top and bottom of the fabric.

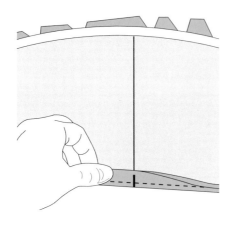

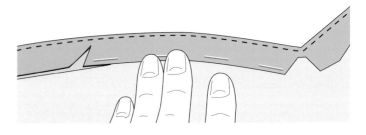

33 Place a staple at the first curve, again through both the top and the bottom seam allowances. It helps to keep everything in line if you also staple at the top and bottom of the joins. Keep checking that everything is correct on the front of the cornice.

34 Place one staple on end of each of the returns, making sure that you have allowed enough tension on the fabric to keep it taut, but not enough to pull in the returns or distort the fabric, particularly if you are using striped fabric.

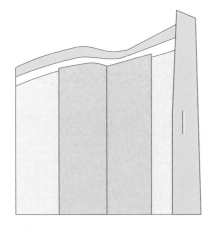

Place staples at regular intervals on the top and bottom edges of the cornice. If you turn the cornice to the right side, it will be immediately obvious if you need extra staples.

35 Trim away excess bulk at the corners. and also at the points where the hinges bend.

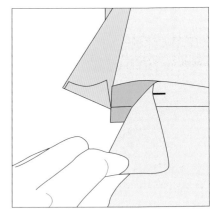

36 Pull the lining down over the back of the wood and pin it in position, turning under the raw edges as you go. Insert the pins, with the heads protruding at right angles to the cornice board. The lining should just cover the machining line of the piping. Make sure that the lining is taut. But not so tight that the returns cannot bend easily.

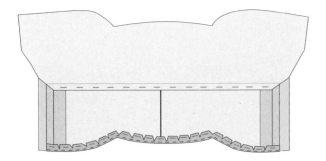

37 Using a circular needle and a very strong thread, attach the lining to the back of the piping strip with tiny slip stitches or ladder stitches.

Use the top bands to attach the cornice to the Velcro applied to the top of the cornice board.

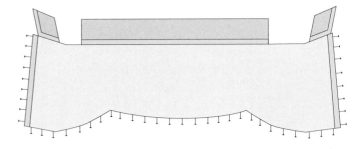

PROJECT 5

The classic tieback

As anyone who makes or purchases curtains knows, tiebacks can really complete the look of a window. They can also be practical in keeping curtains away from a door or French window, though I do find they have one great drawback. If the curtains are tied back each day, they inevitably become creased in such a way that when they are released, they do not hang in good vertical folds. With some fabrics this can even mean that when the curtains are released and drawn together, there is a gap between them. I think it is important to weigh up the pros and cons and if you are making tiebacks for someone else, that they are made aware of the problem and that the final decision rests with them.

Knowing the arguments, I must confess I still prefer the look of curtains with tiebacks where possible.

Materials

Fabric for tieback and piping

Lining

Interlining

Fusible buckram

Piping cord, or alternatively a purchased decorative cord or trimming

Brass rings, if not using fabric loops

Equipment

Scissors

Pins

Circular needle

Fading marker or tailor's chalk

Iron and ironing mat

1 See Technique 25, Measuring for Tiebacks, page 33.

Guide to sizes for stiffened fabric tiebacks

As a rough guide, the following measurements may prove useful. Obviously the size will change according to the type of fabrics, linings and interlinings you are using.

Standard lined curtains			Interlined curtains		
1 curtain	1 width	50-60cm (20-24in)	1 curtain	1 width	70-80cm (27-31in)
	1.5 widths	70-80cm (27-31in)		1.5 widths	80-90cm (31-35in)
	2 widths	80-90cm (31-35in)		2 widths	90-100cm (35-39in)
	2.5 widths	90-100cm (35-39in)		2.5 widths	100-110cm (39-43in)
	3 widths	100-110cm (39-43in)		3 widths	110-120cm (43-48in)

To some extent, the fabric and design of your window treatment will help to dictate the shape you should use for a stiffened fabric tieback. If you are using a fabric-covered cornice, use some of its curves to make a pattern for the tieback. One thing I do find difficult is a completely straight tieback with, say, a border pattern running along it. They never do sit quite as well as the suggested designs on the next page.

115

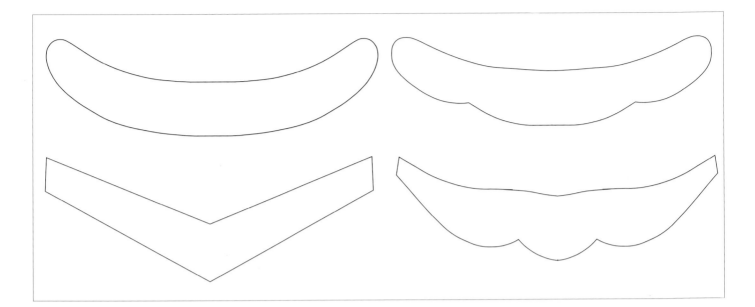

2 The fusible buckram you use should be stiff and recover well after bending around the curtains. Some buckrams are very difficult to cut so I use a pair of good quality kitchen scissors for this task. Other buckrams, though still thick, are easier to cut and I use ordinary scissors (not my best fabric scissors), or an old cutting wheel. Cut the buckram to the exact shape and size you want the tieback to be.

3 Lay the shaped buckram, glue-side-down, onto the right side of the fabric. With a fading marker, or tailor's chalk, held at an angle, draw a line around the edge of the buckram. This will give you a sewing line just under 2mm (⅛in) from the edge of the buckram, which will allow the piping to sit around the edge of the tie-back rather than on the face. This also allows enough fabric for the tieback to bend.

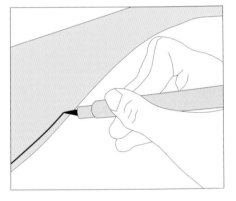

4 I prefer to use a layer of interlining between the fabric and the buckram to give a more substantial look and feel to the finished tieback. Cut out the fabric and interlining, adding a 2cm (¾in) seam allowance all the way around. Cut out the lining to exactly the same size as the main fabric. The exception to this step is if the fabric is

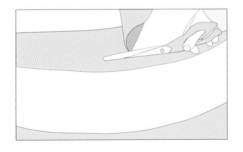

stretchy, it may be better to leave the fabric as a whole piece, pipe on the drawn line, then cut away the excess fabric. This helps to prevent stretching on the edges where the fabric is on the cross and therefore susceptible to movement. Place the interlining beneath the main fabric with the line you have drawn face up.

5 See Technique 74, Cutting Piping Strips, page 70.

6 See Technique 77, Piping with Joining Ends, page 73.

7 See Technique 80, Piping Curves, page 78.

8 See Technique 78, Joining Piping, page 74

9 The piping fabric should always be cut on the cross to enable the fabric to lay smoothly, particularly on the corners, although this can sometimes mean purchasing a piece of fabric of perhaps 75cm (29½in) to 100cm (39in) to enable you to cut long strips. This can seem extravagant, but there are many advantages in having a box of lengths of contrast fabrics to use for appliqué, contrast trims, cushions, etc.

Place the piping, with the cord protruding, on the lower edge of the center of the tieback fabric, so that the machining line will be slightly inside the line you have drawn. Leaving the first 6cm (2½in) of the piping strip free, pipe around the shape. Always be careful to gently ease the piping fabric into place and not to stretch it.

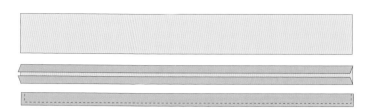

10 If you are using a loop of fabric to attach the tieback to the tieback hook, cut a length of fabric approximately 3cm (1¼in) wide by 40cm (16in) long. This will be sufficient for four loops, enough for one pair of tiebacks. Fold the long raw edges almost to the middle and press. Fold the whole length in half widthways and topstitch it to form a strip.

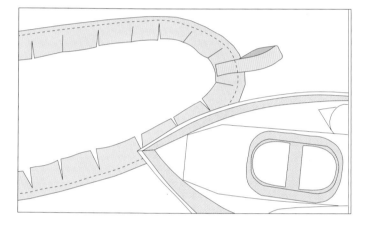

13 Lay the buckram, glue-side-up, onto the piped fabric. Starting at one end of the tieback, turn the piping fabric over the edge of the buckram and press with a steam iron, allowing the iron to rest in one place for a few seconds to melt the adhesive. Repeat the same process at the opposite end then iron the remaining edges. Some buckrams need to be slightly dampened before pressing with the iron. Use a moistened piece of scrap fabric to do this.

15 If you are working to a tight budget, the method of attaching the rings shown below means that the ring set in from the edge of the tieback will cover a cheap metal cup-hook. The ring on the end of the tieback nearest to the wall is attached in the normal way. Stitch the rings into position using buttonhole stitch. If you are using an attractive tieback hook, then the rings should protrude from each end of the tiebacks, so that they are not hidden.

Tiebacks can be further enhanced with rosettes, appliqué, frills, ribbon, braid or fringing attached by hand when the tieback is completed.

11 Cut the piece into four, fold each length in half and stitch one into place at each end of each tieback. Make sure they are placed at an angle.

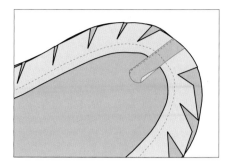

12 On the reverse side of the tieback, trim away the interlining as close as possible to the machining line to cut down on bulk. Cut away approximately two-thirds of the seam allowance of the main fabric and one side of the piping fabric. This leaves the top piece of piping fabric at its full width for attaching to the buckram.

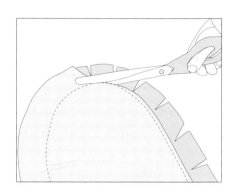

14 To complete the tieback, the back is lined with curtain lining or matching chintz. Place the lining over the back of the tieback and pin it into position. Starting from the center of the top edge of the tieback and working towards each end, fold under the raw edge of the lining, positioning it so that the folded-in edge lies on the stitching line of the piping. Depending on the fabric you are using, you may have to trim or notch the lining a little for a smooth finish. Using a fine, curved needle and a strong thread, stitch the lining to the tieback using ladder stitch.

See Technique 56, Ladder Stitch, page 55.

PROJECT 6

The classic swag and tail treatment

This is such a well-known and popular window treatment, though it is usually seen as complicated to make and best left to the professionals. However, as you will see, it really isn't hard to make. Different fabrics and swag and tail shapes can change the whole look of the treatment, making it suitable for almost any house.

Any style of swag can be made to any size using the following method. However, it really is quicker to make a new template each time than to try and alter existing ones.

Materials

Fabric

Lining

Interlining, if used

Hand-sewing thread

Machining thread

5cm- (2in-) wide Velcro

Equipment

At least one swag board,
20 x 100cm (8 x 39in)

Thick pins

200c (78in) lead weight chain,
as used in curtain hems

Scissors

Ordinary pins

Metre (yard) stick

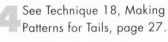

1 See Technique 10, Designing Swag and Tail Treatments, page 21.

2 See Technique 11, Making Cornice Boards, page 22.

3 See Technique 17, Making Patterns for Swags, page 25.

4 See Technique 18, Making Patterns for Tails, page 27.

5 See Technique 40, Cutting Swags and Tails, page 43.

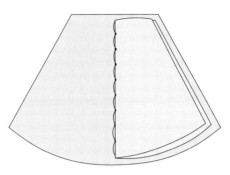

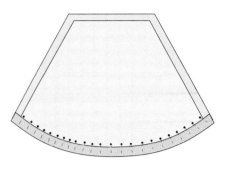

6 For a swag without interlining: right-sides facing, machine the fabric and lining together along the curved edge, taking a 2cm (¾in) seam allowance, and a great deal of caution to prevent stretching. Notch the edge as shown. This allows the fullness to be absorbed into the swag. Turn the swag right-side out and gently press. Now go to step 13, to pleat up the swag.

7 For an interlined swag, the interlining must first be attached to the main fabric. Lay the main fabric right-side down on the table and place the interlining on top of it. The interlining is smaller than the fabric to cut down on bulk. Fold back the interlining to the center of the swag and stitch the two layers together using laying-in stitch. For a large swag two rows of stitching may be required.

See Technique 55, Laying-in Stitch, page 54.

8 Turn the main fabric over the interlining along the curved bottom edge of the swag. Put pins in at right angles to ease in the extra fullness.

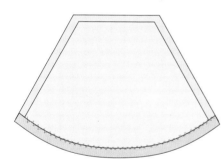

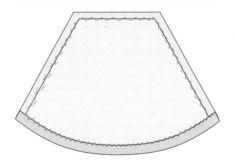

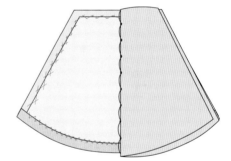

9 Using a small herringbone stitch, 2cm (¾in) wide by 1cm (½in) deep, stitch the bottom hem in place. Make sure that at the lower edge the stitch goes right through all the layers on alternate stitches, leaving a slight indentation on the right side of the fabric. The top part of the stitch attaches to the interlining only.

See Technique 53, Herringbone Stitch, page 53.

10 To prevent the interlining from moving while you are completing the swag, it is best to herringbone stitch all the way around the remaining edges of the interlining, connecting it to the main fabric. Use a fairly large stitch, 4cm (1½in) wide and 1cm (½in) deep. The stitches do not need to go right through to the front of the main fabric, as they are just to hold the interlining in place while completing the swag.

11 Lay the lining on top of the interlining. Fold back the lining and stitch the interlining and lining together. The laying-in stitches should not go through to the main fabric, they merely connect the lining and interlining.

Smooth the lining flat and turn under its raw edge along the bottom hem. About 0.5cm (¼in) of the main fabric should show at the hem. Sew the lining to the main fabric using slip stitch.

See Technique 55, Laying-in Stitch, page 54 and Technique 54, Slip Stitch, page 53.

119

12 I would find it exceedingly difficult to pleat up a swag without a swag-board. First of all, place three pins, preferably the thicker type used for loose covers, at the center of the swag and at each point where the finished end of the swag will be.

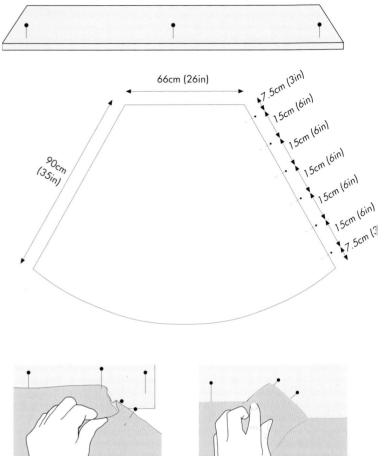

66cm (26in)

7.5cm (3in)

15cm (6in)

15cm (6in)

15cm (6in)

15cm (6in)

15cm (6in)

15cm (6in)

7.5cm (

90cm (35in)

13 The size of a pleat normally varies between 12cm (4¾in) and 18cm (7in). Measure the side of the swag and divide this measurement by the pleat size you want to use. For this example I will use a pleat size of 15cm (6in) and a swag with a side measurement of 90cm (35in).

90cm (35in) ÷ 15cm (6in) = 6 pleats
Side measurement *ideal pleat size*

Starting with half a pleat measurement, put pins into the side of the swag to indicate the pleats. As you can see, this means you will finish at the bottom of the swag with a half pleat again. Repeat the process on the opposite edge.

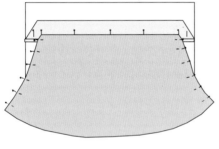

14 With the swag-board on the edge of a table or suitable shelf, place 2cm (¾in) of the top edge of the swag on the swag-board, making sure the centers match and pin to secure. If you are right handed, you will probably find it easiest to start pleating up on the right-hand side of the board.

15 Starting with the first pin on the right-hand side, lift the fabric up above the horizontal edge of the fabric pinned to the board, pivoting on the outer pin. Push the pin marking the pleat line into the swag-board.

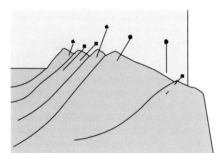

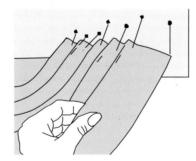

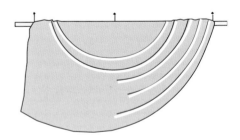

16 Using the same principle, lift each pin and pin the pleat into place on the swag-board, with the top of each pleat level on the board. Make sure that all the pleats are evenly spaced between the end of the flat central part of the swag and the pin at the corner of the swag.

17 Initially the spacing of the pleats can be tricky; getting it right comes with practice. The last pleat sometimes needs to be twisted slightly so that it lies flat, this depends on the curve on the bottom of the swag. The edge of the swag should touch the pin marking the end of the finished swag.

18 Repeat the pleating process on the other side of the swag. I prefer to follow each pleat along from the right-hand side of the swag to the pin on the left-hand side, thereby forming the left-hand pleat.

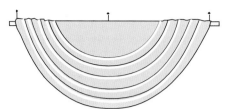

19 This pleating-up process should produce a perfectly shaped swag. However, making swags and tails always involves a little 'tweaking' of the fabric, as you are not dealing with something that is entirely predictable. I have often ended up with the pleats on one side of the swag, usually the left-hand side, placed higher on the board than on the other side, although the swag has looked perfectly level. This is more likely to happen with fairly soft, loosely woven fabric, especially when it is cut on the cross.

20 Tails can also be made with or without interlining, though they should be the same as the swag. With a very difficult fabric, you should turn in the hems, herringbone stitch them in place and attach the lining, as shown for a swag. With a more stable fabric, right-sides facing, simply lay the fabric and lining together and machine around the edges, leaving the top edge open. Turn the tail right-side out and press it before pleating it up.

21 For an interlined swag: with the main fabric right-side down on the table, lay the interlining in position, with an equal seam allowance on all sides. Make a row of laying-in stitches approximately every 30cm (12in) across the tail, especially on a long tail, to prevent the layers of fabric from stretching and spoiling the hang of the fabric.

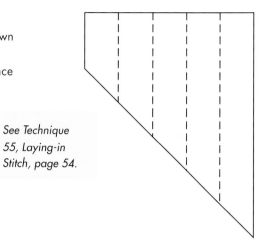

See Technique 55, Laying-in Stitch, page 54.

22 Fold the main fabric over the edge of the interlining along both side hems and the sloping bottom hem and herringbone it into place, in the same way as the swag. Make sure that the lower part of each alternate stitch picks up the main fabric at the front of the tail to prevent the hem from rolling.

See Technique 53, Herringbone Stitch, page 53.

23 Lay the lining in position and using laying-in stitch, stitch it to the interlining, following the previous stitching lines. The stitches themselves should not go through to the main fabric and should start and stop 3cm (1¼in) from the top and bottom edge of the tail.

See Technique 55, Laying-in Stitch, page 54.

24 Turn the hem allowances on the lining under, allowing a very small amount of the main fabric to show at the hem. Slip stitch the lining to the main fabric very neatly. When the tail is folded, both the main fabric and the lining will show, which is why the line of slip stitching must be almost on the edge of the fabric. If you are adding a trimming, it is best to attach it by hand, once the lining has been stitched on. For a really professional look, a braid that matches the trimming should be stitched onto the back edge of the tail, so that when the tail is folded you are not seeing a fringe without a braid heading. Trimming can be sewn down the front leading edge and along the sloping bottom edge or just along the sloping bottom edge, according to the position of the swags in relation to the tails.

25 The next stage is to pleat the tail and for this you need to refer back to your original drawing to find out the what the width across the top of the tail will be when it is pleated up. Lay the tail out on the table with the main fabric facing upwards. Measure the width of the return and mark it with a pin. In this example you need four pleats, so using a calculator divide the width of the remaining fabric by four-and-a-half. So, if the width of the tail, after you subtract the width of the return, is 99cm, (38¼in) divide this figure by four-and-a-half and each section measures 22cm (8½in), with the half section measuring 11cm (4¼in). Along the top edge of the tail, mark the position of the fold lines, with the half-pleat at the leading edge.

See Technique 10, Designing Swag and Tail Treatments, page 21.

17.5cm (7in) 99cm (38¼in)

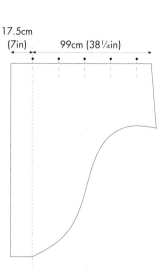

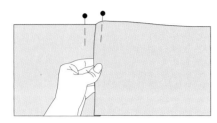

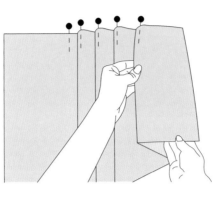

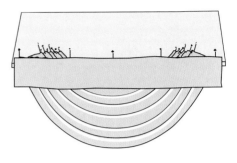

26 Leaving the fabric up to the pin marking the return flat, bring the next pin along across to the return pin. If the pleats are to lie on top of one another, the pins must touch. For a tail with staggered pleats, leave a small space between the pins. The size of this space must be equal for each pleat and the width of all the spaces and pleats must add up to the width of the top of the tail, as shown in your scale drawing.

27 The remainder of the marking pins should be folded across in the same way. This leaves the edge of the half pleat, which is on the leading edge, just covering the folded back of the last pleat.

28 I prefer to cut the top bands on the straight grain of the fabric. When you are attaching the top band to the swag, it is much easier if the swag-board and fabric are both lying flat on the table, rather than the swag hanging over the edge of the table, as for the previous steps. The top band should be laid out flat, with one of the long edges level with the central, flat part of the swag. At each end, the top of the pleats should be visible above the edge of the top band.

See Technique 69, Making Top Bands, page 67.

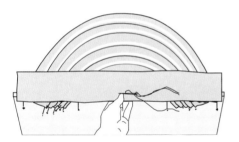

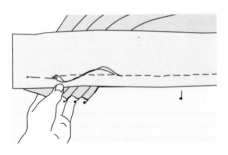

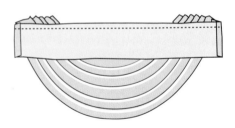

29 Working from the center out to one edge of the swag, and lifting a little of the fabric at a time up from the board, tack all the layers in place using large stitches, a long needle and a double thickness of strong hand-sewing thread. You will need to take the pins out of the swag-board to do this, but it is important to remove them only one or two at a time to keep the pleating in place.

30 Finish off the sewing at one edge, then return to the center of the swag and sew to the other edge. This is easier if you turn the swag-board around so that the swag is facing away from you.

31 When this stage is complete, take out any remaining pins and lift the swag off the swag-board. Machine across the swag, through all the layers.

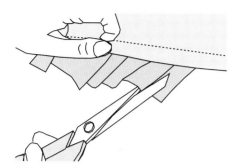

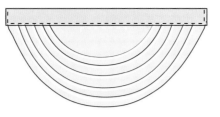

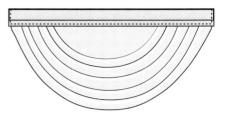

32 To cut down on bulk, the interlining, if used, should be cut back as close as possible to the line of machining. This is done by cutting along the front and back edge of each pleat, then cutting back the interlining as far as possible. The remaining fabric and lining should be trimmed back to 1cm (½in).

33 The raw edges of the top band are turned under, then the top band is folded in half, enclosing all the raw edges. Slip stitch the sides and long edge of the band to the back of the swag, level with the line of machining. I find it quicker to complete the top band by hand, as if you try to stitch it by machine it invariably twists and you have to unpick it anyway.

See Technique 54, Slip Stitch, page 53.

34 Machine sew-on loop Velcro to the top edge of the top band. For a heavy interlined swag I would use 5cm- (2in-) wide Velcro, while a lightweight swag would only require 2cm- (¾in-) wide Velcro. This attaches to strips of the appropriate width of self-adhesive hook Velcro that are stuck to the top of the cornice board.

35 If there are several swags and they overlap, sew-on hook Velcro is also attached to the front of the top band of the underlying swags. As an example, for three swags, with the middle swag lying on top of the other two, the Velcro should be attached to the fronts of the bands as shown.

36 Attaching the top bands to the tails is done in a very similar way to attaching the top band to the swag.

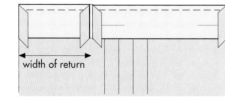

clip tail fabric here

width of return

The only difference is that the tail has to be fitted around the corner of the cornice board, so the top band has to be made in two pieces. Cut two top bands for each tail, both 16cm (6¼in) wide, one the length of the return, the other the length of the pleated part of the tail, both plus seam allowances. With the raw edges aligned, machine the top bands to the tail, taking a 2cm (¾in) seam allowance. Clip the top of the tail between the two top bands to allow it to lie smoothly round the cornice board. Turn in the seam allowances, fold the top bands in half and slip stitch along the edges.

37 To hold the tails to the cornice board and the swags to the tails, sew hook Velcro to the front of the top bands as shown, and loop Velcro to the back in the appropriate positions.

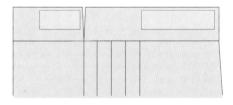

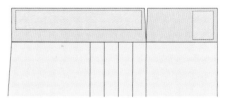

PROJECT 7

The classic Roman blind

Blinds are an excellent way of adding another element to a window treatment. They can be hung behind curtains to give shade and privacy during the day when the curtains are tied back. They will also protect expensive fabrics from the damaging rays of the sun. If you only have dress curtains at a window, blinds are a practical solution to covering the window at night. Used by themselves, blinds are perfect for a more contemporary look or if you are dressing a window with little or no space around it for curtains to stack back into.

I make up three basic styles of Roman blind, all of which vary slightly in the positioning of the slots. For all styles you must draw a diagram of the blind, marking out the position of each of the pockets for rods and D-moulds (weight bars) and the spaces between them.

Materials

Main fabric

Lining

Hand-sewing and machine thread

0.5cm (¼in) wooden or fibreglass rods

5 x2.5cm (2 x 1in) wooden batten

2.5cm (1in) D-mould

Cleat

Cord

Cord guides

As an alternative to the last six items, a specialist blind headrail system can be used

Small plastic or brass rings or quick-release rings

Equipment

Long pins

Long fine needles

Clamps or bricks

Measuring tape

Small ruler

Iron and ironing mat

Scissors

Vanishing marker

1 See Technique 1, How to Draw to Scale, page 12.

2 See Technique 23, Measuring for Blinds, page 31.

3 See Technique 29, Measuring Pattern Repeats, page 36.

4 See Technique 35, Cutting Plain and Lining Fabrics, page 41.

5 See Techniques 35-37, Cutting Plain and Lining Fabrics, Cutting Velvets, Cutting Patterned Fabrics, pages 41-42.

6 See Techniques 41-43, Joining Plain and Lining Fabrics, Joining Velvets, Joining Patterned Fabrics, pages 44-45.

Blind One

This blind has an un-weighted bottom hem with decorative trimming, which shows below the folds even when the blind is raised. This is the style of blind to make if you wanted a cut-away appliqué trim or a shaped hem.

7 The top space in the blind should be 6cm (2½in) longer than the other, standard, spaces to allow clearance for the cord guides. The D-mould is placed up from the bottom of the blind, to add weight while showing the trimming on the hem, even when the blind is drawn up. The bottom space is normally half the depth of the standard spaces, plus the depth of the trimming on the hem. In this example I have added 8cm (3in) for the trimming.

The standard spaces are rarely less than 16cm (6½in) and the larger the blind, the larger the space should be. I have made Roman blinds on very long, narrow windows where the distance between rods was as much as 50cm (20in), but it was correct for that particular window. To prevent sagging, the rows of rings and the cord guides should not be further than 40cm (16in) apart.

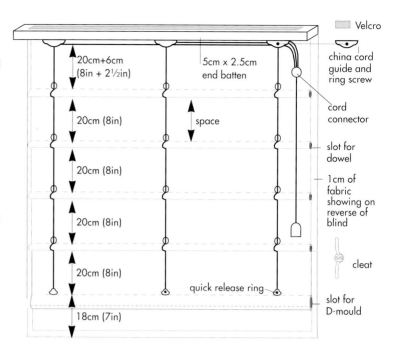

8 This example shows you how to work out the spaces for a blind 124cm (48½in) long, with a cut-away appliqué hem.

124cm (48½in)	- 6cm (2in)	- 8cm (3in)	= 110cm (43½in)
overall finished length	allowance for cord guides	allowance for hem trim	remaining amount of blind to be divided into spaces

For this size of blind, I would usually use a space of 18-20cm (7-8in). Therefore, divide the above figure by the approximate size of the space we want.

110cm (43½in)	÷ 20cm (8in)	= 5.5
from above calculation	approx. size of space	number of spaces

This is perfect, as it gives us five full spaces plus half a space below the D-mould. To check the calculations, add up the figures.

Top space	20 + 6cm (8 + 2¼in)	= 26cm (10¼in)
4 spaces of	20cm (8in)	= 80cm (31in)
Bottom space	10 + 8cm (4 + 3in)	= 18cm (7in)
Total		= 124cm (48¼in)

9 The next example shows you how to work out the spaces for a more complicated, much longer blind 205cm (80in), but with the same amount of decoration showing at the hem.

205cm (80in)	- 6cm (2in)	- 8cm (3in)	= 191cm (75in)
overall finished length	allowance for cord guides	allowance for hem trim	remaining amount of blind to be divided into spaces

For this blind, I would probably use a space of approximately 30cm (12in).

191cm (75in)	÷ 30cm (12in)	= 6.366 (6.25)
from above calculation	approx. size of space	number of spaces.

We are actually looking for a number of spaces to the nearest half space, so we need to round this figure up or down, whichever is appropriate. (If this calculation had resulted in a figure of say 6.8 spaces, I would round it down to 6.5.) That figure can then be used in the next calculation.

191cm (75in)	÷ 6.5	= 29.5cm (11¾in)
from above calculation	number of spaces	size of whole space

Therefore a half space will be 14.7cm (5¾in). Double check the calculation by adding up the figures as before.

Blind Two

A blind with a weighted bottom hem with decorative trimming, which shows below the folds even when the blind is raised. This style of blind can be used for applied trims.

10 The way of working out the positions for the rods for this style of blind is the same as for Blind 1, except that a D-mould is used at the bottom of the blind, in addition to the D-mould that takes the ring. This does not affect the calculations for spaces between the rods, but extra fabric has to be added to form the slot at the bottom of the blind.

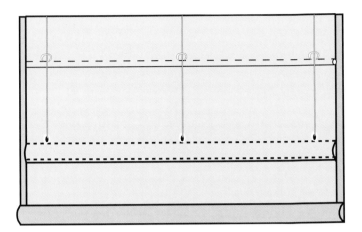

Blind Three

A blind with a weighted bottom hem, without trimming, which is level with the remainder of the folds when the blind is raised.

11 Where blinds do not have any added decoration you may prefer a second D-mould at the bottom of the blind. Many workrooms use only one D-mould, which in this type of blind would be placed at the bottom of the blind, with all the lower spaces equal. If the rings are attached to this bar, it will mean that when the blind is raised the main fabric will show on the window side of the blind. Personally, I don't particularly like to see blocks of main fabric from the outside and, more importantly, this fabric will almost certainly fade. Then, when the blind is let down, you will quickly start to see a faded band across the bottom of it. Therefore, I always use two D-moulds, with the rings attached to the higher one.

In making up, the bottom edges are overlocked and the correct amount (I usually allow 2cm (¾in) then 3cm (1¼in), is turned up to form the slot. I normally stitch this in place by hand.

As you can see from the diagram, the bottom space is now half the measurement of the upper spaces, so a slightly different calculation is needed.

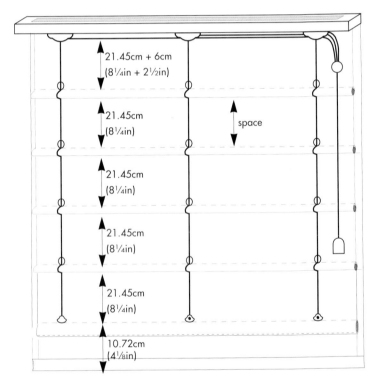

124cm (48¼in)	- 6 cm (2½in)	= 118cm (45¾in)
overall finished length	*allowance for cord guides*	*remaining amount of blind to be divided into spaces*

For this size of blind, I would usually use a space of 18-20cm (7-8in). Therefore, divide the above figure by the approximate size of the space we want.

118cm (45¾in)	÷ 20cm (8in)	= 5.9 (5.7)
from above calculation	*approx. size of space*	*number of spaces*

For this blind, we need to round this figure up or down to a half space (the half space being the amount below the first D-mould).

118cm (45¾in)	÷ 5.5 (5.7)	= 21.45 (8¼in)
from above calculation	*number of spaces*	*size of whole space*

Therefore the half space will be 10.72cm (4⅛in).

To check the calculations, add up the figures.

Top space	21.45 + 6cm (8¼ + 2½in)	= 27.45cm (10¾in)
4 spaces of	21.45cm (8¼in)	= 85.80cm (33in)
Bottom space	10.72cm (4⅛in)	= 10.72cm (4⅛in)
Total		=123.97cm (47⅞in)

12 In most cases, if you are using an applied trim, such as fabric or ribbon, it should be stitched onto the blind before stitching the side hems. With the blind fabric right side down on the table, mark the side hems and bottom hem with a vanishing marker. Alternatively use a small ruler to measure the hems and gently press the fold with an iron.

13 Blind One: turn in 5cm (2in) on the bottom and side hems. Make true mitres at the corners to cut away bulk. Herringbone stitch the side hems in place and ladder stitch the corners.

See Technique 49, True Mitres, page 48; Technique 53, Herringbone Stitch, page 53 and Technique 56, Ladder Stitch, page 55.

14 Blinds Two and Three: turn in 5cm (2in) for the side hems and herringbone stitch them in place. Leave the lower edge raw.

15 Cut the lining to the exact finished width of the blind. Add together all of the measurements given on the illustrations, plus 2.5cm (1in) for each rod pocket and 5cm (2in) for the upper D-mould for the cut length. These illustrations show the lines and spaces for the blind measurements calculated in step 8. For any other blind, revise the spaces accordingly, though the size of the rods and the top batten will not change. If you are folding up the bottom hem of the blind to form a slot for a second weight bar do not forget to allow sufficient lining – I usually allow 5cm (2in).

Place the lining right side down and, using an iron and a small ruler, press 1cm (½in) to the wrong side along the side edges. If the lining is likely to fray, neaten the edges with an overlock or zigzag stitch. Turn the lining over and mark on all the sewing lines for the slots, using a metre stick and a fading marker or tailor's chalk. If you are using a fading marker, a warm iron will restore color should the lines fade too quickly. Excess lining and fabric at the top of the blind will be trimmed off at a later stage.

17 Wrong sides facing, place the main fabric and lining together. Use clamps to keep the layers together and prevent them stretching and twisting. Pin the lining in place, making sure you start to position it at the bottom of the blind, using the slot for the D-mould as your guide (if there are two D-moulds, use the upper one as your guide). Pin the layers together along the lines of the pockets. Slip stitch down both sides and along the bottom of the blind, leaving the slots free. If there is an appliquéd bottom hem, you will only need to hand-stitch the sides, as the bottom edges will remain raw. If you are using a D-mould at the bottom edge, again you will leave raw edges, which are then overlocked to neaten them. Fold and press them under to form the bottom slot and hand stitch along the bottom to give a neater finish on the right side of the blind.

See Technique 54, Slip Stitch, page 53.

16 Fold the lining, bringing two adjacent marked lines together and pinning the fabric, from the front, exactly through both lines. Machine along the lines to form pockets for the rods. Press all the slots towards the bottom of the blind. Stitch at the bottom of the folded D-mould slot through to the main part of the lining to add strength. All the slots should be on the right side of the lining.

18 With all the slots lying flat and facing towards the bottom of the blind, machine on top of the line of machining forming the slot, through to the main fabric. If you have used contrast band or ribbon trim, do not stitch across it. Also machine across the top row of machining for the D-mould pocket. If you prefer to avoid seeing any machining on the front of the blind, you can catch the two layers together by hand. Use small stab stitches, about 2cm (¾in) apart, right across the blind, following the line of machining forming the slot.

Between stitches, run the thread between the main fabric and the lining.

19 Re-measure from the base to the top of the blind and, allowing for a 1cm (½in) turning under the Velcro, trim off any excess fabric. Attach the Velcro by machine. If the blind is to be top fixed with Velcro attached to the front of the batten, it looks unsightly to have two lines of machining showing on the blind. Of course, if the top of the blind is to be hidden by a valance or cornice, this isn't a problem. I have tried many techniques over the years to get round this problem of visible lines of machining. The best method I have found is to place the Velcro right at the very top of the blind and machine very close to the top edge. The bottom of the Velcro should then be hand-stitched to the blind with a strong thread. This method gives a good combination of looks and strength.

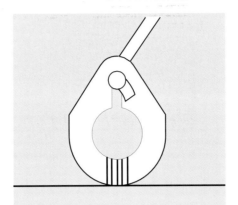

Quick release ring.

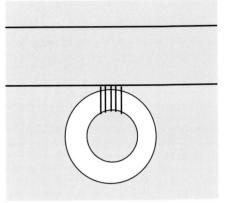

Standard ring, preferably made from clear strong polycarbonate.

20 The rings must run in vertical columns from the cord guides to the D-mould. Attach the rings by hand on the machine line of each slot. Quick release rings are a useful innovation; they enable you to tie a knot in the cord that fits into the groove at the top of the ring. The rings themselves are stitched in position at the top of the D-mould. Their advantage is that if the blind needs to be removed for cleaning it is a simple matter to release the cord and you do not have the problem of tying the cords so that they are level when you re-fit the blind.

21 A blind can be transformed from looking like a single, flat piece of fabric hung at the window into a stylish and creative window treatment by the addition of appliqué.

The appliqué motifs are roughly cut out from a separate fabric, making sure that the design you have picked has good strong outlines with not too many tricky points. Iron these motifs onto medium-weight iron-on interfacing. This lets you cut closely around the design with the minimum amount of fraying and also gives body to the bottom of the blind.

See Technique 99, Making Inserted Borders, page 90 and Technique 102, Making Mitred Borders, page 94.

22 Allow an extra 2cm (¾in) of main fabric and lining at the bottom of the blind, as it is easier to appliqué around the motifs with some extra fabric below them, which is cut away later. When the blind is almost complete, on the right side draw a line to indicate the lowest position for the appliqué. Lay the motifs so that they are almost touching this line.

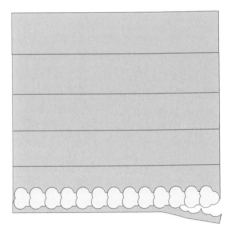

23 Pin or tack the motifs into place, making sure that where the design touches the side hems it will finish with a complete motif. Using a zigzag stitch with a width of 2-3 mm (¹⁄₁₆-⅛in) and a length of 0.3mm (¹⁄₃₂in), satin stitch closely around the design, through the main fabric and the lining, making sure all the raw edges are concealed. Along the base line, cut away the main fabric and lining, leaving an attractively shaped hem on your blind, adding interest and color when silhouetted against a window.

24 Cut a wooden batten to the width of your blind. The batten can be painted to match the wall it will be fastened to.

25 Attach adhesive-backed Velcro to the top or face of the batten, making sure there is no grease to prevent adhesion. As an added precaution, put a staple or tack at either end, where an initial tug could dislodge the Velcro. Following these simple precautions I have worked successfully with Velcro for many years.

26 Place screw eyes, or preferably china cord guides (which will help the blind to operate much more smoothly), on the batten at the top of your rows of rings. Take all the measurements from your original diagram.

27 Insert the wooden rods and battens into the prepared pockets, putting a couple of stitches at either end to secure them if necessary. I do not usually stitch the ends, especially if the blind is going to require frequent cleaning. Attach the Velcro on the blind to the Velcro on the batten.

28 Screw the angle brackets to the wall or window frame, approximately 5cm (2in) from either end of where the batten will sit. If the blind is very wide or heavy, you may need another bracket in the middle. Occasionally it is better to top-fix the blind by drilling and screwing directly through the batten. This is particularly useful if you have UPVC window frames.

29 Cut enough pieces of cord to the correct length; these measurements will vary as they have to travel different distances. Cords travel from the quick release ring, where they are held in place by a knot, up through the rings to the cord guide on the batten, along the other guides and a short way down the side of the window where they are fastened together in a cord connector. A single length of cord with a cord weight is used to operate the blind. Alternatively, you can plait the cords together and use a single cord weight. To cord it up, it is easiest to lay the blind out flat and face down.

30 Place the blind in position and screw through the bracket into the batten to secure.

31 When the blind is in place, screw the cleat to the wall or frame to hold the cord.

32 Another method of hanging blinds is by using a range of specialist tracks which have Velcro permanently attached to their face. Their range is enormous, covering almost every type and shape of window and every weight of blind from lightweight voiles to heavy fabric with blackout lining on electrically operated tracks. This is a huge subject in its own right, so I would suggest you go along to a specialist furnishings store to ask for leaflets.

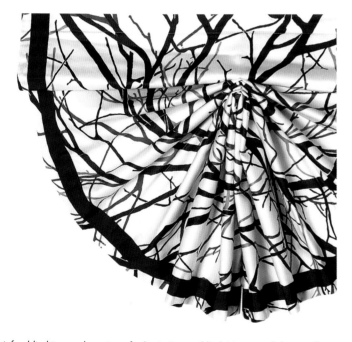

A fan blind is an adaptation of a basic Roman blind. It's unusual shape will add interest to a window. This style of blind works particularly well on tall, slim windows or long, thin french windows, See Project 11, page 141.

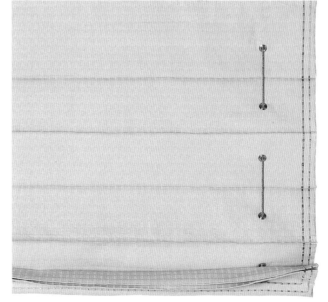

This eyelet blind introduces a much softer, more casual look to a window. It does not have any horizontal rods at all, just stitched folds. See Project 19, page 156.

PROJECT 8

The classic loose cover for a wooden chair

Covering a wooden chair using the following technique totally transforms a junk shop find into an elegant piece of furniture. Remnants or short lengths of fabric, a sewing machine, time and patience are virtually all you need to work this magic for your home. I really don't like the term loose covers: tailored covers is a much more accurate description of describing the way these covers will look if you follow this method carefully.

Materials

Fabric: be certain that the fabric is suitable for the purpose if the chair is going to be used constantly. As a guide ask for a Martindale rub test. A test result of 30,00 upwards means that the fabric will stand everyday use by a family. A test result of under 20,000 means that the fabric is only suitable for occasional use. Also, be certain that the fabric complies with fire regulations in your country.

Equipment

Cloth tape measure

Metre (yard) stick

Loose cover pins: these are much thicker than standard pins and have many advantages. They do not bend in thick fabric, they part the threads, giving a good indication of the stitching line, and they do not fall out as you are moving the cover about while making it up.

Tailor's chalk marker: a fading marker may not be suitable, as the cover may not be completed before the marks fade.

Masking tape

Scissors

1 See Technique 24, Measuring for Loose Covers, page 32.

3 See Techniques 35-37, Cutting Plain and Lining Fabrics, Cutting Velvets, Cutting Patterned Fabrics, pages 41-42

2 With experience, calculating your fabric requirements can be done literally in your head. However, initially draw each piece to scale on paper. If you are using a patterned fabric, to be extra cautious you can draw out the design of the fabric first and place the pattern pieces accordingly. As a rule, I find that a large bouquet design will take between 25% and 33% extra fabric if you wish to place the patterns perfectly and match front borders to the aprons, etc. For the skirt, you will need to allow triple fullness if you are using box pleats that butt up to one another and two-three times fullness for a gathered skirt (depending on the thickness of the fabric). For an apron, you will need to allow sufficient for each separate piece and extra for the kick pleats.

Piping can be cut from the same fabric or from a contrasting color. In either case I rarely use less than one metre (yard) of fabric, simply because you can cut longer pieces and therefore have less joins on the finished cover. Obviously, if you are working to a tight budget you will use less fabric and therefore you will have more joins. A problem with joining piping strips is that with some fabrics, you will find that they wear more quickly at the joins.

4 Cut the fabric pieces according to your measurements, plus 3cm (1¼in) seam allowances all round. I simply cut plain fabric, but I prefer to drape patterned fabric over the chair to place the pattern before cutting and pinning it. I almost always pin the cover right side out, as it is easier to see the pattern. Also, if you make the cover inside out then turn it through to the correct side, you are assuming that the chair is totally symmetrical, which it may not be. To accurately place the border and aprons, I stick a band of masking tape around the legs of the chair, 2cm (¾in) lower than the position of the horizontal piping, and parallel to the floor.

To give you something to push the pins into while fitting the chair cover, take a piece of scrap fabric approximately 6cm (2½in) wider than the chair back and long enough to make the 'sleeve' shown in the illustration below. To within a few centimeters this length is not critical. Place the fabric over the back of the chair and pin each side to obtain a really tight fit.

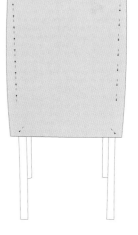

5 Remove the fabric from the chair, machine the pinned edges and turn to the right side. Place the sleeve on the chair. Now you can pin the main fabric pieces to this sleeve to hold them in place while they are being fitted. The fabric pieces pinned around the chair legs are also for pushing pins into.

6 Take the piece you have cut for the outside back and place it on the chair as shown, pinning it to the sleeve and the leg bands.

7 Place the inside back piece on the chair and pin the two pieces together, working from the outside back. When you are pinning loose covers, it is always best to pin the pieces from the side you will pipe: in this instance you will be applying the piping to the outside back.

8 On the inside back, at the top corners, form a dart, as shown, to take up the excess fabric.

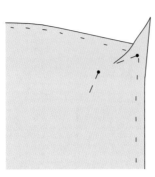

9 Turn up the fabric at the bottom of the inside back to the point where the inside back meets the seat. In order to divide the fabric, to join both the seat and the border to it, make a cut exactly on the corner of the chair. Do not make too deep a cut at this stage, you can always make it a little deeper but you can't cover it up if you cut it too much.

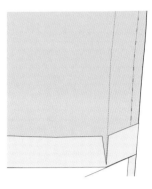

10 Place the seat piece and pin it to the inside back, leaving the outer edges free.

11 Place the border with the bottom edge just to the bottom of the band of masking tape. As seats often slope slightly, this will ensure that the lower edge of the border is parallel to the floor.

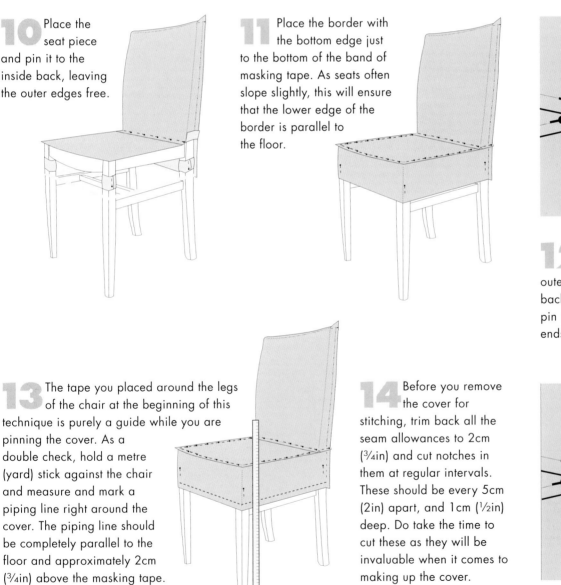

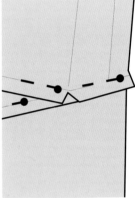

12 Pin the seat to the border. Pin the outer edges of the inside back to the border and also pin the outside back to the ends of the border.

13 The tape you placed around the legs of the chair at the beginning of this technique is purely a guide while you are pinning the cover. As a double check, hold a metre (yard) stick against the chair and measure and mark a piping line right around the cover. The piping line should be completely parallel to the floor and approximately 2cm (¾in) above the masking tape.

14 Before you remove the cover for stitching, trim back all the seam allowances to 2cm (¾in) and cut notches in them at regular intervals. These should be every 5cm (2in) apart, and 1cm (½in) deep. Do take the time to cut these as they will be invaluable when it comes to making up the cover.

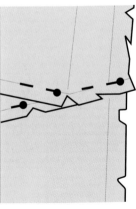

15 Be very accurate with these last two stages; in effect you are forming a jigsaw puzzle, which will be taken apart a bit at a time, piped and put back together. Just as with a good quality jigsaw it should be obvious which pieces fit together and they should do so easily. You will have three things to help you at this stage:

1 You will know that the seam allowance is exactly 2cm (¾in).
2 The loose cover pins will leave a row of pin marks.
3 The notches will help you to align the pieces exactly.

16 Some people really worry when it comes to removing the cover from the chair for piping. They usually think that they have to take out all the pins, then put everything back together again. Nothing could be further from the truth. You do take the whole cover off the chair, but then you just take out one small section at a time, attach the piping to one side then put the section back, with the piping in between the layers. So that you can see exactly which pieces to unpin, some of the following illustrations show the pieces still on the chair. At each stage, it is best to neaten the raw edges by overlocking or zigzag stitching them, as it is impossible to do this neatly when another section has been attached.

17 Remove the pins joining the seat to the front of the inside back, leaving the two side pieces still pinned to the border.

18 See Technique 74, Cutting Piping Strips, page 70.

19 See Technique 75, Joining Piping Strips, page 71.

20 See Technique 76, Piping with Square Ends, page 72.

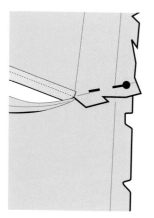

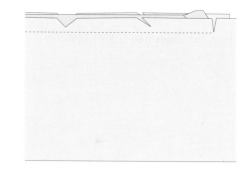

21 On the right side of the fabric, pipe the front of the inside back, as shown.

22 To avoid bulk, cut the cord 2cm (¾in) before the edge of the piping fabric. Gently pull the end of the piping fabric over the end of the cord, as shown, then machine over it to secure the ends.

23 Right sides facing, match up the notches on the piped inside back section and the seat section. On the wrong side, machine as close to the piping cord as possible.

24 The finished section would look like this if you placed it back on the chair. If you are unsure, this is always a useful check, but you will soon gain sufficient confidence to sew the whole cover without resorting to putting it back on the chair to check every section you have stitched.

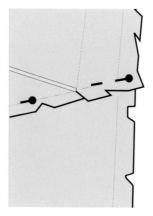

25 The next section to pipe is across one outside edge of the inside back, around the seat and back across the other outside edge of the inside back, as shown by the arrows. The seat section and the inside back section are now joined at every point.

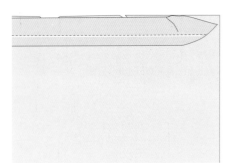

26 In this instance, as with most of the piping on your cover, you need to 'fade' the piping fabric away at the beginning and end of the seam. Cut the piping cord 2cm (¾in) in from the edge of the section and pull the fabric over the cord as shown. This should be a less abrupt end than that shown in step 22. This technique ensures that as little as bulk as possible is introduced into the seam, particularly where two seams cross. Once you have piped this section, match up the notches and attach the border.

27 Remove the outside back section and pipe from the marked line indicating the horizontal piping line on one side, right around the outside back to the marked line on the other side. Match up the notches and attach the outside back to the rest of the chair.

29 The apron skirt for this chair consists of four panels of fabric, one on each side of the chair. Lying under and between them (over each leg of the chair) are four separate kick pleats. Using your measurements, make up four sections of apron, either in the same way as a lined valance, or self line them by simply cutting the fabric to twice the length, folding it in half and machining down both sides. Cut away any bulk, turn through to the right side, neaten the top edges and press.

28 The next step is to pipe the marked line around the chair, joining the piping on one side. I find it best to neaten this lower piped edge of the chair. If you neaten the top of each section of the apron and each kick pleat before it is attached, it removes the need to try and do this through the tremendous bulk once everything is machined together.

See Technique 78, Joining Piping, page 74.

See Project 3, The Classic Valance, page 106.

30 Make up four separate pieces as kick pleats for the corners using the same technique. These pieces should be approximately 15cm (6in) wide and 0.5cm (¼in) shorter than the aprons, so that they do not hang lower than the aprons once they are attached.

31 Right-sides facing, raw edges aligned, pin the four aprons to the bottom of the border. Right-side down, pin the kick pleats over the aprons at the corners. As they sit round the inside corners, pin carefully to ensure they lie smoothly. Machine round the border, through all layers. Press and put the cover on the chair. Because of the bulk, you may find it easier to machine the aprons first, then the kick pleats.

Box-pleated skirt

Cut and join sufficient widths to form the box pleats, adding seam allowances of 8cm (3in) to the length of each piece. Join the pieces, press up a bottom hem of 2cm (¾in) then 4cm (1½in) and machine blind hem or slip stitch. Form box pleats until you have sufficient to go around the chair. Right sides facing, machine the pleated fabric to the piped border, joining the ends in an area camouflaged by a pleat.

See Technique 65, Forming Box Pleats, page 64 and Technique 54, Slip Stitch, page 53.

Frilled skirt

Cut sufficient widths, adding seam allowances of 8cm (3in). Join the pieces, press up and stitch a bottom hem of 2cm (¾in) then 4cm (1½in). Gather the skirt until it fits around the chair. Right-sides facing, machine the skirt to the piped border, joining it in an inconspicuous place.

See Technique 86, Making Frilled Edging, page 83.

PROJECT 9

The classic loose cover for a simple chair

Covering this type of chair is in all aspects, except the tuckaway, done in exactly the same way as the wooden chair. In fact, this style of chair is easier to cover than a wooden chair, as you can push the pins into the upholstery to attach the cover pieces to the chair. The cover will also tend to fit better as the fabric 'grips' the upholstery rather than sliding over the wood. Some chairs of this type do not have a gap between the seat and the back to hold a tuckaway, in which case, follow step 2 rather than step 3.

Materials and equipment:

As for The Classic Loose Cover for a Wooden Chair, page 130.

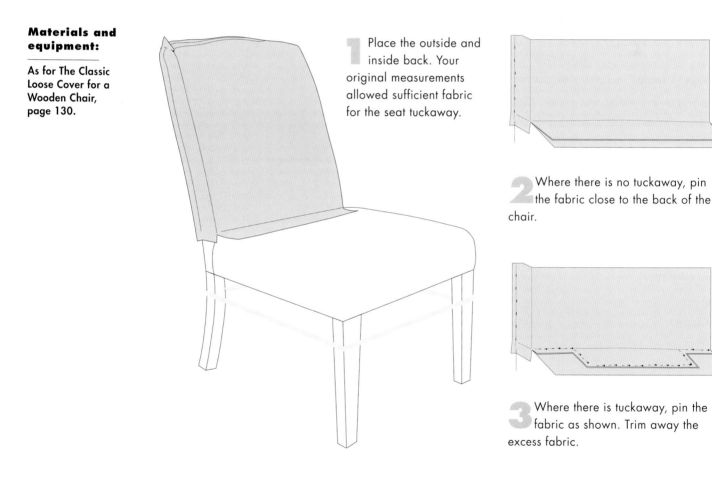

1 Place the outside and inside back. Your original measurements allowed sufficient fabric for the seat tuckaway.

2 Where there is no tuckaway, pin the fabric close to the back of the chair.

3 Where there is tuckaway, pin the fabric as shown. Trim away the excess fabric.

4 Pin the remainder of the cover and notch all the seams well, including the tuckaway seam. Remove the cover when the pinning is completed, the seams carefully matched and trimmed back to 2cm (¾in).

5 Remove the pins from the seam between the seat and the inside back. Make sure you leave the two outside edges of the inside back (which will be attached to the border in due course) still pinned.

6 Turn the cover wrong-side out, then stitch and neaten the seam. If there is a tuckaway, you do not insert piping. Continue unpinning, piping and assembling the cover, including the skirt, as previously described.

135

PROJECT 10

Classic cushions

There is a very simple guideline for cutting out cushions. Measure the cushion pad on one edge (not over the domed part of the pad). The cushion cover should be cut to exactly the size of the pad, then machined taking a 2cm (¾in) seam allowance. So, if you have a pad measuring 46cm (18in) square, cut the cover to 46cm (18in) square, then machine it taking a 2cm (¾in) seam allowance on all sides. The finished cover will measure 42cm (16½in), which will give you a beautiful plump cushion rather than a flat one that has excess fabric at each corner.

Materials

Zip

Piping cord

Machine thread

Fabric for cushion

Fabric for piping

Fabric for frilling, pleating or ruching

Flanged cord or other purchased trim

Cushion pad, preferably filled with curled feather or down, though polyester or hypoallergenic can be used if you are allergic to feathers

Equipment

Scissors or cutting mat, ruler and rotary cutter

Metre (yard) stick

Set square

Square Cushions

1 To cut out a plain cushion cover, or one where the fabric has an all-over pattern, draw a right angle on the fabric with a set square and a vanishing marker. Draw in two sides of the cushion with a metre (yard) stick. Place the set square on the second corner and again, use a metre (yard) stick to measure the third side. Finally, connect the last two points to form the square.

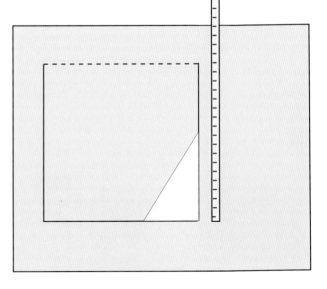

2 If you want to position a design centrally on a cover, draw a horizontal line, with a fading marker or tailor's chalk, through the center of the relevant part of the design. Use a set square to draw a vertical line, again through the center of the design, at right angles to the first line.

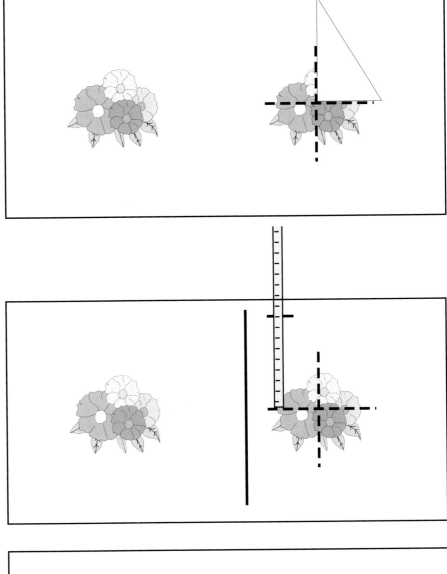

3 Use a metre (yard) stick to measure half the width of the pad out from the central lines.

4 Join the marked measurements to form a square with the design exactly in the middle. Cut out both pieces of the cover and use as many of the following techniques as you wish to embellish the cover.

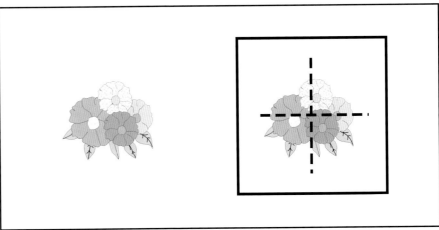

137

5 See Techniques 35-37, Cutting Plain and Lining Fabrics, Cutting Velvets, Cutting Patterned Fabrics, pages 41-42.

6 See Technique 74, Cutting Piping Strips, page 70.

7 See Technique 75, Joining Piping Strips, page 71.

8 See Technique 77, Piping with Joining Ends, page 73.

9 See Technique 79, Piping Square Corners, page 76.

10 See Technique 78, Joining Piping, page 74.

11 See Technique 81, Piping with Flanged Cord, page 78.

12 See Technique 82, Joining Flanged Cord, page 79.

13 See Technique 86, Making Frilled Edging, page 83.

14 See Technique 87, Making Bound-edge Frilled Edging, page 84.

15 See Technique 88, Making Double-frilled Edging, page 84.

16 See Technique 89, Making Pleated Edging, page 84.

17 See Technique 90, Making Ruched Edging, page 85.

18 See Technique 91, Inserting Edgings, page 85.

19 See Technique 92, Inserting Edgings Around a Corner, page 85.

20 See Technique 93, Joining Edgings, page 86.

21 See Technique 94, Joining Ruched Edging, page 86.

22 See Technique 83, Inserting a Zip Between Two Pieces of Fabric, page 80.

23 See Technique 84, Inserting a Zip in a Piped Seam, page 81.

24 Once you have embellished the front section of the cover and put in a zip, you must stitch the two halves of the cover together. Stitch very close to the piping or cord, using the line of machining attaching it to the fabric as your guide. If you can't see a line of machining, you are working on the wrong side of the cover. By pushing very hard with your left hand as you sew, your machining will be positioned inside the piping line of machining. Be very careful at the corners and press the piping or cord towards the center of the cover to allow you to get really close to it. Overlock the remaining raw edges and trim the corners to cut down on bulk before turning the cover right-side out and pressing it.

Round Cushions

1 If you are making a round cushion, place the two sides of the cushion right-sides facing and make notches so that the two sides can be matched together after piping. The notches should only be 1cm (½in) deep.

3 Right-sides facing, put the two halves of the cover together, the back of the cushion will have a zip in the center. With the piping uppermost, match up the notches. This will mean easing in the fabric of the bottom half of the cushion, which has not been gathered by the piping. Stitch inside the piping line of machining to complete the cover. Neaten the edges, turn the cover right side out and press.

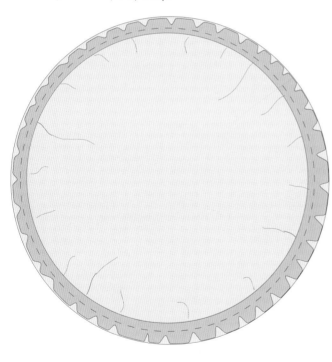

2 Pipe round the cover, pulling the piping slightly to give an almost gathered look. If the fabric is smooth, the finished cushion will have no depth. Notch the piping a section at a time to help it curve before machining it.

See Technique 80, Piping Curves, page 78.

Box Cushions

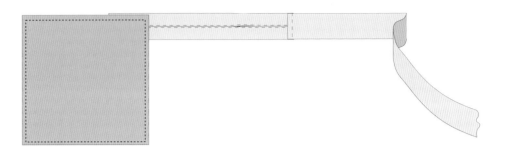

1 Both sides of the cover should be piped, with good square corners and careful placing of the piping to make sure you take up exactly the right amount of seam allowance.

2 See Technique 85, Zip in the Center of a Border, page 82.

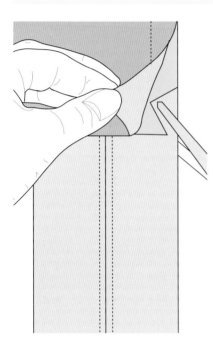

3 The next step is to attach the border and zip section to one side of the cover. Something I find most annoying is covers which have been made with a very short zip, sometimes only across the back. This makes it almost impossible to remove the cushion pad without splitting the stitching at the end of the zip.

Right-sides facing, machine the zip section of the border to one of the piped pieces. Machine almost to the first corner, make certain your line of machining is as close to the piping as possible.

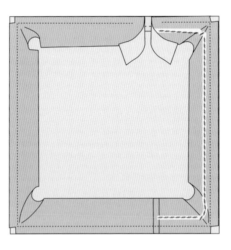

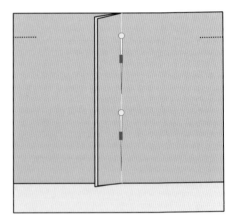

4 Before you reach the corner, raise the piped piece and cut the border section at the same angle as the cut in the piping fabric. Stitch exactly to the corner and, with the needle down in the fabric, twist the cover to start the next side. Make sure you press down on the piping fabric, so that you are as close to the cord as possible. Before machining the second side of the cover, pull slightly on the border fabric. This avoids a small bubble of fabric on the border. Start and stop machining approximately 5cm (2in) from the beginning and end of the border.

5 Once you have attached the border to all sides of the piped piece, join the ends of the border.

6 Pin the ends of the border in place so that they fit the piped piece exactly. Trim off excess fabric and neaten the ends. Press the seam allowances and machine again for strength. Machine the gap closed.

7 Fold the border at each corner of the cover, as shown, and cut a notch a maximum of 1.5cm (⅝in) deep. If you cut it any deeper it will show and it will also fray in time. Lay the cover piece with the border attached on the table and place the other piped section face down onto it. On one side, line up the notches in the border with the corners of the machining line, then machine the two sections together. When you reach the corner, put the needle down in the cover and twist all the fabrics around so that you can line up the next notch with the next corner. Cut away the bulk at the corners, neaten all the edges, turn right-side out and press.

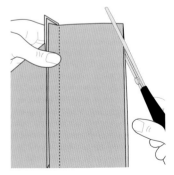

PROJECT 11

Fan blind

Perfect for long, narrow windows or glass door panels, this style of blind can be made in any fabric suitable for a Roman blind but looks particularly stunning in one of the incredible ranges of sheers, burnt outs or voiles now available. Try using it on an arched window where the arched section of the blind remains static.

The addition of a contrast petersham band down the outer edges of the blind helps to really define the shape.

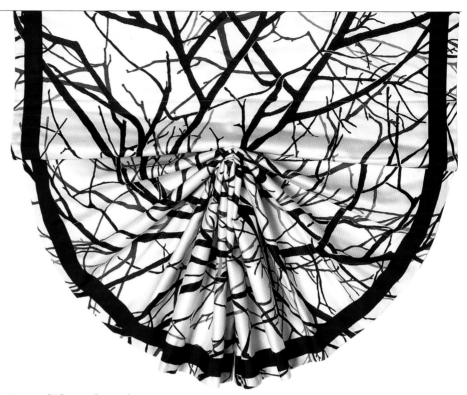

Materials and equipment

As for Project 7, The Classic Roman Blind, page 124.

1 See Project 7, The Classic Roman Blind, page 124.

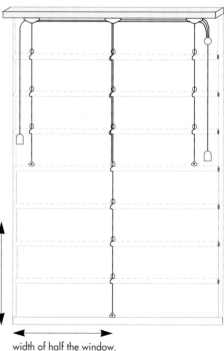

width of half the window.
Take the same measurement up the side of the blind.

The blind is made up in the same way as a standard Roman blind, with equal spaces (apart from the top space), and the weight bar in the bottom. The differences appear when it comes to inserting the rods and installing the blind. I have tried a number of different ways of making this work and after several years have finally decided that the following is the best technique.

The bottom few dowels, and also the bottom rod, are cut in half. It is best to leave a gap of approximately 1cm (½in) between the ends of the rods at the center of the blind to allow the blind to bend into the fan shape.

To decide how many rods to cut, measure half of the width of the window. Take the same measurement up from the bottom of the blind, as shown, and it will give you the minimum height to which you need to divide the rods.

For longer blinds I tend to divide the rod one above the minimum number, as it makes a better fan shape.

With split rods you must sew up the ends of the rod pockets. If you don't, every time you raise and lower the blind the rods will fall out.

The next step is the installation. You will need at least three cord guides and two cleats because the blind is corded in two ways: the one cord is attached down the center of the blind only to form the fan. The second and third cords are attached only to the dowels that are not divided, on each side of the blind, so that the blind has a fan on the lower part and is a Roman blind on the upper part, which in my opinion creates the best effect. If you prefer purely a fan effect you simply divide all the rods and just have one cord through the center of the blind only. The cords

can all be taken to one side of the blind or, as shown above, the cording for the fan effect can be taken to one side and the normal Roman cording to the other. To operate the blind, first raise the Roman section and fasten the cord to a cleat. Then raise the fan section and secure the cord.

141

PROJECT 12

Cuffed goblet-pleated curtain

This is a very attractive heading and can be used with the cuff raised for a static or semi-static window treatment, or with the cuff folded down, showing a contrast lining.

Materials

Fabric

Lining

Contrast fabric

12.5-15cm (5-6in) curtain buckram

Machine thread

Pin-on or sew-on hooks

Equipment

As for Project 1, The Classic Curtain, page 96.

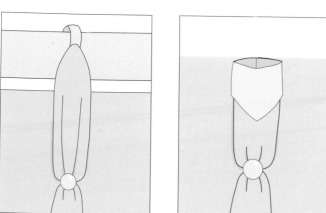

Far left: the cuff standing up, partly covering the pole and ring

Left: The cuff folded down, showing the contrast lining

1 If using a 12.5cm (4⅞in) buckram, add 10cm (4in) to the overall finished length of the curtain to allow for the cuff. You also need a strip of contrast fabric measuring the width of the curtain plus 4cm (1½in) by the following calculation.

12.5cm (4⅞in) *depth of buckram*	+ 10cm (4in) *amount for cuff*	+2cm (¾in) *seam allowance for top of the curtain*	+1cm (½in) *turn under the buckram*	=25.5cm (10⅛in) *depth of contrast strip*

2 See Project 1, The Classic Curtain, page 96.

3 Trim off the top of the curtain to the finished overall length, plus the depth you require for the cuff, plus 2cm (¾in) seam allowance. Cut the buckram to the exact width of the curtain. Cut the contrast band to the same width, plus 2cm (¾in) on each of the short ends to fold over the buckram. Overlock one long edge of the contrast band then lay the buckram on the band, leaving 1cm (½in) at the bottom to turn over the edge of the buckram. Turn this edge over the buckram and machine through all layers, right across the long edge. Raw edges aligned and right-sides facing, place the contrast band and buckram across the top of the curtain and pin them together.

4 See Technique 64, Forming Goblet Pleats, page 63.

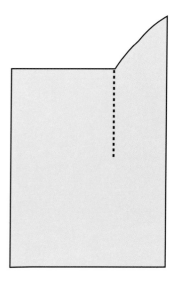

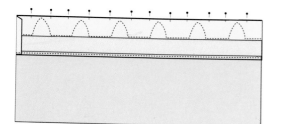

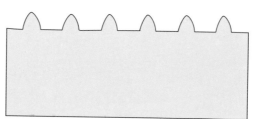

5 Calculate the amounts required for pleats and spaces and use pins to indicate their position, as shown. Make a card template for the shape of the cuff and draw round it in the areas defined for pleats to mark the line of machining.

6 Stitch along the marked line using a small stitch and cut away the excess fabric. Clip the corners and turn the heading through to the right side. The points are soft so that they can form the cuffs. Press gently.

7 Stitch the goblets in position in the normal way and add the hooks. The cuffs can be left up, with the points covering the pole, or turned down and caught with a few hand stitches to show the contrast lining.

PROJECT 13

Pleated valance

This is definitely one of my favorite valances, traditional without being fussy and suitable for windows of almost any width. Because of its proportions, it looks best at a tall window but it is perfectly possible to make it up without a top band, which would be suitable for shorter windows. Allow three-times fullness in the fabric for the best results.

Materials

Fabric

Contrast lining

Piping fabric

Smooth, narrow piping cord

Tieback stiffening

Velcro

Equipment

As for Project 3, The Classic Valance, page 106.

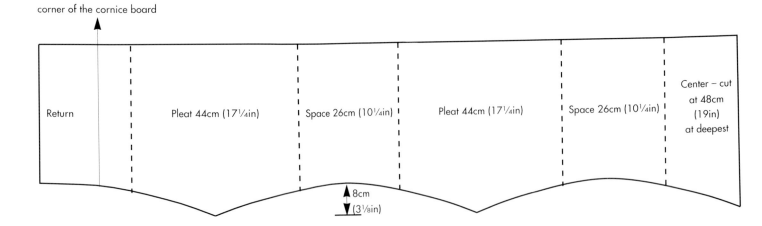

corner of the cornice board

| Return | Pleat 44cm (17¼in) | Space 26cm (10¼in) | Pleat 44cm (17¼in) | Space 26cm (10¼in) | Center – cut at 48cm (19in) at deepest |

8cm
(3⅛in)

1 With a fabric such as the one in the photograph, it is critical that you think very carefully about how to place the design before you start cutting. Adjustments can be made in the width of the flattened areas (spaces) according to your pattern and, of course, the width of the window. The width of the double box pleats can also be adjusted. A panel and border print like the one I have used is ideal for this particular style. The illustration shows half the valance template with the dimensions I have used. These can be used as the basis for your pattern, but they will need to be adjusted according to your dimensions and your fabric. Overall, the deepest part of my valance is 54cm (21¼in), which would be suitable for a window treatment with an overall height of about 270cm (106in) from the top of the cornice board to the floor. So, this valance, at its deepest, should be approximately one-fifth of the depth of the whole window treatment. Cut both the fabric and the contrast lining to your pattern.

2 See Project 3, The Classic Valance, page 106

3 You also need to cut a band, which in this instance is cut to 14cm (5½in), by the width of the board, including returns, plus 2cm (¾in) at each end for seam allowances. Cut one in the main fabric and one in the lining. If I am using a border print, I tend to cut the border from the outer edge that is normally returned to the wall before I start to make up the curtain. I can then use it for the top of valances such as this. or perhaps bordered cushions or tiebacks. If the curtains have sufficient fullness it will be no loss, but to buy an extra few metres (yards) is rather extravagant if you only need a small amount of border.

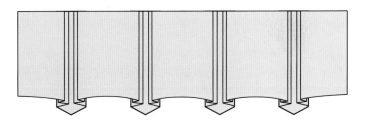

4 Right-sides facing, machine the fabric and lining together down one side, along the bottom edge and up the second side. Trim the corners, notch the curves, turn right-side out and press. Pleat up the fabric and lining until it measures the correct width. The dimensions given allow for double pleats, which should be arranged according to the design of the fabric. Be prepared to spend some time planning and pinning the pleats. Because of the bulk behind the folded pleats, you cannot place a pleat at the corner of the board.

5 Wrong-sides facing, place the lining and main fabric of the band together and cut 1cm- (½in-) deep notches on all edges to ensure that, once they have been separated for piping, you will be able to reassemble them exactly.

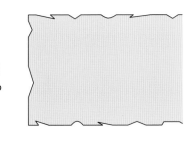

6 See Technique 74, Cutting Piping Strips, page 70.

7 See Technique 75, Joining Piping Strips, page 71.

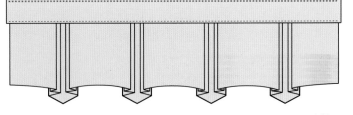

8 Separate the two layers of the band and pipe the top and bottom of the main fabric.

See Technique 76, Piping with Square Ends, page 72.

9 Right-sides facing and raw edges aligned, place the piped section across the top of the valance. Pin the band in position, then machine along the top edge, as close to the piping cord as possible.

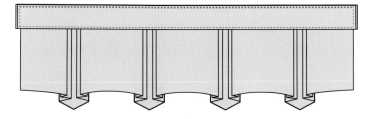

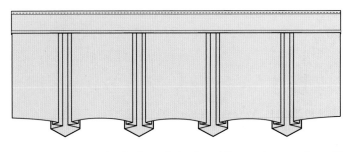

10 Place the lining band beneath the valance with the top raw edges of the valance, main fabric band and lining exactly aligned. If you are not using top bands, machine Velcro to the top of the band lining first.

Match the notches in the band main fabric and lining and machine the long edge on the previous line of machining. Make sure the layers are tucked out of the way and machine up the short edge of the band. Return to the start of the machining, and stitch from the corner up the other edge of the band.

11 Trim away the bulk, pull the band flat and insert the stiff buckram. Turn in the raw edges along the top and hand-stitch them closed. If you are using top bands, do not turn in the raw edges as you will attach the bands to them.

See Technique 69, Making Top Bands page 67.

PROJECT 14

Ruffle-headed curtain

Many fabrics are suitable for this type of curtain, as long as they are not too stiff or bulky. In order to hold the shape at the top, the fabric needs to have a fair amount of body, but fullness is the key factor. The contrast lining can be of a similar weight to the fabric itself, or a contrast chintz or colored lining.

It is quite amazing how much fullness can disappear into this style of curtain. I would recommend that you use approximately three to three-and-a-half times fullness, depending on the thickness of your fabric. In this picture I have used a 6.5cm- (2⅝in-) wide valance rod, which is readily available. However, if you have a rod or wooden pole you wish to use, simply adjust the measurements accordingly. The slot for a rod of this size should be 8.5cm (3¼in) wide, as if you make it tighter you will not be able to push the gathers together successfully. To get the ruffled heading, I left 8cm (3in) above the slot, plus a making allowance of 2cm (¾in).

Materials

Soft 0.5cm (¼in) jumbo cord or a flanged furnishing cord. (Be careful to choose one which is not too bulky or stiff for the fabric.)

Main fabric

Contrast lining

Piping fabric to cover the cord, if not using flanged cord

Equipment

As for Project 1, The Classic Curtain, page 96.

1 See Project 1, The Classic Curtain, page 96.

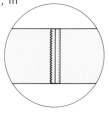

2 I have used two fabrics (one as a main fabric and the other as a contrast lining), of identical weight from the same range. This means they will shrink at the same rate and I can pipe across the bottom of the curtain. If, as is usual, your fabrics are not identical, use the following method. Make a bottom hem on both fabrics. Measure them and trim the tops to the right length.On the right side of the main fabric, pipe up from the bottom hem, along the top edge and down the second side. To save on cost you could pipe the top only. Right-sides facing, machine the curtain and the lining together, close to the cord on all three sides, leaving the bottom hem free.

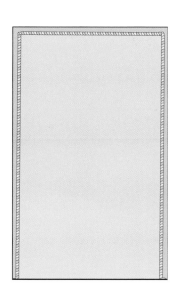

See Techniques 74-76, Cutting Piping Strips, Joining Piping Strips, Piping with Square Ends, pages 70-72.

3 Prepare a strip of fabric the same as the lining of the curtain to form the slot. This should be 8.5 cm (3¼in) wide plus 2cm (¾in) seam allowance at the top and bottom: a total of 12.5cm (4⅞in). The strip should be as wide as the curtain, plus 2cm (¾in) for turnings at each end. In almost all cases you will have to join widths of fabric together. You could 'railroad' it and turn the fabric on its side, but placing fabrics together with the warp and weft threads in different directions is not always a good idea as they may react differently in cleaning.

See Technique 68, Making Slot Headings, page 66.

4 To allow the rod to pass through the rod pocket with ease, use either a straight stitch or, if possible, a zigzag stitch to keep the seam allowances flat. Neaten the two long and two short edges of the strip. Otherwise, in cleaning or washing they might fray, making it difficult to put the curtain back onto the rod.

5 Press under and stitch a 2cm (¾in) seam allowance at each end of the strip. Press under, but do not stitch, a 2cm (¾in) seam allowance at the top and bottom of the strip.

6 Place the strip onto the back of the curtain at the right height, and machine across the top and bottom edges, through all the layers, as close to the pressed under edges of the strip as possible.

7 The rest of the effect is purely in the way the curtains are dressed. Slot the valance onto the valance rod and dress the curtains by pulling the piping towards you to create the ruffled shape.

PROJECT 15

Striped, ruched bolster

This very elegant cushion looks wonderful on a chair or a bed. Once applied, the ruched tape and stripes are treated simply as part of the main fabric, so for the sake of clarity in the illustrations, they are not shown throughout.

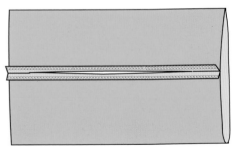

Materials

Feather bolster pad

Lattice-pleat curtain tape

Zip

Main fabric

Contrast fabric

Decorative flanged cord or piping

Two tassels or large self-cover buttons

Equipment

As for Project 10, Classic Cushions, page 136.

1 Measure the circumference of the bolster, pulling the tape measure a little to get a good tight fit. Cut bands of the main fabric the circumference of the bolster plus 4cm (1½in). The contrast bands will be the width of the tape attached to them, so the bands of main fabric must be wide enough to cover the remaining width of the bolster, plus 2cm (¾in) at each end.

The contrast bands should be approximately two-and-a-quarter times the circumference of the bolster pad, by the width of the tape, plus a seam allowance of 2cm (¾in) on each side. Stitch the tape onto the contrast bands and draw up the cords, making sure you secure the ends, until the bands are the length of the main fabric bands. Right-sides facing, sew alternate colored bands together to make a piece of striped, ruched fabric the length of the bolster by the circumference, plus 4cm (1½in).

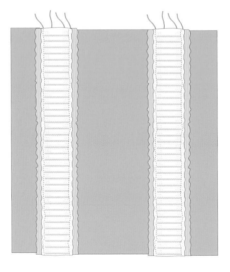

See Technique 59, Applying Standard Tapes, page 56 and Technique 61, Drawing-up Tapes, page 57.

2 Neaten the long sides of the fabric piece and join them, leaving a gap large enough to insert the zip.

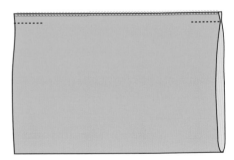

3 Press the seam open carefully, so as not to make crease marks in the rest of the cover.

4 Place the zip in position, with the teeth facing downwards, and stitch it to the seam allowance only on one side. Stitch as close to the teeth as possible.

See Technique 83, Zip Between Two Pieces of Fabric, page 80.

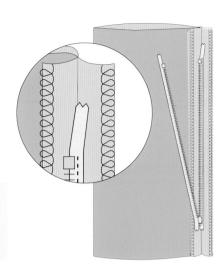

5 This next bit is quite fiddly I'm afraid. Because of the style of this cover, you have to work on the inside of the tube. Pin the fabric to the second side of the zip through all the layers of fabric, seam allowance and zip tape. Carefully machine the second side of the zip, forming a flap to cover the zip itself.

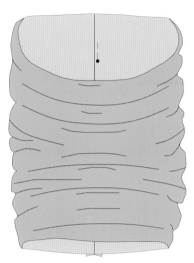

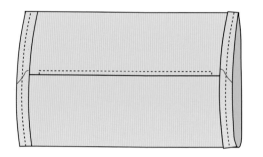

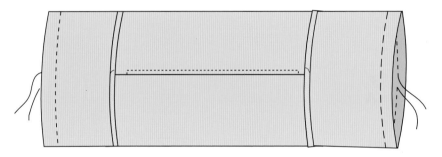

6 Turn the cover right-side out. Apply flanged cord, or piping, to each end of the tube.

See Technique 81, Piping with Flanged Cord, page 78 and Technique 82, Joining Flanged Cord, page 79.

7 Cut two end pieces of main fabric, the measured circumference of the bolster pad, plus 4cm (1½in), by the radius of the pad plus 4cm (1½in). Join each one along the short edges and press the seams open. Working from the side of the piping line, machine the two end pieces to the main part of the cover, lining up the seams if possible, although I sometimes offset them if the fabric is very bulky.

With a strong double thread, run a row of stitches 2cm (¾in) in from the edge of the end pieces. Start with a knot and a double oversew stitch on the wrong side of the fabric. The stitches should be approximately 0.5cm (¼in) long on the right side of the fabric and 1.5cm (⅝in) on the wrong side to give the best effect. This also helps to cut down on bulk while adding depth to the gathers on the right side.

8 Working on the wrong side of the cover, pull the stitches tight. If you are using a key tassel, add it as you are pulling up the stitches, by pushing the tassel loop through the gathered opening to the wrong side of the cover. Wrap the gathering threads around the bunched-up fabric and secure with stitches. Secure the key tassel with stitches as well. Turn the pad right-side out. If you have not used a key tassel, you could hand-sew covered, decorative buttons over the gathered ends of the cover. Insert the bolster pad.

9 I am so grateful for this special tip given to me by an upholsterer friend. If the fabric is very soft, or if you prefer a more tailored look to the ends of the bolster, there is a simple solution. You will need to cut two pieces of 2.5cm- (1in-) thick foam the same diameter as the bolster pad, with a central hole, as shown. When you are cutting the main fabric, add 5cm (2in) to the overall width of the fabric. Make up the bolster cover as described in steps 1-8, then insert the foam pieces at each end, before you put in the bolster pad. The gathers of the end pieces fit nicely into the central hole in the foam, and the foam itself gives the end of the bolster a flatter, neater finish.

149

PROJECT 16

Banner valance

The simplicity of a banner valance enables us to make the most of a special fabric. The fabric I have chosen is a damask design, which I have used as the basis for the decorative embroidery. For this I used a satin stitch, which is available on all but the most basic domestic sewing machines. I have also trimmed the banner with millinery petersham ribbon. This is not often used in furnishings, but I find it an ideal weight and texture to use with furnishing fabrics. The banner is also trimmed with a piped edge for that final, professional touch.

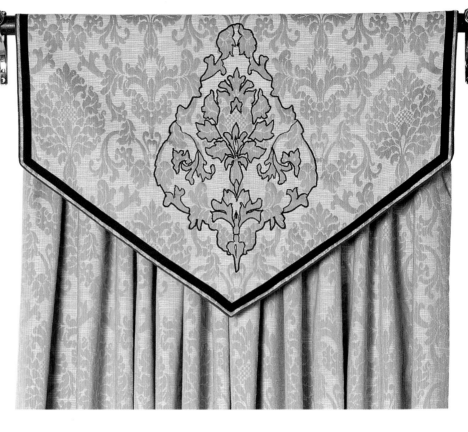

Materials

Main fabric

Contrast Lining

Medium weight iron-on interfacing to stabilise the fabric for embroidery

Petersham ribbon

Piping fabric and cord

Curtain pole

Equipment

As for Project 3, The Classic Valance, page 106.

1 Plan the placing of the design and the dimensions of the banner very carefully, by drawing them out to scale. For a wide window, you will need a number of banners hung together. Cut out the main fabric and the lining and, before separating the layers, cut small notches along each edge so that they can be matched up easily when you assemble the banner.

See Technique 1, How to Draw to Scale, page 12.

2 If you want to embroider decoration, bond the interfacing to the back of the area of the fabric you wish to embroider. Use a stitch width of approximately 3mm (⅛in), with the stitch length adjusted to give you a good, smooth satin stitch. Another thing you may find useful is to loosen the tension on the top thread: although the back of the fabric will not look too good it will give a smoother, more rounded look to the stitches on the front. The lining will hide any untidy stitching on the back of the banner.

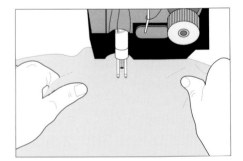

3 When I am using satin stitch, as with appliqué, I do not move the fabric around too much. Instead I 'steer' it, by holding it firmly on both sides rather than holding at the front and back.

4 This illustration shows perhaps the first attempt of one of my students. They always think that the stitches should be at right angles to the design, or, in the case of appliqué, to the edge of the motif.

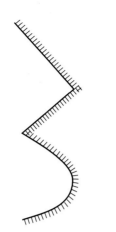

5 However, by allowing the machine to stitch at its own pace, but gently pulling from side to side, you will get a much more natural flow of stitches. Obviously in some areas you will have to turn the fabric itself, but it tends to be a combination of turning and steering.

6 Gently press the back of the fabric.

7 Machine the ribbon, or even a border made out of bands of a contrast fabric, to the valance.

See Technique 96, Making Ribbon Mitres, page 88.

8 See Technique 74, Cutting Piping Strips, page 70

9 See Technique 75, Joining Piping Strips, page 71.

10 Pipe the edges of the banner, being careful not to stretch the cross-cut edges. Do not stitch too close to the cord.

See Technique 76, Piping with Square Ends, page 72.

11 Right-sides facing, match the notches in the main fabric and lining. Stitch round all edges of the banner, as close to the cord as possible. Leave a gap in the stitching, cut away any excess bulk, turn right-side out and press gently. Close the gap in the stitching. The valance is now ready to be hung. The back of the valance should hang slightly lower than the front to show the contrast edge. You could also attach small strips of Velcro to the pole and the underside of the valance to hold it in place.

Simple voile swag

This voile swag always causes a stir when I construct it in front of the audience at lectures. It is so simple, but so quick to do. The dimensions given here are for the sample photographed, which is constructed on a pole 110cm (43in) long.

1 See Technique 38, Cutting Sheer Fabrics, page 42.

2 See Technique 44, Joining Sheer Fabrics, page 46.

Materials

Length of voile

Five pieces of 0.5cm- (¼in-) wide cotton-covered elastic, each 10-15cm (4-6in) long (depending on the diameter of your pole), and tied or stitched into loops

Curtain pole

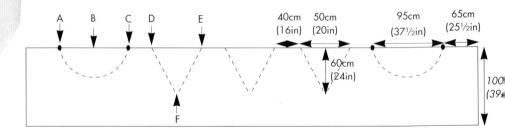

3 The swag is constructed from a straight piece of voile, which has a very small hemmed edge on all sides. The dotted lines indicate where I gather the fabric between my hands. If you prefer you could use a fading marker to mark a guideline, though this may not work on all fabrics.

4 Take point B in your right hand and slowly gather the voile from A to C in your left hand.

5 Your gathering need not be exactly on the line, which is purely a guide.

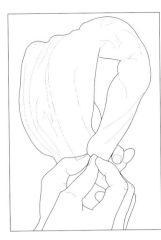

6 Still holding the main part of the fabric in the left hand, fold over the top point (B), and tuck it behind the fabric in your left hand.

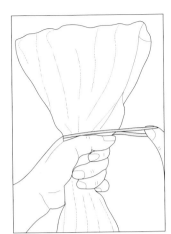

7 Place one of the loops of elastic around the fabric, making sure you catch in B.

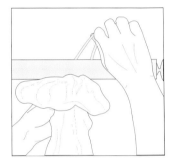

8 At one end, take the elastic behind the pole and around the fabric. The elastic must fit the pole tightly, holding the fabric securely.

9 Pull the fabric gently to make sure it is sitting neatly in the elastic loops. Make sure that the ends are tucked into the elastic.

10 When you have dressed the swag, this bunch will make a large rosette. Repeat the process at the other end of the pole.

11 We now have three 'jabots' to form. Take points D and E and gather the fabric in your hands until you reach point F.

12 Bring your hands together to make a bunch of fabric. Take the top point, fold it to the back and attach to the pole with a piece of elastic in the same way as for step 8. repeat for the other two jabots.

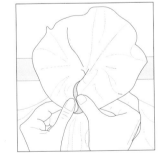

13 Now it only remains to dress the swag. For the large rosettes at each end of the pole, open up the two ends of the fabric bunch, and tuck one inside the other.

14 Repeat at the top of the 'jabots' to form smaller rosettes. Dress the fabric beneath as shown.

15 At the outer edges, gently fold the fabric between your hands to form a tail to complete this rather wonderful, voile window dressing.

153

PROJECT 18

Envelope cushion

This envelope cushion is so simple to make and can be trimmed in endless different ways. It needs a bit more fabric than the average cushion, but the results are worth it.

Materials

Square cushion pad

One piece of fabric 50% larger than the pad

Two triangles of fabric for the cushion back (these could be in a contrast color if preferred as they form the inside of the envelope), each measuring half the square plus 2cm (¾in) seam allowance

Zip

Flanged cord, enough to go right round the main fabric, including joining

Four self-cover buttons

Four key tassels

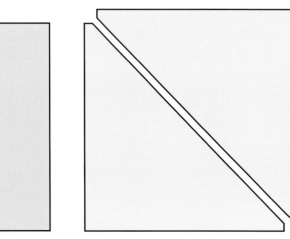

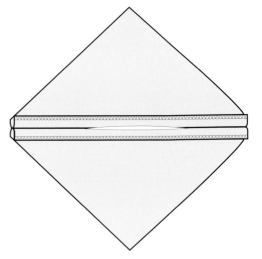

1 The zip goes between the triangles that make up the back of the cover, diagonally across it. If you use a zip horizontally across the back, it will not be hidden when the corners of the cover are brought to the center.

2 Neaten the two edges of the fabric that will be next to the zip. Stitch the two pieces of fabric together, leaving a gap large enough for the zip. Press open the seams and insert the zip.

See Technique 83, Inserting a Zip Between Two Pieces of Fabric, page 80.

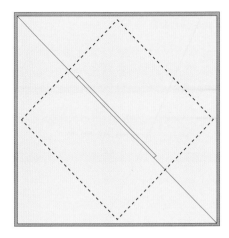

3 Pipe the front piece of the cover with flanged cord.

See Technique 81, Piping with Flanged Cord, page 78 and Technique 82, Joining Flanged Cord, page 79.

4 Place the front and back of the cover together and machine as close to the cord as possible. Trim away the bulk at the corner, turn and press.

5 Place the cushion pad in the center of the cover; the dotted line indicates its position.

6 To complete the cushion, bring the four corners to the center. Use buttons at each corner of the cushion, with key tassels attached, if you prefer, to keep the shape of the cushion.

This cushion was decorated with remnants of braid and velvet ribbon, which were sewn to the front of the cover before it was piped. Fabric loops attached to the corners of the cover hold the buttons, and therefore the corners, of the cover in place.

155

PROJECT 19

Eyelet blind

An eyelet blind is a lovely casual, modern style of blind, which I think particularly lends itself to a 'natural' look. It works well on fairly narrow windows, so if yours are wide it is best to use more than one blind. Although it is made in a similar way to a Roman blind, it is less structured as it does not have any dowels, merely a single weight bar at the bottom edge. The folds themselves are stitched both at the front and the back, which helps the blind to fold well without dowels.

Materials

Fabric

Lining

Eyelet kit

Decorative cord

Sew-on loop Velcro

Adhesive-backed hook Velcro

Equipment

As for Project 7, The Classic Roman Blind, page 124.

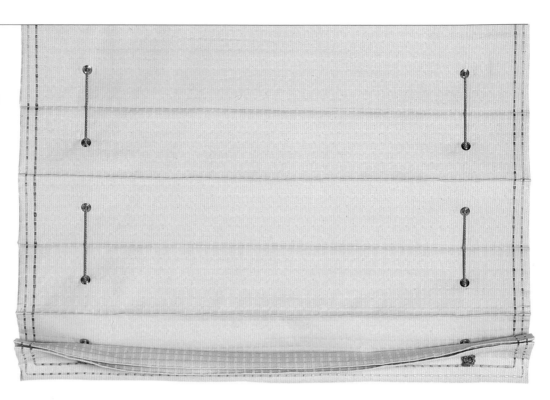

1 The first step, as for most blinds, is to work out the spacing. For this blind it is the spacing between folds, rather than rods, that we need to work out. The following calculation is for an example blind measuring 100cm (39in) wide and a 120cm (48in) in overall length.

120cm (48in)	– 6cm (2½in)	= 114cm (45½in)
overall length of the blind	*allowance for cord guides*	*remaining length of blind*

The distance between the folds in this instance should be about 20cm (8in), and because of the way the eyelets are placed, you will need a half space at the bottom of the blind.

114 cm (45½in)	÷ 20cm (8in)	= 5.7 spaces
remaining length of blind	*ideal space size*	*number of spaces*

Round this down to the nearest half space to give us 5.5 spaces.

114 cm (45½in)	÷ 5.5	= 20.72 cm (8¼in)
remaining length of blind	*number of spaces*	*size of whole space*

This will give us a half space of 10.36cm (4⅛in).

It is always best to double check this type of calculation before cutting the fabric.

Allowance for cord guides	= 6cm (2½in)
Five full spaces at 20.72 cm (8¼in)	= 103.60cm (41¼in)
A half space	= 10.36cm (4⅛in)
Total	= 119.96cm (47⅞in)

I don't think we could make it more accurate than that!

Add on to the length an extra 0.5cm (¼in) for each stitched fold, plus 1.5cm (⅝in) allowance beneath the Velcro, plus 5cm (2in) for the slot for the weight bar. The lining is cut to exactly the same length as the main fabric.

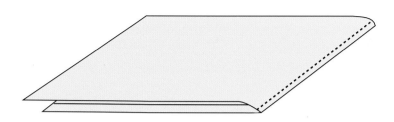

1 See Project 7, The Classic Roman Blind, page 124.

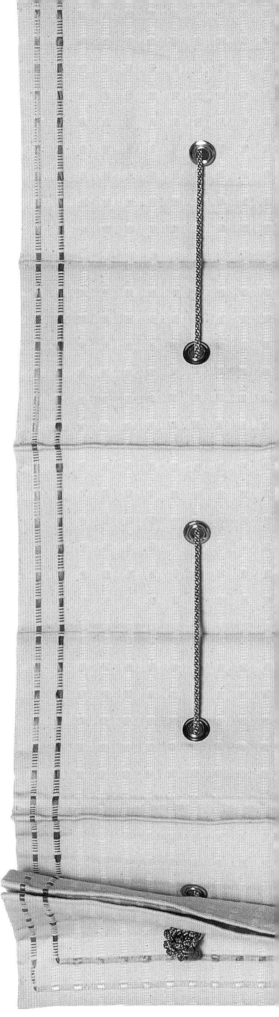

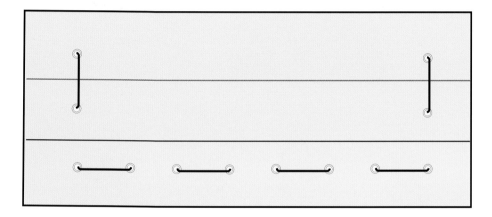

2 Make up the main fabric of the blind. Attach the lining, without rod cases, but machine or hand-stitch the slot for the weight bar. With a fading marker, draw the fold lines across the blind at the calculated measurements. Fold the fabric so that you can machine close to the edge of the fold. Machine alternate folds from the front of the blind, then turn the blind over and machine the remaining folds from the back of the blind. The fold above the weight bar at the bottom of the blind must be machined from the front.

3 The final stage is to put the eyelets in the center of each space of the blind, as shown. Follow the instructions on the kit, working from the front of the blind. The eyelets should be about 15cm (6in) in from the edge of the blind and along the bottom hem there should be an equal number of eyelets.
Before you cord the blind insert the bottom weight bar.

The cord is threaded through the cord guide, which should be placed on the side from which you intend pulling the blind up. Pass the cord down through the eyelets on the first side, along the bottom of the blind, then up the second side. Lastly, the cord passes through both cord guides to join the original cord in a cord weight. A boxwood acorn is fine, though something a little heavier helps to keep the cord in position when the blind is lowered.

As an alternative way of cording up the blind is to place the eyelets down the sides as described, but not across the bottom edge. Thread the cords through the eyelets and then tie a large knot in the cord, below the last eyelet, as shown right. The blind is then operated by two cords in the same way as a classic Roman blind.

PROJECT 20

Eyelet swag

This swag is very simple though very effective. It is made from an rectangle of fabric, but if you prefer you could shape the ends to form a more formal style of tail. Personally I like to leave it a much more informal style of swag. It does not work well on windows over 180cm (74in)wide, unless they are very tall.

Materials

Fabric

Contrast lining

Extra fabric for tabs

Small eyelets kit

Velcro

Equipment

Cornice board

Small hooks

Lead-weight tape

1 See Technique 11, Making Cornice Boards, page 22.

2 Add a strip of adhesive-backed hook Velcro to the back edge of the top of the cornice board and two small hooks or domed screws to the corners, as shown.

3 The next stage is to calculate the cutting measurement and the amount of fabric needed. Staple a strip of scrap fabric to the center back of the cornice board to represent the shortest center point of the swag and to calculate the length of the center tab. (This must be long enough to come from the back of the cornice board, round the fabric of the swag and return to the back of the cornice board.) Pin or staple a length of lead weight chain to one corner of the cornice board. Loop the strip of fabric over the lead weight chain and adjust the curves (which represent the curved front of the swag) until you are happy with them. Remove the lead weight chain and measure it. If this is the first time you have tackled making any form of swag, this technique is also useful as you can stand back from the window and see the finished shape and proportions.

4 From the illustration, right, you can see how to use these measurements to draw out your swag. You may have to join widths of fabric together, but if the pattern is appropriate you may be able to 'railroad' the fabric and use it on its side. The tabs with eyelets will be positioned at a later stage, but have been shown on to indicate their positions.

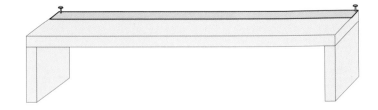

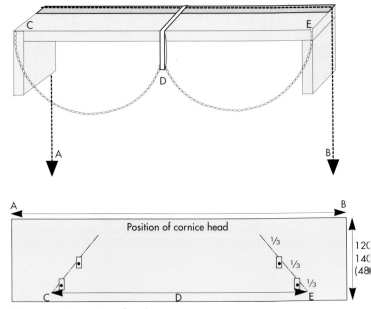

▢ Represents the position of a tab

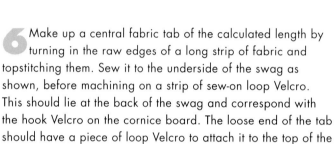

5 Once you have worked out the measurements, cut out the fabric and lining. Right-sides facing, machine them together, taking a 2cm (¾in) seam allowance. Leave a gap to turn the swag right-side out. Press and close the gap by hand.

6 Make up a central fabric tab of the calculated length by turning in the raw edges of a long strip of fabric and topstitching them. Sew it to the underside of the swag as shown, before machining on a strip of sew-on loop Velcro. This should lie at the back of the swag and correspond with the hook Velcro on the cornice board. The loose end of the tab should have a piece of loop Velcro to attach it to the top of the swag, and a piece of sew-on hook Velcro should be stitched in the corresponding position on the top of the swag.

7 Make up four small tabs by machining round three sides, taking a small seam allowance, turning right-side out and pressing them. Turn in the raw edges on the fourth (top) side and stitch them closed by hand. Put an eyelet in the bottom of each tab, as shown.

8 Fix one eyelet to one end of each tab before machining the tabs to the swag in the positions indicated in step 4.

9 Place the swag on the cornice board, with the Velcro on the swag pressed onto the Velcro on the cornice board. Raise the top tab on each side of the swag and put the eyelet over the screw or hook on the top of the cornice board. Repeat the process with the lower tabs and you will form a swag. Take the long central tab from the underside of the swag and bring round and to top of the swag and attach it to the corresponding Velcro. You may wish to make up a larger, decorative tab to complete the center of the swag, as shown in the photograph. This just hangs down over the middle of the swag and is attached at the top with Velcro.

If you prefer to make one large swag, leave out the center tab when working out the measurements.

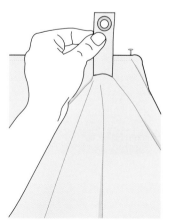

PROJECT 21

Eyelet curtain

Large eyelets have been used for a number of years for shower and cubicle curtains. With the selection of beautiful metal poles now available, they have become a decorative method of attaching a curtain to a pole. They can, of course, be simply attached to the top of the flat curtain, but this has its drawbacks in that when the curtain is closed, the fullness is not evenly distributed. The following method overcomes this problem. Two-times fullness gives you the sort of spacing and width of fold shown in this photograph.

Materials and equipment

As for Project 1, The Classic Curtain, page 96, with large eyelets or grommets instead of heading tape.

1 See Project 1, The Classic Curtain, page 96.

2 Make up the curtain in the normal way, but when it comes to the final length, allow for a band at the top into which the eyelets are inserted. The width of the band will vary according to the size of the grommet and the length of the curtain. The depth should be sufficient to allow for the insertion of the eyelet, without interference from the bulk of any seam allowances. Cut the band to twice the required depth plus 4cm (1½in), by the width of the curtain, plus 4cm (1½in). Press under 2cm (¾in) down both short sides and along one long side of the band. Right-sides facing and raw edges aligned, place the band across the curtain and machine, taking a 2cm (¾in) seam allowance.

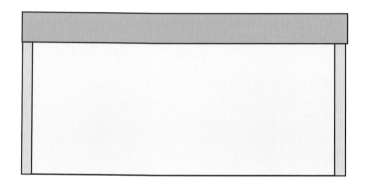

4 Each of the eyelets will be placed in a 'flap' of fabric, similar to those formed when making pinch pleats. The next step is to calculate how much fabric goes into a space and how much into a flap. This is done in just the same way as for pinch pleats, except the ends would be only 3-4cm (1¼-1½in). I would normally use approximately 10cm (4in) in both the flaps and the spaces, as I usually use a 3.5cm (1⅜in) outer diameter eyelet. However, your measurement will depend on the size of the eyelet you are using and the amount of fullness you have in your curtain.

3 Fold the band in half and slip stitch the long, pressed edge to the back of the curtain. Ladder stitch the ends closed.

See Techniques 54-56, Slip Stitch, Ladder Stitch, pages 53-55.

See Technique 63, Forming Pinch Pleats, page 60.

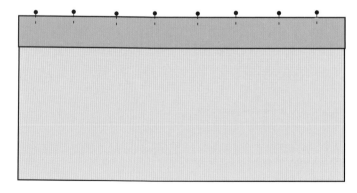

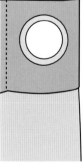

5 Mark the spaces and pleats with pins.

6 Fold the top band to bring two pins together to form the flaps. Machine down the band only.

7 Insert the grommets using the kit, or take the curtain to a company with specialist machinery who can insert them in seconds.

PROJECT 22

Flanged cushion

Materials

Two pieces of fabric each measuring 27 x 50cm (11 x 20in) for the back sections

Nylon zip measuring 35cm (14in)

One piece of fabric measuring 50 x 50cm (20 x 20in) for the front section

Threads for contrast stitching and basic machining

Cushion pad measuring 46cm (18in) square

A flanged cushion is simple yet most effective and economic. It can be made in patterned or plain fabric, used in a modern or a traditional setting and acts as a perfect, simple cushion to mix with more fussy styles. The size of the cushion can be adjusted but I would recommend that the flanged border is adjusted in scale to match the cushion – it does not work well if you have a small cushion with a large flanged border.

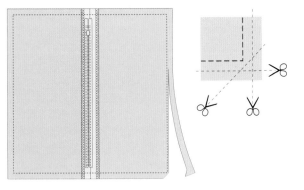

The combination of a mitred border on a flanged cushion, as shown in the photograph, can be very effective. Make up the front of the cushion with a mitred border (see Technique 102, Making Mitred Borders, page 94). Follow steps 1 and 2 below, then stitch round the center section in a matching thread to create the flange.

1 Insert the zip between the two back sections. Open up the zip a little then, right-sides facing, stitch the front and back sections together all the way around the cushion, taking 2cm (¾in) seam allowance.

See Technique 83, Inserting a Zip Between Two Pieces of Fabric, page 80.

2 Trim the seam allowance back to 1cm (½in) to cut down on bulk. Trim away the bulk at the corners as shown. Turn right side out and press.

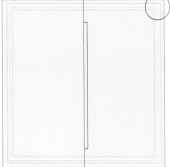

3 On the machine, set a satin stitch width of 3mm (⅛in) and a length of 0.3mm (1/32in). With the edge of the foot against the edge of the cover, machine around the sides in a contrast color. At the corners, stop sewing with the needle in the fabric, turn the cover through 90° and machine down the next side. Repeat this machined line twice more (see detail), making sure you keep the edge of the foot against the edge of the previous line.

4 The innermost line of satin stitch creates the actual size of the cushion, as far as the pad is concerned, so the measurements of the center of the cover should be a little smaller than the size of your cushion pad. Press before inserting the pad.

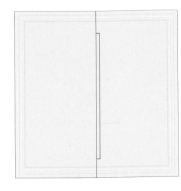

As an alternative to multiple lines of satin stitch, a single line to contain the cushion in the central area makes an attractive, speedy and inexpensive finish for a cushion. A purchased trim can be used to decorate the edge.

PROJECT 23

Grampol swag

This is not really a swag in the true sense of the word, more a cross between an Italian strung curtain and a tail. It is not practical as a working curtain but it is extremely decorative, and it is also economical as it takes virtually no extra fabric for fullness. I think it looks particularly stunning over a working reefed blind. To calculate the necessary measurements, use a length of lead weight tape or a piece of chain pinned to the cornice board.

1 See Technique 11, Making Cornice Boards, page 22.

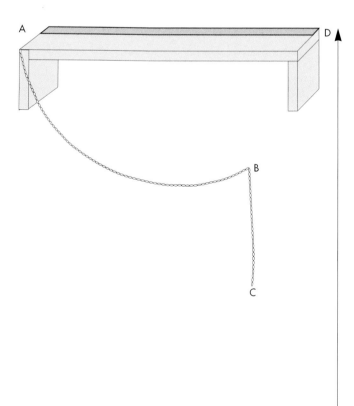

Materials

Main fabric

Contrast lining

Bullion trimming

Fine cord

Lead weight tape

Equipment

Small brass rings

Cord guide

Cleat

2 A is the curved part of the swag.

B is the position of the first ring for the Italian stringing.

C is the point at which the angled bottom hem is cut on one side.

D to E is the longest point of the tail. When cutting the fabric I normally allow 33-50% extra on this measurement, as the tail shortens when the swag is pulled up. This measurement dictates the length of fabric you need to make the swag.

163

3 To calculate the width of fabric you require, add together the measurements of the front of the cornice board, plus four times the depth of the returns. This extra fabric forms the first fold of the swag.

4 Translating all these measurements into a pattern gives you a shape like this.

5 Cut the fabric and the lining to the same size. Right-sides facing, machine them together down both sides and across the angled bottom.

6 Trim the corners, turn the swag right-side out and press it. Then, hand-sew the bullion along the leading edge and the angled bottom, as marked by the arrows.

See Technique 95, Attaching Fan-edge, Bullion and Cushion Ruche Trimmings, page 87.

7 Place the rings, initially by attaching a small safety pin to each and pinning it to the swag, through both layers of fabric. The first pin is placed according to the illustration. The other rings are normally placed 12-15cm (4¾in-6in) apart in a curve to achieve good, deep pleats, though larger windows should have deeper pleats. Once the swag is hung and the cording tested, you may find you need to adjust some of the rings. When you are satisfied they can be stitched in place.

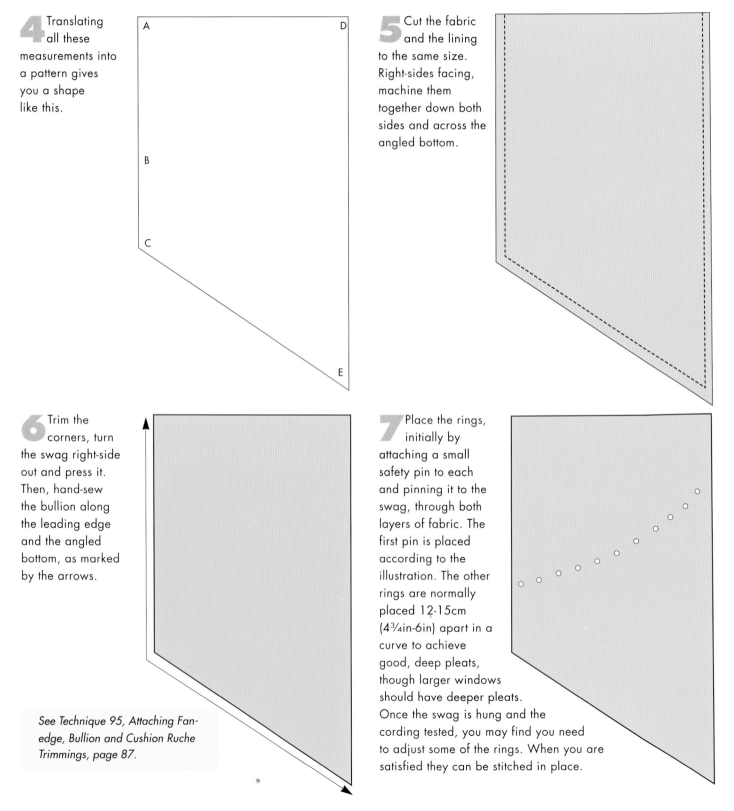

8 This illustration shows how to fold the swag so that it fits around the edge of the cornice board. Cut two pieces of fabric, 2cm (¾in) larger on all sides than the top of the cornice board, to form a top band to suspend the swag from.

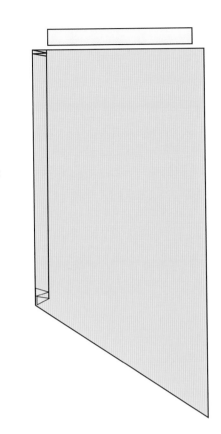

9 Right-sides facing, place the band on the swag as shown, with the first part of the swag set 2cm (¾in) in from the edge of the band. Machine along the short edge to the corner, then turn the swag and machine the long side of the band to the front of the swag. Stitch to the second corner.

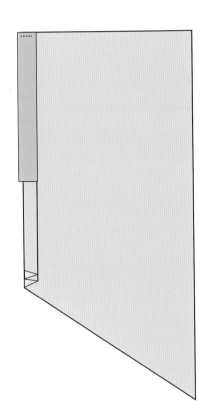

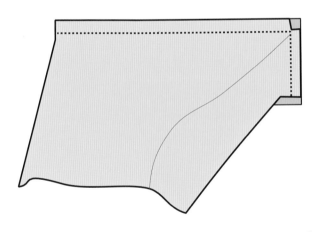

10 Snip the swag at the corners so that it sits smoothly round the band.

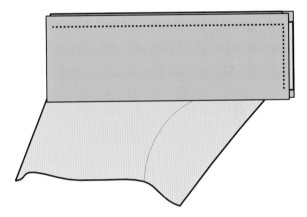

11 The second band piece is then placed face down onto the right side of the swag and the first band and stitched to them along the same line of machining. Be careful not to catch the swag itself in the machining. Cut the bulk away and gently pull on the swag fabric, turning the band right-side out as you do so. You will find you have made a facing that hides all the raw edges and will completely cover the top of the board when fitted. Turn under the seam allowance at the back of the band and sew loop Velcro to the underside, to correspond with hook Velcro stuck to the top of the cornice board.

12 Place the swag on the cornice board. Attach cord to the ring at the leading edge, taking it through the rings to a cord guide on the edge of the window or on the underside of the cornice board. When the swag is pulled up, the cord is attached to a cleat at the side of the window to hold the swag in the correct position.

PROJECT 24
Hooded valance

This is made simply and quickly and, depending on the fabric and the trim you use, it can be a good solution for those looking for a more unusual style to use in either a traditional or modern setting.

The hoods are made individually with a large slot at the top that the pole runs through. The curtains shown are purely dress curtains held back by tiebacks when required. If you want the curtains to draw, use a longer bracket for the pole to extend it away from the wall and a neat corded track behind for the curtains.

The actual length of the hood is dependant on the overall length of your window treatment and the thickness of your pole. The measurements given below are the ones I used for the hoods in the photograph, but it is best to make a mock piece in scrap fabric to make sure the dimensions are correct for your window.

Materials

Main fabric

Contrasting colored lining

Flanged cord

Key tassels

Curtain pole

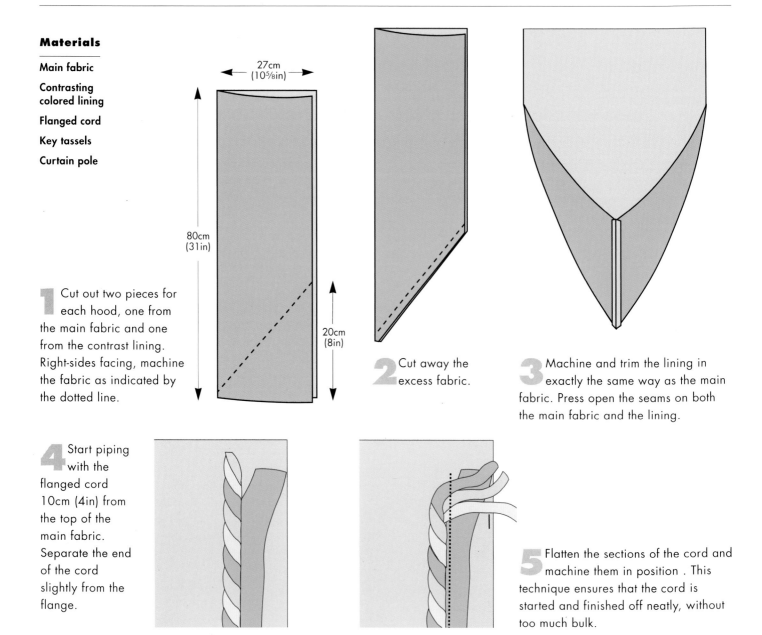

1 Cut out two pieces for each hood, one from the main fabric and one from the contrast lining. Right-sides facing, machine the fabric as indicated by the dotted line.

27cm (10⅝in)

80cm (31in)

20cm (8in)

2 Cut away the excess fabric.

3 Machine and trim the lining in exactly the same way as the main fabric. Press open the seams on both the main fabric and the lining.

4 Start piping with the flanged cord 10cm (4in) from the top of the main fabric. Separate the end of the cord slightly from the flange.

5 Flatten the sections of the cord and machine them in position . This technique ensures that the cord is started and finished off neatly, without too much bulk.

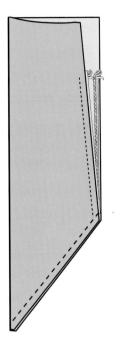

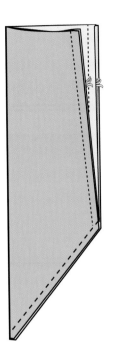

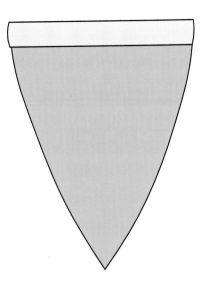

8 Overlock or zigzag the raw edges and turn the hood right-side out. Overlock and turn in the top edges of the main fabric and lining 1cm (½in) and press. Fold the top 9.5cm (3¾in) of the hood (the lining will be uppermost) to the back and hand stitch the turned-in edges to the main fabric at the back to form the slot for the pole.

6 Pipe round the main fabric with the cord, stopping 10cm (4in) from the top on the other side.

See Technique 81, Piping with Flanged Cord, page 78.

7 Right-sides facing, place the lining section inside the main fabric. From the wrong side of the main fabric, machine along the piped edges, starting from right at the top of the hood.

9 Stitch a key tassel to the point of each hood. Thread the hoods onto the curtain pole.

PROJECT 25

Hooded chair

I think this hood design works equally well as an added detail on a loose cover for a simple chair.

Materials and equipment

As for Project 9, The Classic Loose Cover for a Simple Chair, page 135 and Project 24, Hooded Valance, page 166.

1 See Project 9, The Classic Loose Cover for a Simple Chair, page 135.

2 See Project 24, Hooded Valance, page 166.

First of all, cut and pin the loose cover. The hood itself is made in exactly the same way as for the Hooded Valance. Before you start to cut it out in fabric, measure the width of the chair back between the pins and the length you want the hood to be when finished. Once you are happy with the dimensions, cut out and stitch the hood, leaving the top edges raw.

Pin the hood in position on the back of the chair as shown. Trim away any excess fabric at the top of the back, leaving a 2cm (¾in) seam allowance. Once you have checked and notched all the seams, remove the cover and complete it.

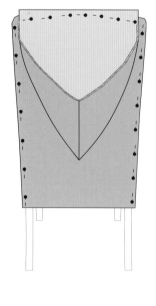

PROJECT 26

Ruched cushion

This is a variation on a very old theme. I wonder how many of you can remember the smocked velvet cushions made using a paper pattern. This version is much less formal with its 'random' ruching.

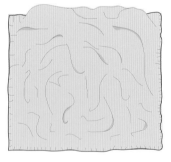

Materials

Cushion pad

One piece of fabric twice the size of the pad for the front

Two pieces the width of the pad by half the depth, plus 2cm (¾in), for the back

One piece of lining the size of the cushion pad

Piping cord

Key tassels

Zip

1 See Project 10, Classic Cushions, page 136.

2 Insert the zip into the center back, taking a 2cm (¾in) seam allowance.

3 Attach the large piece of front fabric to the lining by making a series of small tucks in the edge of the main fabric. Machine the two layers together around the edge of the cushion piece. The front of the cushion should look similar to this illustration.

4 Starting from the center, place the front section of the cushion under the machine and make a few small zigzag stitches with the teeth or 'feed dog' dropped. This will mean that the stitches will be one on top of another, almost like a small bartack. Without cutting the threads, raise the foot, pull the threads and move to the next position. Slowly work out from the center of the cushion, twisting and tucking the fabric to achieve the ruched look. Cut all the excess threads. Pipe around the edge of the cushion, attach the back section and add tassels if required.

PROJECT 27

Reefed blind

Reefed blinds are a wonderful concept, combining the best features of both Roman and roller blinds to create a simple but stunning look. They are best made in a fairly weighty but soft fabric – in other words, fabric that can roll.

As with other soft blinds, the fabric is attached to a headrail. This can be either a wooden batten with adhesive-backed hook Velcro attached to the front edge, or a special metal track with Velcro bonded permanently to its surface. An oval or round bar is inserted into a pocket along the bottom edge.

The rolling action of the blind is achieved with the use of a decorative operating cord. This should be color co-ordinated with the fabric.

Materials

Fabric

Lining, either contrasting or plain

Co-ordinating cord

Weight bar

Heavy cord weight

Eyelets

Small decorative brass rod

Brass buttons

Equipment

As for Project 7, The Classic Roman Blind, page 124.

1 See Technique 1, How to Draw to Scale, page 12.

2 See Technique 23, Measuring for Blinds, page 31.

3 See Techniques 35-37, Cutting Plain and Lining Fabrics, Cutting Velvets, Cutting Patterned Fabrics, pages 41-42.

4 See Techniques 41-43, Joining Plain and Lining Fabrics, Joining Velvet, Joining Patterned Fabrics, pages 44-45.

5 Cut the fabric and lining to the finished measurements of the blind, plus 2cm (¾in) seam allowance all round, plus extra at the bottom hem for the weight bar. Right-sides facing, machine the fabrics together around the side and bottom edges. Turn the blind through to the right side and press it.

6 The slot for the weight bar can either be machined or hand-stitched. If there is any chance of it being seen, I would prefer to hand-stitch it.

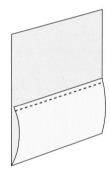

7 For the top of the blind, make up the tabs before you attach the Velcro. Stitch as shown, trim away the corners to reduce bulk, turn right-side out and press.

169

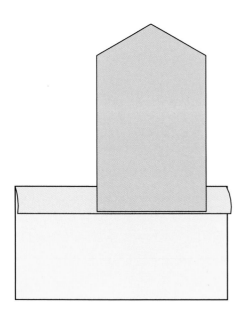

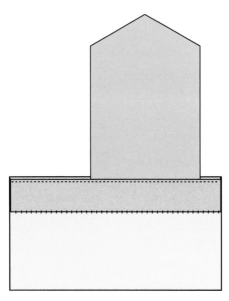

8 Turn over 2cm (¾in) at the top of the blind and place the tabs against the raw edge as shown.

9 Machine the Velcro close to the top edge of the blind through all the layers. Hand stitch the bottom edge.

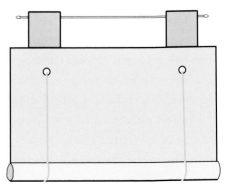

10 As this blind is to roll to the front, the next step is to insert eyelets to allow the cord to pass through to the cord guides behind.

Prepare the batten with screw eyes, or china cord guides if possible, and hook Velcro on the front. Secure one end of the cord to a screw eye before taking it beneath the bottom of the blind, up the front of the blind and through the eyelet to the cord guide. It will then pass through the other cord guides to the cord weight, which for this style of blind should be quite heavy to keep the cords in position when the blind is lowered. You will need two cords for blinds up to 150cm (59in) and three cords for blinds up to 250cm (100in). The outer cords should be a maximum of 25-30cm (10-12in) from the side of the blind.

See Project 7, The Classic Roman Blind, page 124.

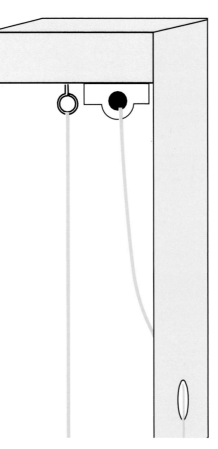

11 The eyelets should be in the right position so that the cord travels in as straight a line as possible.

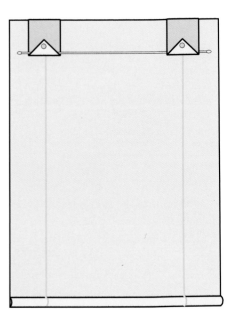

12 Fold up the points of the tabs and secure them with a button. The tabs cover the eyelets and they are weighted to stay in position by the small brass rod running across them.

PROJECT 28

Round, corded cushion

By pulling on the piping cord as you apply it to the fabric, you can make a very attractive cushion which looks almost as though it has a border. To decide how much piping to use and therefore how much you will need to pull on the cord, place a piece around the cushion pad, pulling to make the pad into the finished shape you require. Remove the cord and measure it; it couldn't be simpler.

Materials

As for a normal round cushion, with flanged cord or fabric and piping cord

Self covered buttons or 60cm (24in) of cushion ruche

Strong thread

Equipment

As for Project 10, Classic Cushions, page 136

1 See Project 10, Classic Cushions, page 136.

2 Pulling on the piping cord will give you a surplus of fabric in the center of the cushion.

3 Match the notches on the front and back sections of the cushion and machine them together, from the side of the piping line of machining, easing in the fullness. Stitch as close to the piping line as possible. It is best to leave the zip slightly open when stitching the two sides of the cushion together.

To complete the cushion use a long needle, such as those used by upholsterers (sometimes called a bayonet), and strong thread to stitch through the center of the cushion to pull it in. Attach two buttons, or alternatively you can attach a large ruche rosette, as shown in the photograph.

The zip is placed in exactly the same way as for a normal round cushion.

Before you attach the cord to the cushion, divide its length into quarters with pins. Place pins on the outer edge of the cushion to divide it into quarters too. By matching these pins to those on the cord you will know if you are easing in the correct amount of fabric.

See Technique 98, Making Ruche Rosettes, page 90.

PROJECT 29

Slouch curtain

In my opinion, this style of curtain, in a similar way to tab tops, is for dress curtains only. Both give a great effect but do not draw well, as it is always difficult to arrange the fullness. Having said that, I think that this is a stunning design. The curtain in this illustration has two full widths of fabric; I would never use less than one-and-a-half widths for any type of curtains, even if they are only dress curtains. Any less fullness always looks skimpy.

Materials

Fabric

Lining

Contrast fabric

Sew-on curtain hooks

Equipment

As for Project 1, The Classic Curtain, page 96.

172

1 See Project 1, The Classic Curtain, page 96.

2 Make up the curtain as normal and trim back the top to the finished overall length, plus a 2cm (¾in) seam allowance. Cut four pieces of fabric for the pointed section,

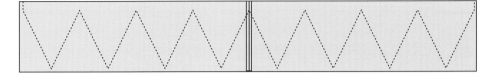

matching the fabric where necessary. Two pieces will be joined together for the front of the pointed section and two will be joined for the lining. Right-sides facing, put the front and lining together.

Mark out the pointed section as shown. The points can be whatever depth you want, but you must have at least 4cm (1½in) of unmarked fabric above them: a 2cm (¾in) seam allowance at the top and sides and 2cm (¾in) to form a band across the top of the points. Machine along the marked line, using a fairly small stitch to prevent the fabric fraying when the excess is cut away.

3 A tip given to me many years ago is that if you are stitching to a point especially if the fabric is thick, make one stitch across at the point (for very bulky fabrics make two stitches).

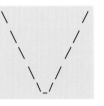

4 Trim off the excess fabric, cutting off the bulk at the points and cutting into the top angles. Turn right-side out and press.

5 Place the pointed section right side down on the wrong side of the curtain. Mark the stitching line as shown. The line should curve downwards towards each point. I used a measurement of 6cm (2½in) from the top of the curtain to the deepest part of the curve. Machine through all layers along the marked line. Trim the seam allowance back to 1cm (½in) and neaten the raw edges.

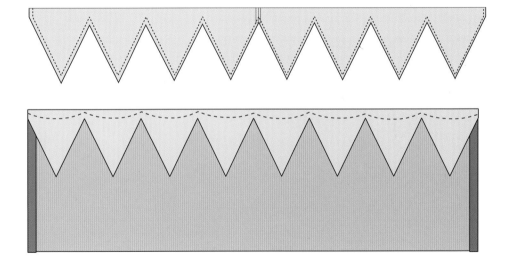

6 Fold the points to the front of the curtain and gently press them. All the neatened edges should be hidden under the top of the pointed section. Attach a sew-on hook to the high points of the heading to enable you to hang the curtain from curtain rings. Alternatively, you could stitch the rings straight onto the curtain.

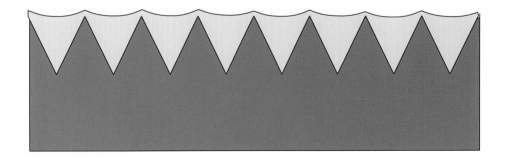

PROJECT 30

Cut-away goblet-pleated curtain

This project has an overvalance that is attached to and moves with the curtain. Although this transforms a straightforward curtain, somehow a normal pencil-pleat heading does not do such a luxurious style justice. An elegant pole, sumptuous fabrics and delightful trims shout out for an equally wonderful heading, such as this one, which I call cut-away goblet pleats.

Materials

Main fabric for the curtain, plus fabric for the overvalance

Contrast lining for the goblets

Curtain lining

Curtain buckram

Pin-on or sew-on hooks

Equipment

As for Project 1, The Classic Curtain, page 96.

1 See Project 1, The Classic Curtain, page 96.

2 See Project 3, The Classic Valance, page 106.

3 Make up the curtain in the usual way until it comes to cutting it to the correct length. Lay it on the table and measure out the correct overall finished length, then add 2cm (¾in). Mark a line on the fabric and lining together to prevent them slipping. Trim away any excess fabric and lining.

4 Make up the top valance with a sateen lining, if possible, to cut down on bulk. The valance should be between one-fifth and a quarter of the depth of the curtain. Attach the trim by hand and right-sides facing, lay the raw edges at the top of the valance to the raw edges at the top of the curtain. Machine all the layers together, taking up only a small amount of seam allowance: this stage is simply to secure all the layers.

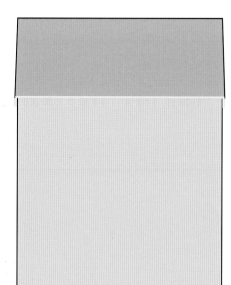

Cut a contrast strip of fabric 3cm (1¼in) wider than the buckram you are using (personally I don't think this type of heading works well on less than 12.5cm [4⅞in] buckram). This allows 1cm (½in) for turning under the buckram and 2cm (¾in) for the seam allowance where it is machined onto the main fabric and lining. Add an extra 4cm (1¾in) to the length of the contrast strip to allow for a 2cm (¾in) seam allowance at each end.

5 Cut a piece of buckram to match the width of the curtain. Overlock one of the long edges of the contrast fabric strip and place the buckram 1cm (½in) up from this edge.

6 Turn 1cm (½in) of fabric over the buckram and machine as shown.

7 Turn in the excess 2cm (¾in) fabric at each end and press.

8 Right-sides facing and raw edges aligned, lay the fabric and buckram strip at the top of the curtain and valance and machine across through all layers, taking a 2cm (¾in) seam allowance.

9 Work out the positioning of the goblet pleats and mark them with pins, as shown.

See Technique 64, Forming Goblet Pleats, page 63.

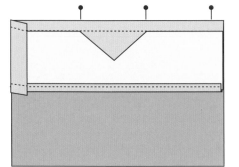

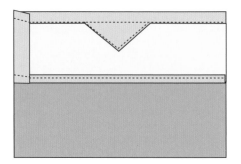

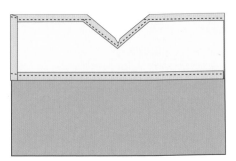

10 Cut a stiff cardboard template for the cut-aways. I find that the deepest part of the cut-away should be just half the depth of the buckram. Place the template onto the pleat areas and mark the cut-aways with a fading marker.

Cut out the areas of buckram only and place the valance or curtain under the machine.

11 Machine reasonably close to the top edge of the buckram. I find it easiest to machine along on the previous line, then into each V shape. This means you have a continuous line, which is simpler than stopping and starting with all the resulting trimming of threads.

12 Trim away the excess fabric and bulk from the corners, notch at the center of the V's.

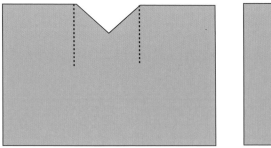

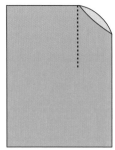

13 Turn the fabric through to the right side and continue as you would normally to form the pleats, except this time the contrast will show and you will have formed a more unusual heading.

Matching the contrast to a color in the design of the main fabric gives a very sophisticated, designer look.

PROJECT 31

Bordered cornice with a cover and a swag

This versatile cornice with its extra cover and swag to ring the changes, shows what can be done with a little fabric and some ingenuity. The cover and swag could be changed according to the season or even for Christmas. The main cornice is made in the normal way, with the addition of a border along the lower edge, on plywood with Velcro at the back of the cornice board. The cover is made on buckram with top bands to attach it to the top of the cornice board.

This swag is attached to the top of the cornice board along its length. The dimensions of the swag template are calculated in the same way as described for a classic swag.

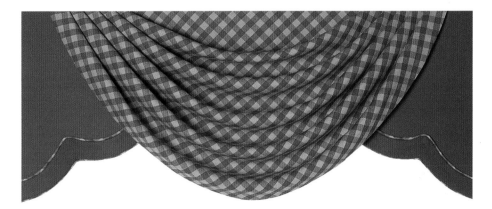

Materials

As for Project 4, The Classic Cornice, page 109 and Project 6, The Classic Swag and Tail Treatment, page 118.

Buckram for the second cornice.

1 See Project 4, The Classic Cornice, page 109.

2 This is a plain un-piped cornice without top bands. Before adding the lining, you are going to add a very effective border to the lower edge. To do this, you need to go back to the original paper template.

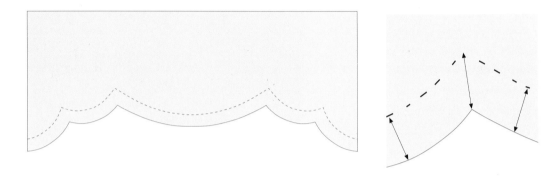

3 Very carefully, measure and then draw a line parallel to the bottom edge of the template. As you can see from the close-up (far right), the points are not the same distance from the lower edge and have to be measured and marked with particular care.

4 Once you are happy with this shape, cut the section out from the remainder of the template.

5 Place the template on the fabric you wish to use for the border and draw along the top and bottom edges.

6 See Technique 74, Cutting Piping Strips, page 70.

7 See Technique 75, Joining Piping Strips, page 71.

8 See Technique 80, Piping Curves, page 78.

9 See Technique 76, Piping with Square Ends, page 72.

10 Pipe the top and bottom lines, as shown, then cut away the excess fabric. If you cut the shape out before piping it you will stretch the edges of the fabric and distort the border.

11 Fold in the outer edges of the border. Place the border on the cornice so that the lower edge can be turned under the edge of the cornice. Staple this edge in position.

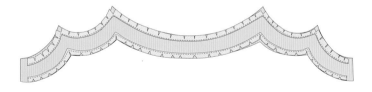

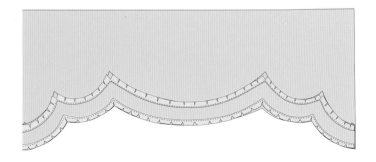

12 On the top edge of the border, notch all the fabrics well, cut away the bulk and turn under the seam allowances leaving just the piped edge showing. Using a circular needle, hand-stitch just below the piping, in the line of machine stitches. This completes the actual bordered cornice.

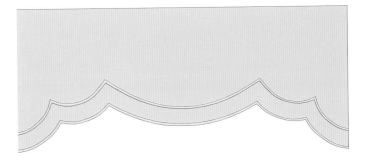

Cornice Cover

13 To make a cover for a cornice, turn to the original paper template (the piece remaining after the border was removed). Place this on top of the cornice to make certain the shape has not been altered in any way (you may need to make some minor adjustments). This additional cornice is made up with buckram, it will have to fit snugly up to the top row of piping on the cornice. You will probably find you have to cut away a little extra along the bottom edge of the template to allow for the two rows of piping. Across the width, you may also have to allow a little extra for bending the new cornice over the original cornice. To enable the buckram to bend correctly at the corners you will have to score it with a sharp point or knife.

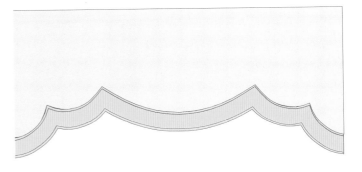

This cover is very simple to make and is a brilliant way of temporarily changing a cornice or adding a new element to an old cornice.

The technique used to cover this second cornice is a mixture of the techniques for making a fabric-covered cornice and a stiffened tieback.

Mark the piping line on the fabric, apply the piping and attach the top bands. Attach the fabric to the buckram by using an iron to fuse them together, as you cannot use staples. Attach the lining by hand.

When you attach the cover you may find you need to secure it also at the outer edges of the cornice. This could be done using a few hand stitches or some small strips of Velcro.

See Project 5, The Classic Tieback, page 115.

Cornice Swag

14 The swag is made in the normal way and is attached to the cornice board using a top band and Velcro.

See Technique 6, The Classic Swag and Tail Treatment, page 118.

Decorative swags are perfect for dressing a room for Christmas. Make them to match the cornice, or even in Christmas fabric.

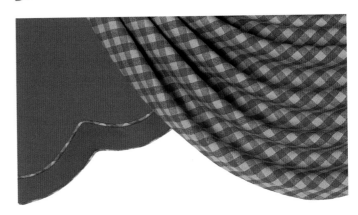

PROJECT 32

Squared cushion

This is a wonderful style of cushion for using up really special oddments of fabric and cord. They can be made to complement and contrast with other soft furnishings in a room for a really smart co-ordinated look. Tassels or covered buttons can be used to decorate the center of the cushion.

Materials

Square cushion pad

Zip

Four squares of fabric the size of a quarter of the pad, plus 2cm (¾in) all round for the front of the cover

Two pieces of fabric half the size of the pad, plus 2cm (¾in) all round for the back of the cover

Four pieces of decorative cord each half the length of the pad, plus 4cm (1¾in) of fabric and piping cord

1 key tassel or a self-covered button to finish the center

Enough piping fabric and cord to go right round the cushion, including joining.

Equipment

As for Project 10, Classic Cushions, page 136.

1 The first stage is to pipe one edge of two of the squares for the front of the cushion. It is important to cut down on the bulk where the cords meet at the center of the cushion and where the cord around the outer edge of the cushion passes over the cord from each square. Separate the cord from its flange for about 2cm (¾in). Place the cord so that the machine line will be positioned 2cm (¾in) in from the edge of the cushion. You will probably have to trim a little from the end of the flanging.

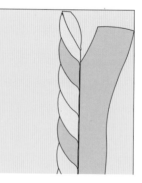

2 Untwist the ends of the cord itself and lay the separate cords flat as shown. Machine across all the ends and continue along the cord.

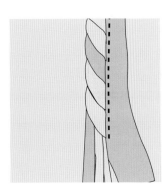

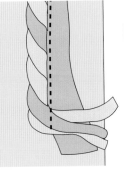

3 Before you reach the end of the square, stop with the needle down in the fabric. Separate the cord from the flange.

4 Unwrap the cords and machine across them to secure.

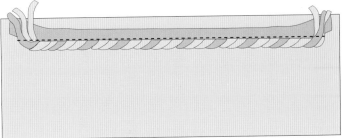

5 One edge of two of the squares should look as shown when you have finished applying the cord.

6 Place the corded edge face-to-face with a plain square. Machine them together from the side where you can see the previous line of machining, stitching as close to the cord as possible.

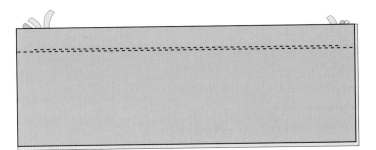

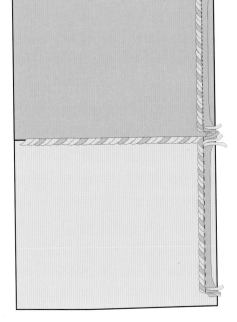

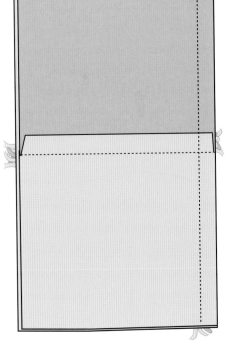

7 The resulting piece should look like this. Make two the same.

8 Machine two more pieces of cord to one half of the cushion front.

9 Place the two halves of the cushion front face-to-face. Machine them together. For a better finish when I am using flanged cord, I frequently turn the piece over and run a third line of machining to get really close to the cord. Complete the cushion in the usual way.

PROJECT 33

Voile curtain with informal pleats

Many of the voiles and sheers available on the market have a weighted bottom hem, which improves the hang considerably. The starkness of the white voile against the black curtain pole is perfectly complemented by the use of a narrow black petersham ribbon, which of course has to be washable for a fabric requiring laundering as often as a sheer.

Sheers are often available in very long lengths (this type of weighted sheer is 'railroaded' or run across the width of the window) which gives you the opportunity to add an over-valance without adding extra fabric. This valance is normally one-fifth to one-quarter of the depth of the curtain.

Materials

Voile; three-times fullness

Thick, washable interfacing

Sew-on hooks

Washable ribbon trim

Equipment

As for Project 1, The Classic Curtain, page 96.

1 See Technique 38, Cutting Sheer Fabrics, page 42.

2 Measure from the bottom hem and place pins on each side to indicate the top of the curtain, From the pin on one side, pull a thread to help you to turn over the top of the curtain accurately. The pulled thread should reach the second side level with the pin.

From this thread, add the depth for the overvalance and again pull a thread at the total length of fabric you require. Include a small seam allowance for the overvalance in this measurement. Trim off the extra fabric.

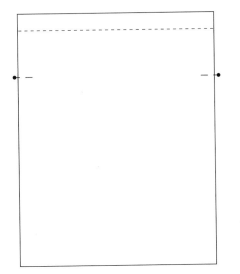

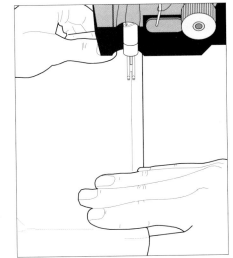

3 Turn in the side hems of the sheer right to the top of the curtain. Hemming voiles is not as difficult as it seems. The secret is to turn in a very small double hem, use a very sharp, preferably blue-tipped needle and a polyester thread. Hold the fabric taut both in front and behind the needle as shown. You will be amazed what a huge difference this makes.

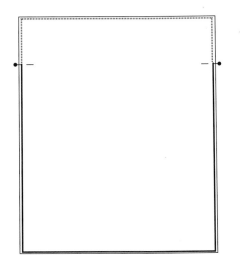

4 Stitch the ribbon to the curtain, covering the side hem stitching. Turn the hem over on the top edge of the curtain and attach the ribbon to the overvalance. In effect this will be on the back of the fabric (shown by the dotted line) as this section will be folded over the front of the curtain.

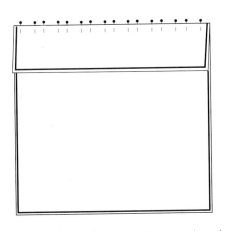

5 Fold over the overvalance and mark the pleats with pins, through the front fabric only. These should be calculated in the same way as pinch pleats, except on a sheer I use approximately 20cm (8in) in the pleats and 10cm (4in) in the spaces.

See Technique 63, Forming Pinch Pleats, page 60.

6 Take a piece of the heaviest weight of soft, washable dress interfacing or fold a thinner version to form a strip of the required thickness. This should measure the depth of the pleat, which should be no more than 8cm (3in), by the finished width of the curtain. With a fading marker, mark the center of each pleat.

7 Place the interfacing between the curtain and the overvalance at one end of the curtain. Anchor with a pin at the side hem and pull together the amount of fabric allowed for a pleat so that the center is on the first marked line. In effect you will have a pleat on the front and back of the curtain. Hold the fabric firmly and stitch though the bottom of the pleat, making sure you catch the interfacing a little. Continue across the curtain, forming the pleats as you go. Ladder stitch the outer edges and attach sew-on hooks.

See Technique 56, Ladder Stitch, page 55 and Technique 73, Attaching Sew-on Hooks, page 69.

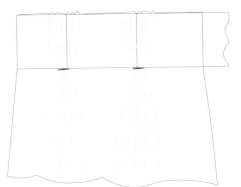

PROJECT 34

Cornice with a shaped top

Occasionally a particular fabric, such as the one used for this cornice, will suggest that a more unusual shape of cornice would look really special. It is so important to be open to interpreting the fabric rather than always having fixed ideas for the finished product, regardless of the design of the fabric. The part of the design I have used in this instance is actually the border taken from the center of the fabric. Sometimes this can be rather wasteful of fabric, but is well worth the cost and you can almost always cut cushions from the waste.

Materials and equipment

As for Project 4, The Classic Cornice, page 109.

1 See Technique 11, Making Cornice Boards, page 22.

2 See 16, Templates for Fabric-covered Cornices, page 25.

3 See Project 4, The Classic Cornice, page 109.

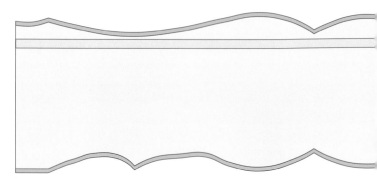

4 With this style of cornice you cannot use top bands to fix it to the cornice board. The Velcro is machined to the lining before the lining is attached to the cornice. If the cornice is very large or heavy you may need to use 5cm (2in) Velcro, which means you will have to add an additional piece of plywood to the cornice board as shown above.

5 Attach the piped fabric to the cornice board in the normal way, stapling on all edges. Attach the lining (with the Velcro machined into position) onto the back of the cornice by hand and staple through the Velcro into the wood to secure it. If you don't staple, the lining and Velcro tend to stretch away from the cornice.

Some fitters use tacks straight through the cornice and then pull the fabric over the nail head. Alternatively a braid or trim attached to the cornice before fitting camouflages any tacks you may use. The drawback of either of these methods is that it is very difficult for a customer to take the cornice down for cleaning or decorating and also occasionally you can get small marks if the fabric is pale or delicate.

PROJECT 35

Tab-top appliquéd curtain

Tab top curtains are hugely popular, though I personally feel they are best used as dress curtains. On high windows they are very difficult to pull, which in turn is not good for the curtain itself. Even if you are using them purely as dress curtains, it can be very difficult to keep them looking neat unless you pleat up the curtain and apply the tabs to the top of each pleat as I have here. For this curtain I have used two co-ordinating fabrics: one is a simple printed stripe the other is made up of alternating stripes and a design of sea shells. This gave me the idea of using the bold stripe for tabs and an applied border and the sea shells for appliqué motifs. I normally allow approximately two-times fullness for this style of curtain.

Materials

Fabric

Lining

Fabric with border and shells

Medium weight iron-on interfacing

Equipment

As for Project 1, The Classic Curtain, page 96.

1 See Project 1, The Classic Curtain, page 96.

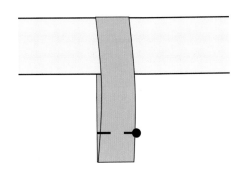

2 I find one of the hardest parts in making tab top curtains is how to measure the length of the curtain, because of the diameter of the pole. I have tried many methods and have finally come up with one that, for me, works every time.

Take a piece of fabric that equals the length of the tab you will be using and place it over the pole with a pin in it to mark the point where it would join the curtain. Take a measurement from this pin to the floor. Then move this tab along the pole and measure in a number of positions.

4 Make up the tabs by folding a strip of fabric in half and stitching down one side as shown. Turn right-side out and press. Fold each tab in half lengthways.

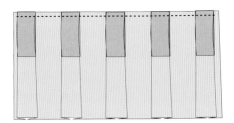

5 Right-sides facing and raw edges aligned, place a tab on the front of each pleat and machine across to secure.

3 Apply the border and the appliqué to the main fabric before turning in the bottom and side hems. Cut strips of fabric for the border, press under the edges and then treat it like ribbon. For the appliqué, cut out the motifs, leaving approximately 1cm (½in) all around the design. Place the motif on the interfacing and press, preferably with a damp cloth or a steam iron. Once you have a good bond, cut around the edge of the pattern: the interfacing will add body and prevent the fabric from fraying. Place the motifs onto the curtain and satin stitch around the edge, making sure you cover all the edges. Hold the fabric firmly at each side and gently steer it.

Make up the curtain in the normal way. Measure, pin and trim off the excess fabric and lining. To pleat up the curtain I used box pleats of 6cm (2½in) (these take up 12cm [5in] of fabric), and spaces of 12 cm (5in). Stitch down only the first few centimeters of each pleat then press flat.

See Technique 96, Making Ribbon Mitres, page 88 and Technique 65, Forming Box Pleats, page 64.

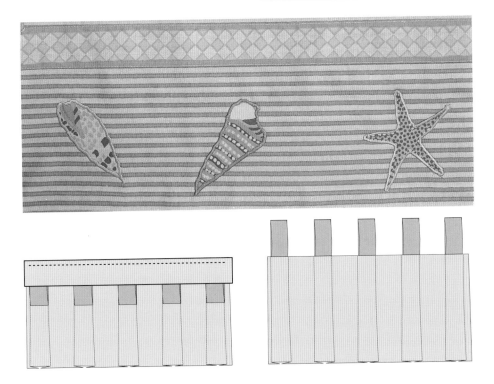

6 Cut a band of fabric to form a facing. This should be the width of the curtain, plus a 2cm (¾in) seam allowance at each end, by 10cm (4in), or longer if preferred: check how it will appear on the outside of the window. Right sides facing, lay the facing on the curtain and machine across, following the line of machining holding the tabs in place. Cut away the bulk, then turn in and press the side seam allowances.

7 Turn the facing to the back of the curtain, which will bring the tabs into the correct position. Turn under the raw edges and pin. Hand stitch along the bottom and side edges to complete the curtain.

Glossary

Buckram – tieback and cornice

A stiffened hessian or non-woven fabric, preferably capable of being attached by applying heat on at least one side.

Buckram – curtain

A white or cream stiffened cotton used at the top of the curtain when making pinch or goblet pleat headings. Much lighter weight than cornice/tieback buckram. Available in iron-on and sew-in forms.

Box pleats

Pleats formed in the normal manner then flattened out and stitched. If the pleats touch, they use triple fullness. Can be used for valances, static curtains and on the skirt of a loose cover.

Cornice

A decorative, fabric-covered board which attaches to a cornice board and forms part of the window treatment.

Cornice board

A wooden structure attached to the wall with metal angle brackets to support a cornice or valance. The curtain rail may be attached to the underside of the board or directly to the wall.

Cross grain or bias cut

Fabric which is cut diagonally, usually at 45° to the selvedge.

Gliders

Plastic or metal devices on a curtain rail which connect the curtain hooks on the curtain to the curtain track.

Hook drop

The measurement from the point at which the hook attaches to the pole or track to the bottom of the curtain.

Interlining

A fabric with a brushed finish which is placed between the main fabric and the lining to add body, aid insulation and assist difficult fabrics to hang in rich folds.

Italian stringing

A row of rings attached to the back of a curtain which are stitched to both the fabric and the lining. A cord is secured to the leading edge, passed through the rings to a cord guide at the side of the window, allowing the curtain to be drawn to one side.

Lining – sateen

A fine, closely woven, usually cotton fabric that protects the main fabric from the sun and adds 'drapability' to the curtains.

Lining – thermal

This type of lining has a special dense layer to add to the draught-proofing qualities of the curtains.

Lining – blackout

This type of lining can be a little heavy for some fabrics or for very large curtains. Often used on Roman blinds within a window recess. Don't expect complete blackout: light will show at the edges and occasionally the stitching lines.

Leading edge

The edge of the curtain which travels across the window.

Lead-weight chain

Small pieces of lead in a polyester and polythene tube that can be placed in the bottom of a curtain. Available in several weights.

Overlap

Centre part of the curtain, which is placed on a special overlap arm on the curtain track to prevent an ugly gap when the curtains are closed

Pattern repeat

The distance from one point on a pattern to the same point further up the fabric.

Pile fabric

Such as velvet or chenille, which has a third thread at right angles to the warp and weft threads.

Piping

A technique to finish seams with a professional touch as well as adding strength. A non-shrinking or pre-shrunk cord is placed in the centre of a folded strip of fabric and stitched into the seam. The fabric is normally cut on the cross or bias.

Return

Part of the curtain which returns to the wall at the end of the curtain rail. This term is also applies to the outer edge of a valance or cornice.

Roman blind

A blind which has no gathers and is completely flat when lowered. Can be hard fold, which has horizontal bars or dowels at the front and back of every fold; soft fold, which has rods only at the back of each fold, where the rings are attached; or casual, with only a bottom weight bar.

Selvedge

The edge of the fabric formed in the weaving process. It frequently shrinks during the life of a curtain and should ideally be completely removed.

Swags

Cut and shaped pieces of fabric, lining and, sometimes interlining, pleated into a top band, creating a formal and traditional window dressing, normally completed with fabric tails.

Tails

Shaped and lined fabric pieces which can be hung at the outer edge of the window when using a valance or swags.

Valance

A gathered or pleated band which hangs in front of the curtain and is attached to the cornice board.

Warp threads

These run vertically from top to bottom of the fabric

Weft Threads

Threads which run horizontally from one selvedge to the other.

Suppliers

Maureen Whitemore Fine Furnishings offers residential and non-residential soft furnishings courses throughout the year in the beautiful English Lake District. Also at The Janome Sewing School near Stockport, Cheshire
A range of fabrics, making-up supplies, workroom manuals and videos are available by mail order. Quarterly newsletter offers innovative soft furnishings ideas and advice.Custom soft furnishings design.
For further information contact:
Maureen Whitemore Fine Furnishings
The Old Church Hotel
Old Church Bay
Watermillock, Penrith
Cumbria CA11 OJN
Tel: 017684 86272
E-mail:
mw@maureenwhitemore.co.uk
Website:
www.maureenwhitemore.o.uk

DOMESTIC SEWING MACHINES
Janome UK
The Janome Centre,
Southside, Bredbury,
Stockport, Cheshire SK6 2SP
Tel: 0161 666 6006
Fax: 0161 494 0179
Also throughout Europe

USA
Janome USA
10 Industrial Avenue
Mahwah
New Jersey 07430, USA
Tel: 201 825 3200
Fax: 201 825 1488

INDUSTRIAL SEWING MACHINES
Brother UK Ltd.
Shepley Street
Guide Bridge
Audenshaw
Manchester M34 5JD
Tel: 0161 330 6531
Fax: 0161 308 3281

Europe
BIE
1 Tame Street
Guide Bridge
Audenshaw
Manchester M34 5JE
Tel: 0161 330 6531
Fax: 0161 330 5520

USA
BIC (NJ)
1 Somerset Corporate
Boulevard
Bridgewater
New Jersey, USA
Tel: 908 704 1700
Fax: 908 704 8235

FABRICS AND WALLCOVERINGS
creation baumann Ltd.
41/42 Berners St.
London W1P 3AA

Textra Ltd.
Barton Mill
Audlett Drive
Abingdon
Oxon OX14 3TZ
Tel: 01235 550 350
Fax 01235 535 906

Whiteheads Fabrics Ltd.
14 Hazelwood Close
Hazelwood Trading Estate
Worthing
W. Sussex BN14 8NP
Tel: 01903 212 222
Contact Helen Orpin for Europe

Cordima UK Ltd.
15/16 Smeaton Close
Severalls Industrial Park
Colchester
Essex CO4 4QY
Tel: 01206 752 575
Fax: 01206 751 200

Anne & Robert Swaffer
Bakewell Road
Orton Southgate

Peterborough
Cambridge
Tel: 01733 371 727
Fax: 01733 371 247

Wilson Wilcox Furnishings Ltd.
Nortonthorpe Mills
Wakefield Road
Scissett
Huddersfield
West Yorks. HD8 9LA
Tel: 01484 864 522
Fax: 01484 864 561

Zoffany Ltd.
17 Church Street
Rickmansworth
Hertfordshire WD3 1DE
Tel: 01923 710 680
Fax: 01923 710 694

Nono Designs Ltd.
Unit A
Marlborough Close
Parkgate Industrial Estate
Parkgate Lane
Knutsford
Cheshire WA16 8XN
Tel: 01565 757 400
Fax: 01565 757 405

Ashley Wilde Designs
Giltex House
Cline Road
London N11 2LR
Tel: 0181 368 6860
Fax: 0181 361 8670

Richard Barrie
PO Box 71
Euroway
Lea Green, St. Helens
Merseyside WA9 4QF
Tel: 01744 851 515
Fax: 01744 812 412

Harlequin Fabrics & Wallcoverings
Cossington Road
Sileby
Leicestershire LE12 7RU
Tel: 01509 813 112
Fax: 01509 816 003

The Isle Mill
12 West Moulin Road
Pitlochry
Scotland PH16 5AF
Tel: 01796 472 390
Fax: 01796 473 869

Hill & Knowles
Palace of Industry
Olympic Way
Wembley HA9 0DB
Tel: 0181 903 8424
Fax: 0181 902 8882

USA
creation baumann USA Inc.
114 North Centre Avenue
Rockville Centre
NY 11570, USA
Tel: 516 764 7431
Fax: 516 678 6848
also throughout the USA

Hinson & Co.
27-35 Jackson Avenue
Long Island City
New York 11101-8817, USA
Tel: 718 482 1100

Europe
Cordima Cordes GMBH & Co.
Postfach 1165
48250 Geven, Germany
Tel: 257 115 244

creation baumann SA
48 rue de Grenelle
75007 Paris, France
Tel: 01 45 49 0822
Fax: 01 45 49 3122
also throughout Europe

SPECIALIST METALWARE
Mykam
Aston, Birmingham
Tel: 0121 333 4443

CURTAIN TAPES, TRIMMINGS AND ACCESSORIES
Rufflette Ltd.
Sharston Road
Manchester M22 4TH

Tel: 0161 998 1811
Fax: 0161 945 9468
*For European stockists, please telephone Export Department on the number above*Conso

(British Trimmings) Ltd.
PO Box 46
Stockport
Cheshire SK5 7PJ
Tel: 0161 480 6122
Fax: 0161 477 1879

USA
Ashbrook & Associates Inc.
1271 N. Blue Gum
Anaheim
CA 92806, USA
Tel: 714 765 5900
Fax: 714 765 5904

VELCRO AND RIBBONS
Selectus Ltd. (Panda Ribbons)
The Uplands
Biddulph
Stoke-on-Trent ST8 7RH
Tel: 01782 522 316
Fax: 01782 522 574

Europe
Societe des Textile
3 Rue de Seville
F 68302 Saint Louis
France
Tel: 3 8970 2222
Fax: 3 8969 9885
also Switzerland

CURTAIN TRACKS AND BLIND SYSTEMS
Silent Gliss Ltd.
Star Lane, Margate
Kent CT9 4EF
Tel: 01843 863 571
Fax: 01843 864 503

also situated worldwide including:

Silent Gliss International AG
Worbstrasse 210
Postfach 76
3073 Gumligen
Bern, Switzerland
Tel: 31 958 8585
Fax: 31 958 8586

Silent Gliss Corporation
4F Sanko Bldg
No 28 Sakamachi
Shinjuku-ku
Tokyo 160, Japan
Tel: 3 3350 4809
Fax: 3 3350 4334

Silent Gliss USA Inc.
Bay Creek Church Road
PO Box 405, Loganville
GA 30249, USA
Tel: 770 466 4811
Fax: 770 466 4814

SWISH AND KIRSCH PRODUCTS
Newell Window Fashions UK
Lichfield Road Industrial Estate
Tamworth
Staffordshire B79 0DX
Tel: 01827 642 42
Fax: 01827 598 16

Europe
Newell Window Fashions
Waterloo Office Park
Dreve Richelle 161 Batiment N
1410 Waterloo, Belgium
also throughout Europe

STIFFENINGS, INTERFACINGS AND INTERLININGS
Freudenberg Nonwovens LP
(Vilene)
Lowfields Business Park
Elland
West Yorkshire HX5 5DX
Tel: 01422 327 900
Fax: 01422 327 998

Edmund Bell & Co. Ltd.
Belfry House
Roydsdale Way
Euroway Trading Estate
Bradford BD4 6SU
Tel: 01274 680 000
Fax: 01274 680 699

Europe
Freudenberg Faservliesstoffe KG
BA Interlinings
D-69465 Weinheim, Germany
Tel: 6201 805710
Fax: 6201 883067

USA
Freudenberg Nonwovens LP
3440 Industrial Drive
Durham
NC 27704, USA
Tel: 919 620 3900
Fax: 919 620 3930

SPECIALIST WHOLSALERS OF FURNISHING ACCESSORIES, HARDWARE AND WORKROOM SUPPLIES
Hallis Hudson
Bushell Street, Preston
Lancashire PR1 2SP
Tel: 01772 202 202
Fax: 01772 889 889

South Africa
H Delahunt CC
Diane House
28 Mandy Road
Reuven
Johannesburg
PO Box 38053
Booysens 2016, South Africa
Tel: 11 683 3301
Fax: 11 434 1618

SEWING THREAD AND HABERDASHERY
Coats UK Ltd.
Netherplace
Newton Mearns
Glasgow G77 6PP
Tel: 0141 616 1050
Fax: 0141 616 1062

Europe
Coats Limited
Desford Road
Enderby
Leicester LE9 5AS
Tel: 0116 275 2020
situated throughout Europe

USA
Coats American
Two LakePointe Plaza
4135 South Stream Blvd
Charlotte
North Carolina 28217, USA
Tel: 704 329 5930
Fax: 704 329 5929

AUTHOR'S ACKNOWLEDGEMENTS
All the many colleagues and true friends that I have made in this great industry – for the encouragement and support that they have always offered so freely.

Nessie, Alwyn, Alwyn and our Geordie Clan, who are always there.

Karen and Fran, who work so tirelessly in our mail-order company.

'Les Girls': Ann, Helen, Mary and Avril, who assist me so ably in the preparation of my international seminars.

Stewart Coxhead, my good friend and business manager.

Frances Eva Mary Thompson, the most talented soft furnisher I have ever known who taught me so much.

Judi Goodwin, who taught me that a blank page is not so frightening.

Everyone at Janome, who believed in me right from the beginning.

Les Edwards, Gail Parker, Ken Paveley, Pete Randall and Grace McNamara.

Dian Garbarini and all involved in Drapery Pro.

Matthew Dickens for his talents and for turning the hard work of a photography shoot into fun.

Roger Daniels for the amazing transformation from my drawings and jottings on disk.

A special thanks to Kate Haxell for her patience with a first time author; Kate Kirby and all at Collins & Brown for their help and belief in this venture.

Last but not least Paul and Rick Fry and Steve Smith, who have dragged me into the age of computers, without which this book most definitely would not have been written.

Index